MASTERING SOFTWARE PROJECT MANAGEMENT
Best Practices, Tools and Techniques

MURALI CHEMUTURI
THOMAS M. CAGLEY, JR.

Copyright ©2010 Copyright J. Ross Publishing

ISBN-13: 978-1-60427-034-1
Printed and bound in the U.S.A. Printed on acid-free paper
10 9 8 7 6 5 4 3 2 1

Library of Congress Cataloging-in-Publication Data
Chemuturi, Murali, 1950-
  Mastering software project management : best practices, tools and
techniques / by Murali Chemuturi and Thomas M. Cagley Jr.
    p. cm.
  Includes index.
  ISBN 978-1-60427-034-1 (hardcover : alk. paper)
  1. Computer software--Development. 2. Project management. I. Cagley,
Thomas M., 1956- II. Title.
  QA76.76.D47C478 2010
  005.1--dc22   2010019185

Phone: (954) 727-9333
Fax: (561) 892-0700
Web: www.jrosspub.com

CONTENTS

FOREWORD

When a software project fails, the impact to an organization can be significant. The losses the organization experiences may be financial, the project's failure may negatively impact the organization's credibility with customers, or the organization may lose market position and competitive advantage. As of this writing, the latest statistics from the 2009 Standish Group CHAOS report state that "44% were challenged which are late, over budget, and/or with less than the required features and functions." This is an alarming number. It represents a dismal trend and is in fact an increase in the number of failures, representing the highest failure rate in over a decade.

Although the reasons for these failures vary, there is every reason to believe that some of these failures are directly attributable to ineffective software project management. Furthermore, it is safe to assume that in nearly all of these failures, project management played at least a minor role. Show me a failed project and I will show you a failed project manager or process.

Does the blame for a failed project always rest on the project manager's shoulders? Can organizational behaviors be blamed for some of these failures? Can a customer or client cause a project to fail? If we concede that, from time to time, there are some extraordinary causes of failure that are outside the boundary of a project manager's control, plenty of fingers are still left pointing at ineffective project management skills, practices, techniques, and technologies.

So, what is at the heart of these project failures? Is it the skill level of the individual project manager? Is it the result of unavailable or inaccurate project data? Is it a lack of training or a lack of a proper project management practices?

To state the obvious, it is essential that software development organizations focus their attention on improving the state of their project management practices. More to the point, there is enough collective experience and understanding that we can now acknowledge and identify software project management best practices.

This is in fact what Murali Chemuturi and Tom Cagley have accomplished in *Mastering Software Project Management: Best Practices, Tools and Techniques.* They have compiled their collective experience and wisdom and have presented it in a practical, clear, and concise format that is of value to a new project manager as well as more experienced project managers. The authors present the process and the philosophy behind the methodologies and techniques of software project management.

The introduction to the book quickly puts context around the authors' working definition of a software development project and the classification of a software project, which includes the software development life cycle, approach-driven software, software maintenance, agile software development, and Web-application development. The authors are clear — this book addresses software project management utilizing a process-driven approach.

Their project management framework comprises four core elements: acquisition, initiation, execution, and closure. In the four chapters that discuss these core elements, we learn about various workflows and best practice activities and are given helpful tools and techniques. The book is formatted in such a way as to be useful as an educational text as well as a practical reference guide for the practitioner.

Mastering software project management is about gaining control through the use of reliable and meaningful information. The authors have addressed the importance of control with insightful chapters on planning, scheduling, and change management. Once again, they present process flows, useful templates, and guidance on how to execute the best practices they have outlined.

Software project management best practices would not be complete without a chapter on agile development. The authors drive home the point that for an organization to achieve success, the organization must first embrace the agile philosophy. Here, too, the authors discuss how to plan and control the workflow in an agile environment.

Chapter 12 discusses pitfalls and best practices and begins with an important observation regarding how best practices may be viewed in an organization. The authors point out that management is unique to an organization based on that organization's culture. And while producing positive results is an important aspect of management, of greater importance is that the results are achieved with optimal costs, productivity, quality, and morale. In their words, "... it is necessary for organizations to adopt best practices and avoid the pitfalls to grow and prosper."

And perhaps, quite possibly, the authors have saved the best for last. There are ten appendixes that focus on project management intangibles, such as Appendix C, dealing with the art and science of managing people, in which the authors discuss such topics as delegating and managing your superiors. Appendix

B addresses the practice of making decisions. Appendix E centers on issue resolution. The list goes on to include other relevant topics such as productivity, measures and metrics, and customer satisfaction. Yes, all of these topics should be considered to be part of a comprehensive discussion on mastering software project management.

This book should be required reading for all software project managers and for those organizations that struggle with late and costly project implementation. The advice and processes so rigorously detailed in this book should become the de facto standard for improving an organization's development practices.

— **David Herron**
Vice President of Knowledge
Solution Services
David Consulting Group, USA

PREFACE

Before we talk about software project management, we need to understand the terms *project* and *management*. Once we understand these two terms and how they relate to each other, we can apply them to the field of software development. In the subsequent chapters and appendices, we strive to define and explain and then to show just what software project management is.

Software projects are initiated, planned, and executed at two places. The first is within the same organization that is going to use the end product; the second is in an organization specialized in developing software that will be used by other organizations. In this book, we are not considering hobby projects although they can use the techniques in the book also. Projects can also be called internal projects and external projects. Internal projects are those with an end product that is used within the same organization; external projects are those with an end product that is used by another organization. We will expand on these terms in subsequent chapters.

Our focus in this book is on the management of software projects that are tightly planned, monitored, controlled, and executed. These projects could be internal or external projects.

This book is not geared to help you pass exams of any kind or to receive certification. Rather it helps you pass the examination conducted by life and to achieve success in software project management. This book is based on our experiences: experiences gained through academic efforts, reading books and literature, and managing and observing real-life projects. What we have learned has been plowed back in to fine tune our theories. This book is a result of that fine tuning and is something akin to the expression "What they don't teach you at Harvard."

We will be glad to receive your feedback and promise to usually respond in one business day. We can be reached at murali@chemuturi.com and t.cagley@ davidconsultinggroup.com.

ABOUT THE AUTHORS

 **Murali Chemuturi** is an information technology and software development subject matter expert, hands-on programmer, author, consultant, and trainer. In 2001, he formed Chemuturi Consultants, his own IT consulting and software development firm. Chemuturi Consultants help software development organizations to achieve their quality and value objectives. The firm provides training in several software engineering and project management topics, such as software estimation, test effort estimation, function point analysis, and software project management, to name a few. Chemuturi Consultants also offers a number of products to aid project managers and software development professionals, such as PMPal, a software project management tool, and EstimatorPal, FPAPal, and UCPPal, a set of software estimation tools.

Prior to starting Chemuturi Consultants, Murali gained over 15 years of industrial experience in various engineering and manufacturing management positions. He then gained over 24 years of information technology and software development experience. His most recent position prior to forming Chemuturi Consultants was vice president of Software Development at Vistaar e-Business Pvt., Ltd.

His undergraduate degrees and diplomas are in electrical and industrial engineering. He holds a MBA and a postgraduate diploma in computer methods and programming. Murali also has several years of academic experience, teaching a variety of computer and IT courses, such as COBOL, Fortran, BASIC, computer architecture, and database management systems.

He is a member of IEEE, a senior member of the Computer Society of India, and a Fellow of the Indian Institute of Industrial Engineering as well as a well-published author in professional journals.

Thomas M. Cagley, Jr. is vice president of consulting for the David Consulting Group. He is an authority in guiding organizations through the process of integrating software measurement with model-based assessments to yield effective and efficient process improvement programs. He is a recognized industry expert in the measurement and estimation of software projects. His areas of expertise encompass management experience in project management, development methods and metrics, quality integration, quality assurance, and the application of the Software Engineering Institute's Capability Maturity Model Integration® to achieve process improvements.

Tom has over 20 years experience in the software industry and has been a consultant since 1997. He was previously metrics practice manager at Software Productivity Research. Earlier, he held technical and managerial positions in different industries as a leader in software methods and metrics, quality assurance, and systems analysis. He is a frequent speaker at metrics, quality, and project management conferences.

Tom blogs about software development and management topics at www.tcagley.wordpress.com and edits a podcasts of essays and interviews entitled Software Process and Measurement Cast (www.spamcast.net). The blog and podcast serve as a platform to share information with the development industry and to foster a continuing dialog. Sharing and dialog are the means of paying it forward.

He is a member of the International Function Point Users Group and is a Certified Function Point Specialist. He is currently the immediate past president of IFPUG and previously served as the chair of the IFPUG Conference Committee and director of Conferences and Education.

Tom has a B.S. from Louisiana State University and has done extensive postgraduate work at Cleveland State University, Case Western Reserve University, and Kent State University.

Web Added Value™

Free value-added materials available from
*the Download Resource Center at **www.jrosspub.com***

At J. Ross Publishing we are committed to providing today's professional with practical, hands-on tools that enhance the learning experience and give readers an opportunity to apply what they have learned. That is why we offer free ancillary materials available for download on this book and all participating Web Added Value™ publications. These online resources may include interactive versions of material that appears in the book or supplemental templates, worksheets, models, plans, case studies, proposals, spreadsheets and assessment tools, among other things. Whenever you see the WAV™ symbol in any of our publications it means bonus materials accompany the book and are available from the Web Added Value™ Download Resource Center at www.jrosspub.com.

Downloads available for *Mastering Software Project Management: Best Practices, Tools and Techniques* consist of free software project planning templates; a demo version of an integrated and collaborative software project managment tool called PMPal, which is valid for 180 days; TestPal, a free, fully functional tool useful for test effort estimations and test case design; and PET, a free personal effectiveness tool.

1

SOFTWARE PROJECT BASICS

INTRODUCTION

Human endeavor, from its earliest hunter/gatherer roots, was carried out in teams, each with a hierarchy of roles. As civilization progressed, the need for structure and rules increased. A large farm is a team organization based on a simple hierarchy of an owner, overseers, and employed laborers. The Industrial Revolution created factories which required more complex hierarchies, both within teams and between teams. Factories aggregated the production of goods for consumption into concentrated units capable of greater productivity. To achieve this great jump in productivity, rules were developed to effectively run the factories. These developments were the genesis of the art and science of managing production, which has been called *production management*.

Classification of organizations. The type of production can be used to classify organizations based on the *manner* in which goods are produced. The categories are:

- Mass production: continuously produces the same products
- Batch production: produces goods in batches; each batch is similar, but not identical
- Flow process production: production of chemicals, pharmaceuticals, and fertilizer products, generation of electricity, etc.
- Job order production: produces tailor-made goods (i.e., goods are produced only when an order is received)

Initially, management texts focused on *mass production, batch production,* and *flow process production systems* (also known as "made to warehouse" production systems). In *made to warehouse* production systems, goods are produced and stored in warehouses for distribution. The significant feature of mass production and flow process production is that the rate of consumption/demand *equals or exceeds* the rate of production for the product. In batch production, the rate of production *exceeds* the rate of consumption/demand for the product. The goal of production management is to balance both rates.

Production management texts, however, did not address organizations such as ship building, aircraft manufacturing, heavy equipment manufacturing, etc. These organizations are known as job order production or *made to order* organizations. In *made to order* organizations, items are produced only after an order is received.

By leaving out job order "shops," management texts also excluded organizations that constructed buildings, highways, and other infrastructure facilities. These types of organizations are certainly not serial production organizations even though they create wealth and employ people. Their work was classified as *projects.* Some knowledge, however, was gathered and released under the title of *project management.* Job order production system organizations latched onto this concept and became project-based production systems.

Presently, management theory addresses organizations in two basic categories: production organizations and service organizations. The art and science of managing these organizations has metamorphosed from *production management* to *operations management.*

Similarly, we can categorize organizations by the *nature* of their operations:

- Continuous operations: organizations with fixed facilities that carry out *similar* operations day after day continuously and produce products for stockpiling in warehouses (real or virtual)
- Project operations: organizations with fixed but flexible facilities that carry out *dissimilar* operations from day to day and produce only against a customer order

More and more organizations are moving toward project operations due to market forces, which put emphasis on individual preferences while reducing costs. Gone are the days of the famous words of Henry Ford, Sr.: "You can have the car of any color as long as it is black."

The project operations category has seen significant development over the past few years under the title "mass customization." Mass customization blends aspects of continuous and project operations.

Having put the concept of project operations in an historical perspective, see Table 1.1 for a comparison of continuous operations with project operations. Mass customization walks the line between the two extremes identified in Table

Table 1.1. Comparisons of Continuous Operations with Project Operations

Item Number	Aspect	Continuous Operations	Project Operations
1	Product design	Designed once: updated as needed/dictated by market forces	Designed for every order received
2	Trigger for commencement	Marketing asks for the product	Customer's order triggers commencement
3	Planning	Periodic: annual, quarterly, monthly, weekly, etc.	Order-wise as well as periodic
4	Workstation design	Low cost: to produce one type of component	Potentially higher cost: versatile workstations to produce a wide variety of components
5	Required education levels for staff	Low: needs to understand instructions and can be easily trained (leads to a flatter training curve)	High: needs to be able to interpret drawings/instructions and may require longer training (leads to a steeper learning curve)
6	Products	Batches of identical products	Products range from similar to (but never identical to) to radically different
7	Types of workstation operations	Mostly repetitive with little variety	Mostly nonrepetitive with wide variety
8	Specialization	Highly feasible	Limited specialization
9	Planning	Planning utilization of facilities becomes more predominant and important	Planning development of the product becomes predominant, while facility utilization planning becomes less important
10	Organizational structure	Hierarchical mostly	Mix of hierarchical and matrix organization
11	Customers	Repetitive customers possible to a high degree	Normally one-off customers with low probability of repeat order for same product

1.1, typically with most of the benefits of each, but with a greater reliance on self-directed teams that make hierarchies and matrix organizations very nervous.

Description of a project. Let's now examine what comprises a project: a project is a temporary endeavor with the objective of manufacturing (producing or developing) a product or delivering a service, while adhering to the specifications of the customer (including functionality, quality, reliability, price, and schedule) and conforming to international/national/customer/internal standards for performance and reliability. Translation:

- A project is a temporary endeavor.
- A project has a definite beginning and a definite ending.
- No two projects will be identical, although they may be similar.
- Each project needs to be separately approved, planned, designed, engineered, constructed, tested, delivered, installed, and commissioned.
- A project may be stand-alone or a component in a larger program.
- A project is executed in phases, with an initiation phase and one or more intermediate phases and a closing phase.
- Many projects have a transition phase (e.g., handover to customer).
- A project may extend through a maintenance phase.

A software development project (often shortened to *software project*) has the objective of developing a software product or maintaining an existing software product. Software development projects have several general attributes, including:

- The project has a definite beginning and a definite end.
- The project deliverable is functional software and related artifacts.
- Activities that may be included in a project are user and software requirements, software design, software construction, software testing, acceptance testing, and software delivery, deployment, and handover.
- Activities not included in a project are the activities of project selection/acquisition and post-handover.

Some of the more unique attributes of software development projects include:

- The primary output is not physical — in the sense that the primary deliverable is functional software and no tangible components are delivered — almost everything is inside a computer.
- Process inspection does not facilitate progress assessment — functional software or at least the code is the real measure of progress. In a manufacturing organization, one can see semifinished goods. The proof of work being performed is in the noise made by machines. In a software development organization, visual assessment is not enough to ensure that a person is performing. One needs to walk through the code being developed to ensure that the person is working.
- Despite significant progress in software engineering tools and diagramming techniques, they do not rise to the level of precision of the engineering drawings used in other engineering disciplines.

- Professional associations in software development and standards organizations have not defined standards or practices for developing software as has occurred in other engineering practices. The International Organization for Standardization (ISO) and the Institute of Electrical and Electronic Engineers (IEEE) have defined a number of standards, but these standards are not at the same level of granularity as other engineering standards.
- Although significant improvements in software development methodologies have been made, these methodologies are still largely dependent on human beings for productivity and quality. Tools are available to help in development or testing, but they still have not been able to rise to the level set by the standards and tools used in fabrication/inspection/testing in other engineering disciplines. In other engineering disciplines, tools are available that shift the onus for productivity/quality from human beings to the combination of tools and process. Most would agree that an average-skilled person can achieve higher productivity/quality with tools than a super-skilled person without tools.

Therefore, the rigor of planning is all the more important in software development than in other engineering projects — planning is a critical tool to keep a project focused. In other engineering projects, a simple schedule based on PERT/CPM (Program Evaluation and Review Technique/Critical Path Method) would suffice, whereas in software development projects, increased rigor and more planning documents are required (planning documents commonly required are described in subsequent chapters).

TYPES OF SOFTWARE PROJECTS

Software development projects (SDPs) are not homogenous. They come in various sizes and types. Some examples will help us gain an understanding of the breadth of SDPs:

- An organization desires to shift a business process from manual information processing to computer-based information processing. This project will include studying the user requirements and carrying out all of the activities necessary to implement the computer-based system
- An organization desires to shift a business process from manual information processing to computer-based information processing. The organization does not want the software be developed from "scratch." It wants to use a commercial off-the-shelf software (COTS) product. This

project will include implementation and perhaps some customization of the COTS product to make it appropriate for the organization.

- An organization has a computer-based system that needs to be shifted to another computer system because the existing system has become obsolete and support to keep the obsolete system in working condition is no longer available. This project could include porting the code, training users, and testing the new implementation.
- An organization has a computer-based system and desires to shift it from a flat file system to a RDBMS-based system (relational database management system). Activities will include data conversion in addition to other activities.
- An organization has a computer-based information processing system and needs to effect modifications in the software or add additional functionality. Activities include adding functionality and making required modifications in the software of a third party (if required).
- An organization has developed a computer-based information processing system and wants to get it thoroughly tested by an independent organization. Activities will include testing and interfacing between the organizations.

These examples barely scratch the surface of the breadth of software projects — and new project types keep coming in. In all cases, however, the projects concern software, but the tasks, activities, and therefore the work in each of the projects are vastly different.

CLASSIFICATIONS OF SOFTWARE PROJECTS

Software projects may be classified in multiple ways (Figure 1.1). For example, software projects may be classified as:

- Software development life cycle (SDLC) projects
  - Full life cycle projects
  - Partial life cycle projects
- Approach-driven software development projects
  - "Fresh" development (creating the entire software from "scratch")
  - COTS product customization/implementation
  - Porting
  - Migration
  - Conversion of existing software to meet changed conditions such as Y2K and Euro conversion

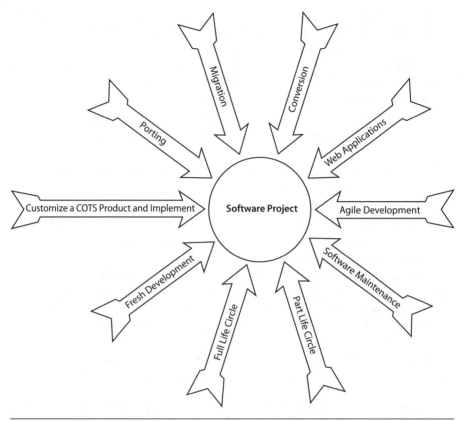

Figure 1.1. Software project types.

- Maintenance projects
  - Defect repair
  - Functional expansion
  - Operational support
  - Fixing odd behavior
  - Software modification
- Web application projects
- Agile development projects

Let's now discuss each type of software project in greater detail.

Based on Software Development Life Cycle

Full life cycle projects. A full life cycle project is a project that traverses the entire arc of the methodology being used: starts at the beginning and ends at the end. One problem when discussing a full life cycle project is that there is no standardization concerning what constitutes a software development life cycle (SDLC). Generally agreed is that user requirements analysis, software requirements analysis, software design, construction, and testing (regardless of what they are called) are parts of a SDLC. Some of the components of an SDLC that remain in question include:

- A feasibility study determining whether the project is worthwhile
- Special testing that is beyond unit testing, integration testing, system testing, and acceptance testing
- Implementation, including installation of hardware, system software, application software, etc.
- Software commissioning, including creating master data files, user training, pilot runs, parallel runs, etc.

In many instances, when the end product is used within the same organization, these four components are considered part of an SDLC. Alternately, in other circumstances, these components are excluded for organizations that specialize in software development and/or develop software for use by a different organization (unless contractually included or part of a software as a service architecture).

In this book, we exclude these four components. We assume that a full life cycle project is one that starts with user requirements and ends with the delivery of software. Therefore, all post-delivery activities and pre-user requirement activities are not considered to be within the scope of this book.

Partial life cycle projects. Partial life cycle projects are those that include only a portion of the SDLC. In partial life cycle projects, any number of permutations could occur, including:

- Testing projects in which the scope of the work involves conducting the specified or necessary software tests on the software product to certify the product (Unit testing and code walk-through are normally *not* included in this type of project.)
- Independent verification and validation (IV&V) projects in which projects go beyond mere testing, including code walk-through and other forms of validation to determine the efficiency of coding
- A project divided between two or more vendors based on the specialty to derive the advantages of best practices developed through specialization which can lead to defining the project by phase or by combination of phases, such as:
  - Requirements analysis
  - Design
  - Software construction
  - Testing

Approach Driven

Fresh or new software development projects. Fresh or new software development projects are identical to full life cycle development projects previously discussed.

COTS product customization/implementation projects. Numerous popular COTS products are available in the marketplace. Examples include the implementation of ERP (enterprise resource planning software, e.g., by SAP and PeopleSoft), CRM (customer relationship management), SCM (supply chain management), EAI (enterprise applications integration), and data warehousing software. Typical phases in these projects include:

1. Current system study: a review of the present system
2. Gap analysis: a comparison of the current system to the COTS product
3. Customization report: a discussion of the desired levels of customization of the system
4. Statement of work: definition of the required customization of the COTS product
5. Design: how the software will accomplish the task
6. Construction and integration
7. Testing
8. Custom code integration: integration of the code bases (in some cases it can include building a layer over the COTS product and integration of custom developed code into the source code of the COTS product)
9. COTS source code modification (rare)
10. Implementation
11. Training: instruction of users (all classes required) in usage of the system, troubleshooting, and operations and maintenance of the system
12. Transition of the system

Many variations of these phases are also possible for COTS projects.

Porting. Porting projects deal with moving software from one hardware platform to another hardware platform. Porting projects can include:

- Changes in programming language
- Differences between implementations
- Manual intervention to make the existing software work on new hardware without issues

Project execution work in a porting project involves:

1. Documenting the differences between the two versions of the programming languages
2. Developing a software tool to make corrections in the code based on the details mentioned above (Sometimes, vendors of the programming language supply this type of tool.)
3. Execution of the software porting tool to make all possible corrections
4. Manual correction to make any specific corrections needed
5. Conducting the specified software tests
6. Modifications to the software engineering documents required to reflect the changes made in the software
7. Conducting acceptance testing
8. Delivery of the software

Migration. Oftentimes, new versions of programming languages and databases are released. For example, Visual Basic has gone through many versions: from version 1 to 6 and then the release of the next set as 2003, 2005, and 2008. Similarly, Oracle has gone through upgrades: up to version 11. Operating systems have also been upgraded. For example, Microsoft has had many upgrades including MS-DOS, Windows, 2 and 3, and then 95, 98, 2000, XP, Vista, and now Windows 7. When upgrades are released, upgrading software may become necessary:

- To take advantage of new features and facilities provided in the newly released version
- Because an older version is no longer available when additional hardware or system software is installed or the existing software does not function well on the new software (In these days of multitier Web-based software architectures, an upgrade of any tier may necessitate migration!)
- Because limitations existing in an older version are removed in the new release and the existing software needs to be upgraded to remove the limitations

Upgrades are typically due to the ever-changing environment and the increasing needs of an organization. Of course, if the configuration of hardware and software remains exactly same, and the existing software is meeting the user's needs, the software would not need to be upgraded. A new version, however, could contain additional features and facilities that are totally absent in an older version. Therefore, a software tool cannot be used to make the changes that are necessary to port the software. To take advantage of new facilities and features available in the newer version, manual changes are typically required and involve:

1. Studying the new version
2. Deciding which new features are desirable and need to be implemented
3. Developing a functional expansion design document detailing the new features being implemented in the existing software
4. Running and upgrading the software (if an upgrade tool is provided by the vendor)
5. Implementing the functional expansion design in the software coding and incorporating necessary software changes (may also include correcting the existing code)
6. Conducting all the tests necessary to ensure that the software delivers all the functionality it was supposed to before migration and all the functionality that is designed for the new software
7. Conducting acceptance testing and delivering the software
8. Data migration involving (sometimes the project scope may include data migration):
   - Mapping the old database schema to the new database schema
   - Developing software/locating tools provided with the new database (if any) to migrate data from the old database to the new database
   - Running the tools to migrate data from the old database to the new database
   - Arranging for data entry in the new database for those fields that are absent in the old database, but present in the new database
   - Testing the database for known cases using the software, comparing the results with the desired results, and making necessary changes so that the new database is correct
   - Integrating the database with the software

Specific migration projects may have different activities from the activities described above.

Note: Porting and migration projects are similar. There is no strict distinction between the two. Therefore, these two terms are sometimes used interchangeably.

Conversion. Year 2000 (Y2K) and Euro conversion projects are excellent examples of conversion projects. Using a Y2K project as example, the work includes verifying all programs for code limitations and then making any necessary modifications. Typical activities in a conversion project include:

1. Studying the existing software and specifications of the necessary conversion

2. Preparing a conversion guidelines document detailing the procedure for incorporating the required modifications in the software
3. Developing a tool (if feasible) to automatically incorporate the modifications in the software
4. Running the tools or hand coding the changes
5. Performing a manual walk-through of each program to locate the remaining required modifications and implementing them
6. Conducting unit testing (and other tests as specified or as necessary)
7. Conducting acceptance testing
8. Delivering the software

In Euro conversion projects, some countries that did not make use of decimals in their financial software had to incorporate decimals as well as provide for the use of the Euro symbol.

Maintenance

Software maintenance projects are major money makers for software development organizations that are dependent on outsourcing. We need, however, to relax the specific beginning and ending requirements to call software maintenance a *project*. In a software maintenance project, generally there is a contract between the parties to take care of a specific application for a given period of time, e.g., 1 or 2 years, but a contract can be extended as long as both parties remain satisfied with each other's performance or as long as the application is in commission. An overall contract would specify:

- Billing rates
- Mode of requesting work
- Service level agreement (SLA) specifying the priorities and turn-around times
- Persons authorized to initiate/authorize work requests, accept deliveries, give clarifications
- Escalation mechanisms
- Billing cycles and payment schedules

This list could go on forever, depending on the specific needs and the "pain" of the organizations.

Normally, a maintenance work request (MWR) triggers software maintenance work. An MWR can be known by other terms, depending on the organization:

- Program modification request (PMR)
- Program change request (PCR)
- Defect report
- Software change request

Again, this list can also go on forever.

Contractually, an MWR is expected to have proper authorizations and to have them in advance. However, for an immediate need, a telephone call, a fax, or an email can also be used and later regularized through raising an MWR, i.e., post-facto (although frowned upon as potentially leading to loss of control).

Work included in a software maintenance project is classified into five types: defect fixing, operational support, fixing odd behavior, software modification, and functional enhancement.

Defect repair. Defect fixing work involves fixing a reported defect. A defect may be classified as:

- Critical (a "show-stopper")
- Major (hinders smooth functioning of work)
- Minor (mostly a nuisance; work is not affected)

Typically, defect fixing has an associated SLA in which the turnaround time for each class of defect, based on priority, is defined (i.e., the time between when a defect is reported until the time it is fixed, the regression test is completed, and the software is handed over to production). Sometimes, the turnaround time can be as little as hours or minutes, depending on the application and the needs of the organization. Normally, the maximum turnaround time for fixing a defect would be about 2 days. In a defect-fixing scenario, follow-up and progress reporting are frequent and close together. Generally, the steps in fixing a defect include:

1. Studying the defect report
2. Replicating the defect scenario in a development environment
3. Studying the code
4. Locating the defect
5. Fixing the defect, conforming to code change guidelines
6. Arranging for peer review and implementing feedback (if any)
7. Arranging for independent regression testing and implementing feedback (if any)
8. Delivering the fixed code to production for implementation in the production system
9. Closing the request

Functional expansion. When additional functionality is required in existing software, functional enhancement is the tool to achieve it. Functional enhancement work is generally of longer duration and may range from a calendar week upward. Work included in functional enhancement includes:

- Adding a new screen or report
- Adding additional processing functionality (e.g., quarterly/half yearly/ yearly processing)

- Adding a new module in the software
- Integrating with another software
- Building interfaces with other software
- Adding new hardware and building an interface to the new hardware in the existing software

Functional expansion generally fits the full SDLC model in which the project leverages the full software engineering process and the project management process and can be treated as an independent project if the duration is sufficiently long enough. The level of process rigor required is typically driven by risk. Each organization has a different definition of a project that should be treated as a functional enhancement project. For example, in one organization, a functional enhancement project is defined as "work with the duration of one person-month of effort or more," while in another, the definition of a functional enhancement project is "40 hours of effort."

Operational support. Operational support is similar to defect fixing. Many times, operational support requires immediate attention. Activities under operational support include:

- Running periodic jobs (end of day/week/month)
- Taking backups
- Restoring from backups
- User management functionality (including creation, deletion, and suspending of user accounts and changing access privileges, etc.)
- Providing "hand-holding" assistance at a specific workstation
- Extracting data and producing an ad hoc report on an urgent basis
- Providing a temporary patch so that operations may continue
- Investigating operational complaints

Again, the list of activities is long and varied.

Fixing odd behavior. In large, complex software systems, and in systems that have been in existence for many years and have undergone software maintenance (e.g., defect fixes, software modifications, and functional expansions), random defects may often crop up under some circumstances, but not in others. These random defects are generally difficult to replicate in a development environment. One reason is because the defect occurs in the field and the person witnessing the defect does not note the chain of events that caused the defect. So until the defect becomes chronic, it might have been handled as an operational support activity and not have been recognized as defect. Such puzzling defects can be placed in the odd behavior category of software maintenance. Odd behavior can be caused by the application software or the system software, a client workstation or a virus, network security, or a combination of all of these. Diagnosing and correcting odd behavior issues may take longer than a week because correcting odd behavior is similar to conducting research. General steps in fixing odd behavior include:

1. Studying the odd behavior report
2. Trying to replicate the behavior scenario in a development environment
3. Studying the code
4. Listing all possible alternative reasons for the reported behavior
5. Reviewing the code for each alternative for possible opportunities for improvement
6. Iterating/eliminating all causes, one by one
7. Fixing all possible opportunities for code improvement
8. Arranging for peer review
9. Arranging for independent regression testing
10. Delivering the software to production for implementation of improved code in the production system
11. Waiting for another report of the identical odd behavior and repeating all the above steps.
12. Keeping the request open through a period of observation

Software modification. Software modification work is the bulk of software maintenance in most organizations. Modification of working software is necessitated due to:

- Changes in requirements mainly due to changed conditions occurring over a period of time
- Changes in business processing logic
- Convenience for users
- Changes in statutory requirements

Often, modifications include changes to reports, changes to screens by moving around data fields, adding or deleting a data field or two, or some other small enhancement. Steps in the process of software modification include:

1. Studying the software modification request
2. Analyzing the existing software to identify components that require modification
3. Preparing a design modification document and obtaining approval from appropriate executives
4. Implementing the approved design modification in the code
5. Arranging for peer review of the modified code

6. Arranging for independent functional testing of the modified functionality — to ensure that it conforms to the approved design document — and implementing feedback (if any)
7. Arranging for independent regression testing and implementing feedback (if any)
8. Delivering the modified artifact to production for implementation in the production system
9. Closing the request

Web Application

Web projects refer to Web-based application development projects. Web projects differ from other projects because they have more than two tiers:

- Presentation tier
- Database server tier
- Application server tier
- Web server tier
- Security server

A Web application consists of:

- HTML pages that include graphics to enhance the "look and feel" of the Web pages
- Backend programs for data manipulation
- Middleware programs for application server or rules engines
- Middleware programs for security management
- Other application-specific programs

Another notable feature of Web applications is that backend programming and middleware programming may be in different programming languages and may require persons with different skill sets, even for the same project. Another request is for independence from databases and Web browsers, which necessitates coding routines that are not oriented toward functionality. Additionally, a Web application needs to be developed so that it facilitates an easy change of code. Environmental changes that have nothing to do with the organization, e.g., a new security threat, the release of a new browser, or the upgrade of an existing browser, etc., can also trigger software maintenance in a Web application — even though the functionality remains unaltered. Web-based and client server projects have a very similar profile.

Agile Development

Agile software development refers to a group of software development methodologies based on iterative development, in which requirements and solutions evolve through collaboration between self-organizing, cross-functional teams. (Agile project management is discussed at length in Chapter 11.)

CONCLUSION

Software projects are basically projects with a definite beginning and a definite ending, except that the final end product delivered is not physical. Software projects come in various types and sizes. Product maintenance in software is also treated as a project — unlike physical product maintenance. This chapter defines software projects as well as enumerates the different types of projects, laying a foundation for better assimilation of the science and art of software project management. Subsequent chapters will deal with the subject of software project management, building on this foundation.

2

APPROACHES TO SOFTWARE PROJECT MANAGEMENT

Software *project execution* has two components, namely, software engineering and management. *Software engineering* consists of all of the technical activities that are performed to build the project deliverable (the "just build it" activities). Software engineering deals with constructing the components, integrating them, verifying them, validating them, and finally combining all of the components into a product and convincing the customer to accept delivery of it. *Management* facilitates software engineering so that the project deliverable is completed on time, efficiently and effectively, and without defects.

ALIGNMENT OF SOFTWARE ENGINEERING METHODOLOGY WITH PROJECT MANAGEMENT METHODOLOGY

There are two general schools of thought about the linkage of the software engineering and management methodologies: tightly coupled and loosely coupled.

   Tightly coupled. One school of thought maintains that both of the methodologies are *tightly coupled* and that management is *completely dependent* on the software engineering methodology adopted for building the project deliverable. Therefore, project management needs to be *tightly interlaced* with software engineering.

Note: In some software engineering methodologies, such as agile methods, the distinction between software engineering and project management is somewhat blurred. In this situation, the argument is that the SPM or software project manager acts as a coach because the primary responsibility of an SPM is to be the voice of the people and a leader rather than a director.

Loosely coupled. In the other school of thought, the two aspects of software engineering and management are *loosely coupled*, but they do *influence* each other. Therefore, each aspect needs some amount of *tailoring* to suit the other. Additionally, in this school of thought, project management is considered to have multiple objectives, with the primary objective being to build the deliverable. Other objectives include management of the schedule, productivity, quality, resources, morale, customers, and profit. In the loosely coupled school of thought, an SPM is to be a manager first and to be aware of the software engineering methodology second.

Briefly, software engineering methodologies include waterfall, incremental, spiral, object-oriented, use case-based (unified modeling language), and agile methods of various types. These methodologies are also commonly referred to as SDLCs (software development life cycles). Agile methods include extreme programming (XP), scrum, clear case, feature-driven development, test-driven development, dynamic systems development, rational unified process (RUP, the agile version), adaptive software development, and pragmatic programming. Agile methods, with the exception of RUP, encourage only the development of the minimal required documentation associated with the software's development. RUP, however, is an exception because RUP is a detailed software engineering process that includes levels of documentation that are similar to other types of methods.

The alignment of the project management methodology to the software development methodology is driven by a number of factors, such as organizational size and the form of software engineering used on a particular project. For example, in a small organization in which the owner is a technical person who is actively involved in project activities, the management methodology can *completely align* with the software engineering methodology. In other cases, e.g., when types of projects and project management styles are more varied, using disparate software engineering methodologies, then aligning the project management methodology completely with the software engineering methodology, is problematic.

A *completely aligned* project management methodology is suitable for smaller, more homogenous organizations, while less homogenous organizations should have a project management methodology that is *decoupled* from the software engineering methodology of the project. Because the methodology of software engineering used on a project has an impact on project management, each project will need to have the management methodology tailored to some extent to align with the software engineering methodology.

THE AD HOC METHODS-BASED APPROACH

By definition, ad hoc methods are not documented and are dependent on the involved parties. In an ad hoc method approach, a software project manager (SPM) is given almost absolute control within a general policy framework that tends to be rather flexible. In organizations that allow ad hoc methods, management typically dictates policy and then modifies the policy as necessary or when convenient. In this situation, often the management style also reflects the personality of the leader of the organization. Management driven by the personality of the leader is classically referred to as "hero-driven" management. In organizations with hero-driven management, success is more luck than process supported.

Advantages of the ad hoc methods approach are that it:

- Fits a dynamic environment
- Allows the leader to have absolute control
- Is perceived to allow very fast response to environmental changes
- Can be the least costly, and the most profitable, methodology (with a well-seasoned SPM *and* if nothing surprising happens)
- Is perfect for pinning the blame for failure on one person (Always have your CV ready!)
- Reduces process overhead activities to nearly zero (e.g., process definition, maintenance groups, measurement, and analysis)
- Permits the principle of "unity of command" to be implemented (can be a great motivator for people involved in a project)
- Leads to a sense of "heroism" in management styles

Disadvantages of the ad hoc methods approach are that it:

- Creates uncertainty in the workplace
- Fosters a leader-centric environment rather than an environment driven by organizational and project goals
- Centralizes authority: lose the leader, lose the project
- Results in outcomes being unpredictable (because they are person-driven)
- Focuses on people monitoring rather than on overall project monitoring
- Causes organizational bandwidth (the capability of the organization to handle multiple projects concurrently) to be dependent on a leader's capacity (to manage multiple projects simultaneously, work long hours, etc.)
- Causes growth in an organization to be limited by the capacity of an SPM

- Leads to deterioration of morale in the workplace due to the encouragement of an undesirable, ego-driven environment (e.g., encourages an increase of self-serving sycophants)
- Hinders (or makes impossible) the development of leaders from within the organization (employees work in their own "cocoons")
- Hastens the inevitability of failure of human endeavors

All in all, the ad hoc method approach might produce some grand successes, but these successes are not sustainable. Because of the inevitability of failure in human endeavors, the impact on the organization can be severe: failure cripples an organization — from which it may not recover. Despite the risks, however, ad hoc approaches to software project management continue to be adopted by a significant number of organizations.

THE PROCESS-DRIVEN APPROACH

Organizations using a process-driven approach are characterized by having documented processes for all activities. Individuals must also be knowledgeable in the processes that concern them to be effective and efficient.

An organization that adopts a process-driven approach to software project management recognizes that the onus is on the organization *as well as* the individual SPM for ensuring continued project successes. The organization facilitates the execution of projects by providing the processes, the tools, a knowledge repository, the training, and expert assistance as needed to help the SPM(s). In other words, the organization's infrastructure enables successful execution of projects by the SPM. In addition to facilitation, the organization also has the responsibility of project oversight, monitoring, measurement, and benchmarking and effecting improvements in processes, tools, and the knowledge repository to continuously keep the organization well honed.

Each SPM is responsible for executing projects while diligently conforming to defined processes provided by the organization. SPMs also are responsible for providing feedback, suggestions, and support for the organizational initiatives in continuous improvement of processes, tools, and the knowledge repository.

In a process-driven organization, the organization and the SPM work in a close-knit manner, complimenting each other's efforts. The goal of the process-driven approach is to achieve uniformity across the organization in project execution regardless of the SPM involved. An often-mentioned benefit of the process-driven approach is that it enables the free movement of people from project to project with no discernable impact on project execution.

Advantages of a process-driven approach to software project management include:

- Minimizes the person-dependency of project management
- Enables a beginner in project management to perform like an expert and an expert to excel
- Facilitates the "plowing back" of experience gained from project execution into the process (As a result, every project execution enriches the process.)
- Equips everyone with the best practices in the process culled from project execution.
- Monitors projects rather than people
- Involves the organization in project execution and organizational expertise, not only from the process, but also from senior executives whose considerable experience influences project execution and supports its continued success
- Provides uniformity of project execution across the organization, irrespective of the people involved in the project, which leads to organizational maturity
- Facilitates measurement, resulting in fair performance appraisals, which makes possible real morale improvement in an organization (Having measurements also facilitates benchmarking the organizational performance with similar organizations and enables improvement thereof.)
- Builds the basis for predictability in project execution
- Enables all-round participation; iteratively drives an organization toward excellence
- Promotes the recruitment and induction of new people into projects because process-driven processes facilitate raising newcomers' performances to acceptable levels quickly

All in all, a process-driven approach facilitates person-independence in project execution, while facilitating process improvement and moving toward uniformity in project execution across the organization — characteristics that tend to foster organizational excellence.

SO, WHAT *IS* THE RIGHT APPROACH?

The field of software development is characterized more by diversity than by homogeneity. Therefore, attempting to prescribe one "right" approach is neither feasible nor appropriate. Although this book deals with software project management from the viewpoint of an organizational approach to software project management that utilizes a process-driven approach, we will briefly describe the characteristics of the ad hoc approach.

The Ad Hoc Approach

An ad hoc approach will serve well organizations in which:

- The organization is small.
- The number of SPMs in the organization is small (e.g., two or three). Having a few SPMs facilitates resolution of differences between the methodologies adopted by the SPMs through progress-monitoring meetings. Small organizations do not need to have a set of documented project references. The senior manager can ensure uniformity through personal intervention and act as the resolution mechanism when there are differences of opinion.
- The number of concurrent projects is five or less. Having a small number of projects also makes resolution of differences in project execution easier.

Most organizations that evolve in an organic manner start small, typically beginning with an ad hoc approach to software project management. As the organization grows and takes on more projects, the workload increases, putting pressure on the human resources. As this pressure on the human resources builds up, two things can happen: the organization buckles under the pressure and moves toward stagnation, failure, and closure or the organization moves toward a process-driven approach.

The Process-Driven Approach

When an organization embraces a process-driven approach, it first adopts a process improvement philosophy and the development of processes to cover project management. Then the organization moves on to address additional organizational areas and movement toward a more mature process — which would seem to be a natural progression. However, embracing a process-driven approach proactively when an organization is at the "take-off" stage is better than having to be forced to do so by the complexity created from the sheer volume of work.

But Is a Process-Driven Approach the Right Choice?

Some organizational activities are already process-driven. For example, in almost every country, through statutes, financial accounting is the first activity to adopt a rigorous process, especially in companies or organizations that handle funds from the public. Strict internal controls and external verification through audits are also mandatory. In addition to auditors, other statutory groups act as "watchdogs" over these organizations.

Human resources (HR) departments are often the next area that adopts a process-driven approach. The need for a process-driven approach in HR departments, however, results from the need to ensure *fairness* to candidates approaching the organization for employment and to ensure that the right human resources are supplied within the organization. Additionally, the unionization of workers as well as other statutes enacted to ensure fair working/hiring conditions increase pressure on organizations to adopt a process-driven approach in their HR departments. In these two examples, each department has an objective of ensuring fairness, but their main objective is to deliver actual results.

In the project environment, however, the aspect of fairness in delivering results is not mandated by any statute. Thus adopting a process-driven approach for reasons of fairness is optional, which leads some organizations to disapprove of a process-driven approach. In these organizations, some even go so far as to say that *any* process-driven approach is a restriction of their freedom to act creatively. In organizations that do not practice process-driven management, but prefer ad hoc methods of project management, often heard are statements such as "results at any cost" and "by hook or by crook." Other statements that indicate an ad hoc project management approach are hearing a senior manager tell subordinates, "I do not know (or care) how you do it — but I want it by ...."

If all of the "heroic" types are curtailed, and a true factory approach replaces a project-oriented environment, when success is realized, all of the stakeholders are heroes, not just a few individuals! Continued success leads to the organization becoming "heroic" as well. As a result, all of the employees perceive that they are wearing the "crown of a hero" — something all organizations striving for excellence pursue. Organizational success belongs to its people. For example, employees of organizations such as IBM, Microsoft, GE, etc. often feel heroic, while employees at other less successful organizations have "chips on their shoulders" and often are jealous of these heroic organizations.

Conversely, an organization that adopts the ad hoc approach produces heroes by luck or chance, while a process-driven organization makes everyone in the organization a hero/heroine! An organization that adopts an ad hoc approach may survive on the heroics of its employees, but a process-driven organization runs like a well-oiled machine, without the necessity of wide-scale heroics by anyone.

From the beginning, however, software engineers have resisted any move toward adopting a process-driven approach. For example, the waterfall model was the first process-driven approach to software development, but in today's environment, more people continue to hate the waterfall model rather than to love it. As a result, many other approaches, namely, rapid application development (RAD), joint application development (JAD), incremental, and agile methods (e.g., XP, scrum), were developed to replace the waterfall methodology. Although methodologies come and go, and some are forgotten, interestingly the waterfall model is still in the mix.

Even today, strong resistance to the process-driven approach continues and numerous write-ups continue to extol the virtues of ad hoc approaches to project management. So our advocacy of the process-driven approach is fraught with the prospect of stiff resistance. Still, we believe that the process-driven approach is a means to assure project success — the first time and almost every time. We think the process-driven approach ensures organizational success in the short term as well as in the long term.

In a Process-Driven Approach: What Process and How Much?

Once we decide to adopt a process-driven approach, the next questions to address are what type of process should we adopt and how deeply should the process penetrate into organizational functioning?

When deciding about the type of process to use, there are two predominant, popular, process standard frameworks: ISO 9000 (of the International Organization for Standardization) and CMMI (Capability Maturity Model Integration of the SEI, the Software Engineering Institute of Carnegie Melon University). ISO covers the entire organization, while CMMI covers activities that are specifically relevant to software and hardware products. Both frameworks advocate a process-driven approach. The nuts and bolts may differ, but the main premise remains similar. Although, there are other frameworks, these two are predominant.

So, what does a process-driven approach contain? From a simple point of view, a process-driven approach consists of:

- Processes for carrying out the activities
- Agencies responsible for carrying out the activities
- Processes for ensuring that quality is built into the deliverables
- Agencies responsible for assuring quality in the deliverables
- Processes for defining and maintaining organizational processes
- Agencies responsible for defining and maintaining organizational processes
- Processes for measuring and analyzing the process performance
- Agencies responsible for measurement and analysis of process performance

In short, a process-driven approach contains *defined methods* for carrying out the work as well as the *checks and balances* necessary to ensure that the processes deliver results and that everyone adheres to the processes.

A simple framework for project management is comprised of project *acquisition*, *initiation*, *execution*, and *closure*. Once acquired, project processes and project management processes begin with project initiation followed by project execution and project closure. Thus, at the project level, there should be project management processes for:

- Project initiation
  1. Review and revision(s) of preliminary estimates
  2. Identification and acquisition of necessary resources
  3. Finalization of service level agreements (SLAs) between various stakeholders of the project
  4. Preparation of project plans
  5. Conducting induction training for team members
  6. Kickoff of project
- Project execution
  1. Work management
  2. Configuration management
  3. Quality management
  4. Productivity management
  5. Team management
  6. Customer management
  7. Measurement and analysis
  8. Project monitoring
  9. Reporting and escalation
  10. Project delivery
  11. User training
  12. Documentation
- Project closure
  1. Release of project resources
  2. Documentation of best and worst practices as well as lessons learned in the project
  3. Identification of reusable components and documentation of their design and usage
  4. Updating of the skills database
  5. Updating of the knowledge repository with lessons learned and best and worst practices
  6. Updating of the code library with reusable components
  7. Conducting the project postmortem
  8. Conducting a knowledge-sharing session
  9. Release of the software project manager (SPM)

In addition to project acquisition, initiation, execution, and closure, which are the core phases of project management, the organization also has a role in ensuring the success of projects; hence, project management should also have organizational-level processes for:

- Project acquisition
  1. RFP (request for proposal) scrutiny (a feasibility study in the case of internal projects)

    2. Cost estimation

    3. Proposal preparation and submission

    4. RFP follow up

    5. Obtaining the order (obtaining budget approvals in the case of internal projects)

- The PMO (project management office)
  1. Project initiation
     - Identification of software project manager (SPM)
     - Allocation of resources for the project
     - Finalization of SLAs (service level agreements) between various stakeholders of the project
     - Kickoff of project
  2. Project execution
     - Project monitoring
     - Exception reporting
     - Measurement and analysis at the organization level
  3. Project closure
     - Takeover of project records
     - Coordination of knowledge sharing
- Measurement and analysis
  1. Measurement procedures
  2. Analysis procedures
  3. Process capability determination procedures
  4. Metrics reporting procedures
- The training process
  1. Identification of organizational training needs
  2. Fulfilling skill gaps uncovered during training needs analysis
  3. Maintaining a skill database for all organizational human resources
  4. Maintaining a training material repository as part of the organizational knowledge repository
  5. Taking ownership for maintaining the organization at the cutting edge of the organization's chosen area of expertise
- The knowledge repository process
  1. Identifying components of the organizational knowledge repository
  2. Designing, building, and maintaining the organizational repository
  3. Periodically carrying out cleanup of the repository
- Process engineering group processes
  1. Defining and maintaining organizational processes
  2. Defining process and quality audit processes
  3. Defining roles and responsibilities

- Software engineering processes
  1. Requirements processes
  2. Software design processes
  3. Software construction processes
  4. Software testing processes

With the exception of the software engineering processes, all of these processes will be discussed in detail in subsequent chapters.

Briefly, software engineering processes describe the technical side of software development. There are several methodologies for software engineering; however, a detailed description of these methodologies is beyond the scope of this book. In subsequent chapters, however, we will discuss the *influence* that each of these methodologies exercises on software project management.

3

SOFTWARE PROJECT ACQUISITION

The first activity in software project management is the acquisition of a project. Project acquisition is an activity carried out primarily by a business acquisition team with the assistance of a technical team. (In smaller organizations, project acquisition can be conducted by a single person or a team, depending on the distribution of labor. Key to remember is that the tasks required to seek out and acquire the work must be accomplished by someone — whether by a single person or by a team is immaterial.) Deciding on the project to be undertaken is a very important strategic activity because the decision made will have a huge influence on the organization's financial health and profitability. Project acquisition should therefore be a *collaborative* activity between the business acquisition team, technical team, finance team, and senior management. The focus of senior management is from a strategic perspective.

Two typical project acquisition scenarios are acquisition from an *external client* and acquisition from an *internal source*. Each of these scenarios has a different workflow.

FROM AN EXTERNAL CLIENT

In a scenario in which a project is acquired from a prospective client (an *external* organization), the project is to be a revenue-generating device. Characteristics of a project from a prospective client include:

- The project will result in revenue for the acquiring organization from the external client.

- The software product resulting from execution of the project will be used or resold by the external organization.
- The external organization will impose stipulations on quality, schedule, and cost.
- End users will typically *not* be directly accessible to the software development team. (The development team interacts with the end users via a proxy.)

Project acquisition from a prospective client follows several steps:

1. The request for proposal
2. The proposal
   - Software estimation
   - Delivery commitments
   - Pricing the proposal
   - Preparing the proposal
3. Negotiation
4. Contract acceptance

These steps will now be explained in greater detail. The process of acquiring a project from an external customer is also depicted in Figure 3.1.

The Request for Proposal

Usually, project acquisition begins with an RFP (request for proposal), or alternately with an RFI (request for information), from a prospective client. An RFP is obtained from a prospective client by the organization's business acquisition team. (Because obtaining an RFP is a core marketing activity, obtaining an RFP is therefore not covered in this book.) The RFP document normally contains the following:

- Name of the prospective client and other details about the client
- Name of the project and other details about the project
- Contact details for the project coordinator of the prospective client
- Scope of the work and terms of reference
- Bidding details, including the format of the bid document (either a single-bid system, technical bid and financial bid in *one* document; or a two-bid system, technical bid and financial bid in *two* different documents and submitted separately); any requirements for a bank guarantee/earnest money deposit toward project execution warranty; etc.
- Procedure for evaluating bids that are received by the prospective client
- Important dates, including the date for requesting clarifications; the date for submission of bid; the date for awarding of the project; etc.

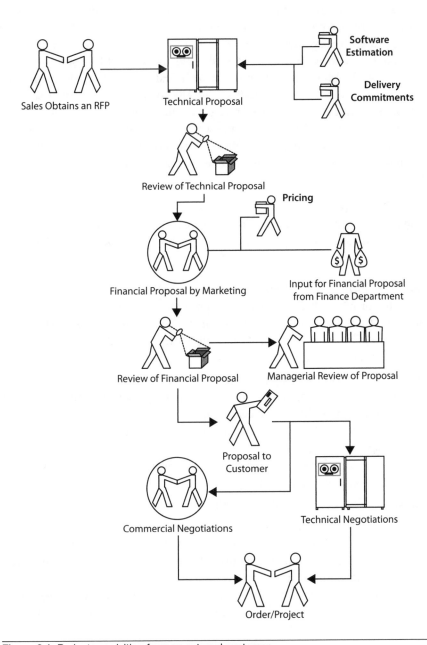

Figure 3.1. Project acquisition from an external customer.

Usually, the business acquisition team initially reviews an RFP to ensure that the information contained in the RFP is complete. Next, the RFP is passed on to the project management office (PMO) or to the head of the technical team responsible for delivery to clients. Then the RFP is assigned to a software project manager (SPM) for preparation of the technical proposal. To determine the feasibility of execution, the SPM reviews the RFP to ensure that areas describing the scope of work and the terms of reference and suggested technology, if any, are complete. Then the SPM prepares the software estimate for the project. Other components of the estimate (e.g., hardware, business processes, etc.) are handled by the appropriate project managers or management groups.

The Proposal

Arriving at the proposal includes *software estimation, delivery commitments, pricing the proposal*, and *preparing the proposal*, which will now be explained in more detail.

Software estimation. Software estimation is carried out at this point to set a price for the proposal. Estimators need to keep in mind that software estimation *assists* project pricing, but is *not the same as* project pricing. Project pricing is a commercial decision. (Pricing methods will be described later in this chapter.) Software estimation has four dimensions:

- Estimation of the *size* of the software product to be produced
- Estimation of the *effort* in person hours or person days that will be required to develop the specified software product
- Estimation of the *cost* that will need to be expended to execute the project
- Estimation of the *duration* (schedule) in calendar days or months that are necessary to execute the project

At this stage, the purpose of software estimation is to:

- Assist in the pricing decision (because the software development effort is a major cost component in the price of the project)
- Estimate the resources required to execute the project (human, machine, money, and duration)
- Assist the decision makers in determining whether the organization has adequate bandwidth in terms of resources to execute the project as detailed in the RFP
- Assist the decision makers in making delivery commitments to the prospective client

Many methods are used to develop an estimate, ranging from parametric models to relational estimates. Usually, the SPM carries out the software estimation based on the organization's software estimation process. The estimates are then subjected to peer and managerial reviews. After implementing the review feedback, if any, and closing the review reports, the SPM submits the software estimate directly to the requestor or makes it a part of the technical proposal. (Software estimation is an independent subject and hence is not covered in this book. A suggested source of additional information on this topic is *Software Estimation — Best Practices, Tools and Techniques* by Chemuturi.[1])

Delivery commitments. Delivery commitments are usually a part of a technical proposal, but as in project pricing, keep in mind that delivery commitments are also a commercial decision. Delivery commitments depend on:

- The prospective client's requirements/urgency
- The competition (which might offer shorter delivery commitments)
- The possibility of a future project that will require the release of resources from this project
- Any other specific reason

Note: The schedule should not be influenced by the above considerations. If a shorter schedule is committed to by the decision makers, explore ways to meet the commitment: either by the infusion of more resources or more expert resources, or by subcontracting a part of the project, or by the project team taking on more stress.

Pricing the proposal. Pricing is a complex interaction of various factors, including commercial considerations, the perceived necessity/desirability of acquiring the project, the opportunity at hand, and pricing models — considerations which dictate pricing for a project. Pricing strategies include:

- *Order book position*: If an organization's order book is empty (no ongoing projects at the present or none in the near future), the organization might price a project low, so that at least the project will pay the organization's variable costs. Conversely, if the organization's order book is full (at the present as well as in the near future) and it does not wish to expand its capacity, the organization might price a project high.
- *Necessity to obtain an order*: Sometimes winning a particular order is critical for reasons other than just the need to fill the order queue. In this situation, an organization might price a project just low enough to win the bid. Reasons for this scenario include:
  - The project will open up avenues of future business.

- The project will provide significant visibility.
- The project will generate significant free publicity.
- The project will provide an opportunity to train a number of the organization's resources (personnel) in a cutting-edge technology, from which the organization can win future orders at higher margins.
- The project will result in the organization gaining a foothold in a new and lucrative market.

- *Desirability of winning the order*: Sometimes an organization does not desire to obtain the order, but must pursue a particular client's business for "political" reasons. In this situation, one strategy is to price the project so high that the organization is certain *not* to win the bid. Reasons for this scenario include:
  - The organization does not have the technology to execute the order.
  - The organization does not wish to do business with the client (perhaps the client is slow to pay or otherwise has a bad reputation), but there is a strong business reason to answer the RFP.
  - The project involves obsolete technology or technology that is becoming obsolete, causing the organization's resources to be disinterested in the project or unwilling to work on it.

- *Stiff competition in the field*: The organization might price a project with a bare minimum profit margin just to compete with other organizations.

- *Monopolistic:* Sometimes an organization is in the unique position of being the only supplier of a product or service. In this situation, the organization exploits (skims) the opportunity and gets as much revenue from the order as possible. In this situation, pricing is focused on maximizing the return from the project.

- *Oligopolistic:* An organization might collaborate with other vendors in the market to establish one price for a product or service that is profitable for all of the vendors involved. (The authors note that this strategy is of questionable legality, especially in North America and Europe, but oligopolistic activity does occur; therefore, it is included for completeness.)

- *Repeat orders.* The organization offers a service to an existing customer at a price that is fair to both the organization and the customer.

- *New market opportunity.* If an order facilitates entry into a new market — either geographical- or domain-based — the organization will establish pricing in a manner that maximizes its chances of getting the order.

Let's now look at the pricing models that are applicable to software projects. Pricing models are a means of implementing a pricing strategy. Any strategy can leverage one or more pricing models. Some popular pricing models that are available to free-to-price organizations (i.e., organizations not constrained by a government statute when setting prices or situations in which market forces set pricing) include:

- *Time and material pricing*: Time and material (T&M) pricing involves agreeing on an hourly rate for each category of human resources engaged in the project and then charging for these resources based on the actual time spent on the project. Time spent is assessed using time sheets that have been approved by the client. (T&M pricing also includes other expenses. For example, travel expenses incurred by human resources on activities that have been approved by the client are charged at the actual cost incurred by the human resources.) Although economic pressure appears to be moving more contracts to a *fixed-price* model, the T&M model is still in existence.

- *Cost plus*: Cost plus is a typical model in project pricing. In cost plus pricing, an organization accounts for all of the costs and then adds a reasonable profit to the final cost. The costs of the vendor are transparent to the purchaser. The cost plus pricing model is commonly adopted between partners who have a strong, long-standing bond. For the most part, cost plus pricing is a fixed-price model, sometimes with a provision for cost escalation for changes that are requested and approved by the client.

- *Opportunity*: In the opportunity pricing model, pricing depends on the opportunity presented by a potential purchaser. If the purchaser has no choice but to buy from a single selling organization, the organization can charge top dollar. Conversely, if there is too much competition, the organization might charge a lower price. The organization might even price a project at a loss if a prestigious project would provide significant publicity to the organization. Within the opportunity pricing model are two variants:
  - *Penetration*: A new entrant into a market adopts penetration pricing in a market that is already overflowing with existing providers. To gain a foothold in such a market, a new entrant charges lower prices as an incentive to motivate purchasers to entrust the project to the new entrant. Sometimes the penetration pricing model is known as *introductory pricing*.
  - *Skimming*: Skimming or high-margin pricing is used by an organization that has an advantage, such as being an "early bird" in an emerging market. The organization charges higher prices before

their competition enters the market; then, once competition is firmly established, the organization lowers prices.

- *Going rate*: The going rate pricing model is adopted by organizations in fields in which there is abundant competition and the price for a particular product is well known to purchasers. The going rate pricing model entails pricing a product (or service) at a price that is similar to the competition. (T&M pricing is typically dictated by the going rate for the cost of human resources.)

- *Monopolistic*: Monopolistic pricing is a variant of going rate pricing. In the monopolistic model, the seller promotes a unique feature of its product and thus prices the product higher or lower than the going rate. Monopolistic pricing is frequently used when a two-bid system (technical bid and financial bid) is adopted by a purchaser.

- *Oligopolistic*: The oligopolistic pricing model is used in a market that has a limited number of suppliers. Suppliers collaborate (sometimes by forming an association) to establish a fixed price for a product and then to enforce that price — the price is the same from all suppliers. (*Note*: This strategy is of questionable legality, especially in North America and Europe, but oligopolistic pricing activity does occur and therefore is included for completeness.)

- *Transfer*: The transfer pricing model is adopted by two departments that are within the same organization. In this scenario, only the *actual cost* is transferred from one department to another. Transfer pricing is also known as a *chargeback* model.

- *Loss leader*: Loss leader pricing is adopted by organizations that are trying to lure clients away from their current vendors. In the loss leader pricing model, an organization provides a product (or service) at a *loss* to a customer, speculating that as a result of the pricing strategy, increased additional business from this customer will offset the losses. Alternatively, an organization may offer free publicity or a prestigious status to new buyers, which might result in new business from other potential buyers.

Because an RFP presents a project opportunity for an organization, a business acquisition team considers the opportunity from a business perspective and then decides how best to utilize the opportunity. Remember from an earlier discussion that pricing and estimation are two separate scenarios that are generally handled by two different areas in an organization.

Although every organization has its own pattern of implementation, project pricing typically follows a stepwise process:

1. The *technical team* prepares the software estimates (software size, software development effort, and software development schedule) and presents them to the business acquisition team.
2. The *business acquisition team* prepares the cost estimation and presents it to the finance team.
3. The *finance team* suggests a floor price to the marketing team, below which the project will not be attractive financially.
4. The *business acquisition team* coordinates pricing with *senior management* (in some cases there might be a pricing committee) and determines:
   - The price to be offered to the potential client
   - The negotiation margin (if negotiations are foreseen)

The price for a project proposal, therefore, is set by an organization in a *collaborative, step-by-step* manner (with, of course, organization-specific changes in the methodology). Larger organizations have a higher degree of formality, with committees, meetings, and approvals, whereas smaller organizations have a lower degree of formality, engaging in consultations with the concerned agencies. Although the steps listed above are a simplification of the process used in large organizations, by and large they are the major steps taken to determine the project price.

Preparing the proposal. The business acquisition team uses the approved price and then prepares the proposal in the required format (either the format of the organization or the format specified by the prospective client), arranges for peer review and managerial review, and obtains formal approval for the proposal document. The approved proposal document is then submitted to the prospective client. The business acquisition team follows up with the prospective client until either the project is acquired or is lost to a competitor.

A proposal is usually a multipage document that has two separate parts (even if both documents are submitted in the same envelope): the technical proposal and the financial proposal.

A technical proposal. A typical technical proposal usually contains the following sections:
- *Title page*: Include a title page containing the name of the project, revision history, the date of the proposal, and the prospective client's name.
- *Contents*: List the contents of the proposal.
- *Introduction*: Include information about the organization submitting the proposal and the context of the proposal.

- *Scope of work*: Include a detailed scope of the work as given in the RFP; any subsequent clarifications issued by the prospective client; and any additional information that the organization may wish to provide.
- *Approach and methodology*: Describe the proposed execution of the project; the methodology to be adopted for executing the project; and the project management methodology.
- *Deliverables*: List the deliverables to the client that are expected from the project.
- *Approvals required from the client*: List the artifacts that need to be approved by the client during project execution, including the timeline required for approvals.
- *Schedule for project execution*: Depending on specifications from the prospective client or the organization's standards, a schedule can range from a detailed structure that mimics the project to a list of major milestones with dates (or the number of calendar days from the commencement of the project).
- *Software estimation*: When mandated by the client, include the software size, development effort, development cost, and a detailed schedule. (Software estimates are *not* submitted with a technical proposal unless they are mandated by an RFP.)
- *Inclusions*: Describe all of the software engineering activities that are proposed to be performed to derive the specified deliverable.
- *Exclusions*: List all of the software engineering activities *not* proposed to be performed during the project execution. Also list any software components that are *not* being included in the deliverables.
- *Responsibilities*: List responsibilities of the vendor and the vendee for all major activities proposed to be carried out during project execution. The responsibility for each activity can be a *primary* responsibility for one party and a *secondary* responsibility for the other party or responsibility can be primary for both parties.

A *financial proposal*. A typical financial proposal usually contains the following sections:

- *Fee*: State the fee for the project.
- *Fee exclusions*: List items that are *not* included in the proposal and items that are *not* included in the project fee (items such as travel, master data file creation, data migration, pilot runs, etc. that may not have been included in the proposal or the fee for the project).

- *Validity period*: State the period during which the fee offered will be maintained.

- *Payment terms*: Include any advance fees required; interim payment schedules that are based on period/milestone /delivery requirements; performance guarantees or retention holdbacks; and any penalties for delayed payments.

- *Intellectual property rights (IPR)*: For any deliverables, specify the IPR restrictions on all parties, including the software produced. IPR may rest with the client or with the developer. If a third party component is used, the specific IPR may rest with the party from which the component is procured. All of these aspects should be described in the proposal.

- *Force majeure clause*: Specify remedies for extreme conditions should they become a reality during the period of project execution (general strife, war, floods, earthquakes, etc.)

- *Software tools or components to be supplied by the client*: A project may require the use of specialized software tools, components, or system software. If the client is expected to supply such software or components, specify this requirement.

- *Facilities*: Should the vendor's staff need to work at the client's site, describe the logistics requirements for the workplace that are to be provided for the vendor's staff at the client's site. Specify what organization will be responsible for expenses that are incurred for reasons related to logistics.

- *Price escalation clause*: Costs may increase, especially for long-duration projects or software maintenance projects. Include an escalation clause that sets out the conditions on which a price escalation would be based; when the price escalation would be effected; and the mechanisms that would be used to fairly make a decision about a proposed price escalation.

- *Arbitration and jurisdiction*: Describe dispute resolution mechanisms so that if and when a dispute arises, all parties will understand how a dispute will be resolved, including the arbitration and legal processes. The arbitration/jurisdiction clause should include the conditions under which recourse to arbitration/legal actions may be taken. Additionally, arbitration/jurisdiction clauses typically include names of qualified arbitrators who may be approached to resolve a dispute and the courts of law that have jurisdiction to hear and award judgments.

- *Consequential liability*: Define the limits of the vendor's consequential liability (sometimes called *special damages*) should such liability become applicable.
- *Other*: Include any other items that are relevant to the financial aspects of the proposal.

Negotiation

In negotiating, the client's finance team, assisted by the client's technical team, conducts price negotiations with the vendor's business acquisition team. As in most negotiation situations, give-and-take occurs. For example, the vendor might offer to give some type of discount (price, scope, technical changes, etc.) or the client might place an order after making amendments that would include changes in scope and duration. (Decisions about the maximum amount of discount that can be offered, the minimum duration in which the project can be completed, etc. should be made by the vendor prior to conducting negotiations.) During the negotiation process, decisions are made "across the table" to clinch the deal.

Three familiar bidding scenarios are public bidding, private bidding, and a synthesis of the two. Each scenario has a different perspective:

- *Public bidding*: In a public bidding scenario, a prospective client posts an RFP on the Internet or in the press and invites bids from all organizations that meet the criteria contained in the RFP.
- *Private biding*: In a private bidding scenario, two options are possible:
  - An RFP is raised on multiple prequalified vendors.
  - An RFP is raised on only one prequalified vendor. (This scenario occurs when an established relationship exists between a client and a vendor.)
- *Synthesis biding*: In a synthesis bidding scenario, open solicitation is combined with the use of a strong core of favored/preferred vendors.

Public bidding. In a public bidding scenario, a two-bid system is usually used (a financial bid and a technical bid). Bids are evaluated based on the criteria specified in the RFP. Proposals are taken as "final." Usually no negotiations are conducted for the purposes of price or technical bargaining. (An exception in price bargaining would be in instances in which a client's budget has been overshot by all bidders. An exception in technical negotiations would be in situations in which no bidder has offered a complete technical solution.) In a public bidding scenario, technical proposals from all of the vendors are evaluated first to shortlist those vendors that fulfill all of the technical requirements and provide the best technical solution. Then, the financial bids from only the shortlisted vendors are considered. Usually, the lowest financial bid is selected from among the shortlisted vendors.

Private bidding. In a private bidding scenario, especially when raised on only one vendor, price negotiations are usually applied (whether for actual cost or functionality). In a private bidding scenario, because there is an existing relationship, more transparency is expected from each party (less is expected, however, from an external client). In multiple-bid scenarios, even though all of the vendors are prequalified, price negotiations are applied to get the lowest price or to get what is perceived to be the highest quality product. Sometimes the client expects a discount in return for their continued trust in the vendor. Therefore, arriving at a price, including the software size and effort, is derived through negotiation. The private bidding type of pricing tends to cause a business acquisition team to build a "buffer" into the price so that a discount expected by the client can be offered, but planned profitability is still retained.

Synthesis biding. No typical scenario exists for synthesis bidding. The scenario is rather ad hoc in nature. Synthesis bidding is similar to a private bidding scenario, but to obtain the best technical solution at the lowest possible price, new vendors are brought in to put pressure on existing vendors. The final winner of the project order is usually an existing vendor, although awarding a project in favor of a new vendor is not ruled out.

When negotiations have been successfully completed in an external project, the client places the order to execute the project with the selected vendor.

Contract Acceptance

Once the order to execute a project has been received from the client, and upon receipt of the order, the business acquisition team reviews the order to ensure:

1. Price, delivery date, and payment terms are in agreement with those specified in the order.
2. All terms and conditions agreed upon and those specified in the order are in agreement.
3. Any new conditions are inserted in the order.
4. The scope of work is as agreed.

If new concerns are raised, the business acquisition team may need to renegotiate with the client to resolve all contentious issues. In some cases, an order acknowledgment letter is given to the client as a final means of completing the deal. In disputes, the RFP, the proposal, the order, and the order acknowledgment are crucial legal documents. Hence, exercise extreme care when preparing these documents.

FROM AN INTERNAL CLIENT

In this section, *internal project* refers to two scenarios:

- An organization whose main business *is not* software development: The organization desires to computerize operations of one of its functional departments. The in-house software development department is to develop the necessary software.
- An organization whose main business *is* software development: The organization desires to computerize operations in one of its departments. The in-house software development team is to develop the necessary software.

In both of these scenarios, the common factor is that the software is intended for internal use within the *same* organization. The software might even be used by the software development team itself. The characteristics of an internal project include:

- The resultant software product is not for delivery to an outside organization.
- No direct revenue for the organization will result from this project.
- Project expenditures are treated as a cost to the organization.
- Expected benefits are reduced cost of operations, improved quality, reduced turnaround times, etc.
- End users of the developed software are within the same organization and therefore are accessible to the software development team.
- The project commences with a feasibility study and ends when the software is installed and "goes live" for use by the end users or the project is cancelled. (These types of projects typically go from a development mode to software maintenance mode.)

Expenditures for development of the software and computerization are normally (depending on the cost and applicable rules for capitalization in the locale) treated as capital expenditures and go through the organizational process for sanctioning a capital expenditure budget. Approval of a budget and allocation of funds for the project are usually considered to be sufficient permission for commencement of a project. Steps in acquiring a project from an internal source include:

1. Conducting the feasibility study
2. Preparing the proposal
   - Software estimation
   - Delivery commitments
   - Proposal preparation

3. Finalizing the proposal (from discussions with the end user department or other budgetary groups)

Each of these steps is now described in greater detail.

The Feasibility Study

A feasibility study is usually conducted by business analysts or systems analysts from the software development team. The analysts study the existing system, the documents, and the current process being used.

User requirements. In a feasibility study, the goal of the analysts is to elicit the user requirements for the new software product from the designated end users of the proposed system. Based on the user requirements, the study ascertains the technical feasibility of executing the project.

Technology requirements. The feasibility study determines the technology to be used, including the databases, the software development platform (such as the programming language, software development tools, Web server, application server, etc.), and the hardware and system software requirements. These requirements determine if any new hardware and system software needs to be procured.

Software development approach. The feasibility study determines the possible software development approach. For example, based on the user requirements, can a COTS (commercial off-the-shelf) product with customization be used or does the software need development from "scratch?"

Type of execution. The feasibility study specifies whether the project can be executed *in-house* or if it should be *outsourced*. Based on the requirements, if outsourcing is required, the analysts specify the extent/portion of work to be outsourced. For example, in some cases, a part of the software may need to be outsourced; yet at other times, the entire software needs to be outsourced. Creation of the master data files using data entry may also need to be outsourced.

Tangible and intangible benefits. The feasibility study also determines tangible and intangible benefits expected to accrue from the proposed project.

At this point, typically a "ballpark" estimate of the overall cost of the project has also been made. The estimate is comprised of:
- Cost of hardware and system software
- Cost of software development
- Cost of creating master data files or cost of data migration

- Cost of training resources in the new system and cost of change-management activities (activities that are necessary to change operations from the existing system to the new system)
- Any other relevant costs

A feasibility report containing the results of the feasibility study is prepared. A feasibility report usually contains the following sections:

- *Title page*: Provide revision and approval history.
- *Contents*: List the contents of the feasibility report.
- *Project preliminaries*: Provide the name of the project, departments affected, cost center, contact persons, etc.
- *The project*: Describe the project.
- *Probable benefits*: Describe the probable benefits expected from the project as well as the possible negative impacts of not implementing the project.
- *Cost estimates*: Provide the ballpark cost estimates for the project.
- *Proposed technology*: Describe the proposed technology and the reasons for selecting the technology over other competing technologies.
- *Implementation strategy*: Describe the project implementation strategy, including the need for outsourcing (if any), the amount of outsourcing, and the expected duration.
- *Appendices*: Include the following:
  - User requirements document
  - List of persons interviewed for eliciting requirements
  - List of documents referenced
  - Details of estimates
  - Analyses for arriving at probable benefits, technology proposed, etc.
  - Any other relevant material

The feasibility report is submitted to management (or to a capital expenditure approval committee) for consideration and for allocation of budget funds. The approving authority, be it senior management or the capital expenditure committee, considers all competing proposals for available funds for capital expenditure. Capital budgeting techniques such as return on investment (ROI), net present value, and internal rate of return, etc. are used to select and prioritize competing projects. The approving authority then grants (or denies) approval for the project based on the availability of allocable funds and the strategic needs of the organization. If approval for the project is received, the next step in an internal project is preparing the proposal.

Note: Prepare the proposal in line with the *approved* budget. Budget approval can be granted *in full* for an entire project as detailed in the feasibility report or for only *a part* of the project. When budget approval includes only the first few phases of a project, approval for the next phases is not considered until after completion of the sanctioned work.

Preparing the Proposal

Proposal preparation for an internal project is comprised of the software estimation and the delivery commitments for the sanctioned activities as contained in the revised budget. These activities are described in the section on acquisition of an external project; hence, the description of these activities is not repeated here.

The proposal for an internal project is subjected to a peer review and a managerial review and is then submitted for approval by the client — in this case, the head of the user department. For the organization, the proposal forms the basis for carrying out the work and making deliveries of the software product to the end user department. For the end user department, the proposal is used to plan activities to support execution of the project as well as to conduct the follow-up activities needed to effectively make use of the delivered software product.

Finalizing the Proposal

The proposal is discussed with the internal client to ensure that all of their requirements as approved in the budget are met and that the proposed expenditure and timelines meet their expectations. Any feedback received is implemented in the proposal. Once the proposal is approved by the internal client, the project is ready for execution.

Note: In internal projects, the emphasis is not on price, but rather on functionality, expenditures, and meeting required timelines. More, actually *maximum*, transparency is expected and demanded because both parties are from the same organization. Closer scrutiny of project details is also likely.

Some closing words. Whether a project is from an external client or from an internal source, project acquisition is a preliminary, prerequisite step in project execution. Once the project is acquired, the next step in project execution is project initiation. The next seven chapters will describe the initiation, planning, execution, execution control, change management, scheduling, and project closure phases of software project development.

REFERENCE

1. Chemuturi, Murali. *Software Estimation Best Practices, Tools & Techniques: a Complete Guide for Software Project Estimators* 2009. Ft. Lauderdale, FL: J. Ross Publishing.

4

SOFTWARE PROJECT INITIATION

INTRODUCTION

If asked to name one step that is crucial for the success of project execution, the answer would have to be a *well-executed software project initiation*. A software project that begins well has a much greater probability of being successful than a software project that begins poorly. Why is this statement true rather than merely being a truism? Because *beginning well* is far more than just being the most obvious best situation — *beginning well* is vitally important. Why? Because certain mistakes that are committed during the initiation of a project do not lend themselves to corrections as the project progresses.

A project that starts out on the "right foot" is well on its way to being successful! In fact, proper preparation for a project's execution "journey" is as important as the project's goal.

INITIATION ACTIVITIES

The software project initiation phase begins after an organization acquires a project from a client. The objectives of software project initiation ensure that:

- Ownership for project execution, project delivery, and customer acceptance is entrusted to a software project manager.

- The software project manager is provided with support commitments from the service departments in the organization.
- The project starts out on the "right foot."
- To ensure success, the experience of the organization is brought to bear on the project.

Ownership of the initiation activities is shared between the organization and the software project manager (SPM). Usually, an organization that is geared up for executing software development projects has a department or group that is entrusted with the responsibility of acting as the repository of project records and charged with initiating and closing projects. So, who should perform these roles? In some organizations (usually smaller ones), the person who heads up delivery has this responsibility. In larger organizations, however, a group or a department known as the PMO (project management office) is charged with the responsibility for being the repository for project records and for initiating and closing projects. Although this book focuses on the PMO model, management of the various activities — whether by an individual or a PMO — is not as important as that the activities are actually accomplished.

During the initiation phase, in a model that has a PMO and an SPM, the PMO and SPM have specific responsibilities. The PMO:

- Identifies the SPM
- Prepares the project dossier and provides the dossier to the SPM
- Coordinates allocation of resources for the project
- Assists the SPM to obtain the necessary service level agreements (SLAs) from other departments in the organization
- Assists the SPM with the project kickoff meeting

The SPM:

- Studies the project specifications and ensures that they are complete
- Refines project estimates based on new knowledge:
  - Reviews the estimates prepared during the project acquisition phase
  - Revises and updates the estimates with details provided in the order received from the client (or the details as approved by management for internal projects)
  - Prepares revised estimates if specifications have undergone a major change since the last estimation
  - Performs software estimation if an estimate was not performed during the project acquisition phase (includes software size, effort, cost, and schedule)

- Identifies necessary resources and raises requests for them:
  - Human resources
  - Hardware resources
  - Software resources
  - Facilities
  - Connectivity (networking, security, and the Internet)
- Prepares project plans (depending on the organization, some of these plans can be created by the teams that are directly responsible for the activities described):
  - Project management
  - Configuration and change management
  - Data management
  - Risk management
  - Quality assurance
  - Project execution and delivery schedule
  - Product integration
  - Deployment
  - Induction training
  - Handover
  - Issue resolution
- Sets up the development environment:
  - Facilities
  - Hardware
  - System software and the development tool kit
  - Information-sharing directories
  - Networking and Internet facilities (as needed by the project)
  - Work allocation and execution mechanisms
- Arranges for project-specific skill training for project team members (If needed, training needs may include programming languages, application tiers, RDBMSs, the development tool kit, etc.)
- Organizes the project team into its constituent functions: module teams, quality control teams, database team, etc.
- Trains the project team on all aspects of project execution as specified in the project plans
- Conducts a project kickoff meeting with other relevant departments and obtains commitments for project-specific service levels and issue-resolution mechanisms

Organizational-level (PMO) and SPM-level activities will now be examined in greater detail.

PROJECT MANAGEMENT OFFICE-LEVEL ACTIVITIES

Organization-level (PMO) activities include SPM identification, project dossier preparation and handover, coordination of the allocation of project resources, and assisting with setting/obtaining SLAs and the project kickoff meeting.

Identifying the Software Project Manager

Once the project is sanctioned and approval to begin the project is received (in the form of a management approval, a purchase order from a customer, or a letter of intent), the PMO identifies an SPM. Identification of an SPM considers several subjective and objective factors:

- Availability
- Past experience in a pertinent functional domain
- Expertise in a pertinent technical domain
- The capability to handle the size of the present team
- A willingness to handle the project

Preparing/Handing Over the Project Dossier to the Software Project Manager

The PMO that is handling the responsibilities for project initiation at the organization level (or in the absence of a PMO, the individual) prepares a project dossier and hands it over to the SPM. The project dossier contains:

- The project initiation note (The PIN contains basic information about the project. The PIN is typically the first document in a project dossier.)
- The RFP, the proposal, and the purchase order (or the approval in the case of an internal project)
- Technical specifications of the project as stated and agreed upon with the customer
- Important project milestones and the commitment dates
- Other requirements, such as communication mechanisms, progress reporting formats and intervals, and escalation mechanisms
- Pointers to past experience, such as the results of similar projects to bring organizational experience to bear on project execution (Include estimates, project plans, design documents, and project retrospective information.)
- Invoicing information for external projects
- Any other relevant data for initiating the project

Table 4.1. Sample Project Initiation Note

Project Name	Development of Software for Materials Management
Project ID	DP/2008/MM/001
Project description	Develop software for a materials management function, including procurement, warehouse management, and inventory control
Start date	1-Oct-08
End date	1-Feb-09
Project manager	John Smith
Person-months (efforts)	56
Resources: software	To be identified after estimation
Resources: hardware	To be identified after finalization of estimation by SPM
Reference documents	1. Technical specifications 2. Documents for project XYZ 3. Metrics data for project XYZ
Created by/date	PMO/15-Aug-08

The dossier is the *initial* set of documentation for the project. The dossier (also known as a project notebook as well as a number of other terms) will evolve over the life of the project. Often the physical aspect of the dossier (also known as instantiation) can range widely: from a physical paper to wiki or SharePoint websites. The physical form of the documentation is far less important than the actual coalescing of information about the project. Documentation should be done in a manner that permits the SPM and the project team to derive knowledge from the data. The project is executed against the backdrop of information included in the project dossier. A sample PIN is shown in Table 4.1.

Coordinating Allocation of Project Resources

In many organizations, the PMO acts as a clearinghouse for resource requests created by the SPM and arranges for resources to be allocated to the project. The PMO monitors the allocation of human resources on projects to identify:

- Resources that are not allocated to any project
- Resources that are allocated to other projects, but are likely to be available to fulfill resource requests raised by the SPM
- Resources that are allocated to other projects, but are being used as a resource buffer

Note: The resource activities described above are commonly monitored by the PMO; however, many different organizational models can also accomplish these activities. In a small organization, a department manager might manage this type of resource monitoring and allocation informally (in his/her head), whereas in a growing organization that is encountering the complexities of managing projects across continents (some say, "rearing their ugly heads"), specialization such as the PMO structure becomes a tool to increase efficiency.

The human resources identified as not allocated, allocated and available, or held as a buffer are reserved for possible allocation to the project. The PMO then interacts with the SPM and other key players to determine timing and the availability of resources to firm up the allocations.

At times, identified and available resources are determined to be inadequate to meet the needs of the project. In such situations, the PMO arranges for additional resources in coordination with different departments of the organization, using the techniques described, for each type of resource:

Human resources. The PMO coordinates with the human resources (HR) department to arrange for additional human resources. The HR department has several alternatives:

- Recruit from the market
- Hire temporary workers from a consulting company
- Hire part-time workers
- Borrow workers from a sister company or division
- Ask existing resources to work extra hours

Computer resources. The PMO coordinates with the systems administration department to arrange for additional computer resources. The system administration department may choose from one or more alternatives:

- Procure new systems/hardware from the market
- Rent systems or hardware
- Request that employees work in shifts and share resources

Monetary resources. The PMO coordinates with the finance department to arrange for the additional financial resources. The finance department obtains additional financial resources from:

- An advance from the customer
- Leveraging the financial reserves of the company
- Borrowing from the market
- Asset sales (e.g., accounts receivables can be packaged and sold on the open market)

If delivery commitments cannot be met with the present level of resources, the PMO assists the SPM by finding and infusing additional resources. Other options that the PMO (or some other management model that is being used) might suggest include:

- Seeking expert guidance to achieve better productivity
- Investigating the appropriateness of using automation tools to speed up the project if adding resources or improving productivity is not feasible (Introducing new tools in an important project sometimes increases risk.)
- Coordinating with the business acquisition team to renegotiate the time lines if all else fails to meet the requirements of the project

Simply put: The role of the PMO is to assist the SPM with obtaining the necessary resources to ensure success of a project.

Assisting the Software Project Manager in Obtaining Necessary Service Level Agreements from Departments in the Organization

SLAs for each project are negotiated between the SPM and the service departments (HR, finance, networking, and systems administration). At the request of the SPM, the PMO coordinates setting up meetings with outside resources and ensures that an amicable resolution is achieved between a project activity and the responsible service department. A sample SLA is shown in Table 4.2.

Assisting the Software Project Manager with the Project Kickoff Meeting

In consultation with the SPM and all project stakeholders, the PMO:

- Determines the date for the kickoff meeting
- Coordinates and ensures that all project stakeholders are represented at the project kickoff meeting
- Assists the SPM in getting project stakeholders to accept the roadmap that has been laid out for project execution and in ensuring that project stakeholders support the project
- Formalizes the kickoff meeting by recording the minutes of the meeting (including issues and action items) and circulating the minutes to all stakeholders

SOFTWARE PROJECT MANAGER-LEVEL ACTIVITIES

SPM-level activities include ensuring that the project specifications are complete; reviewing estimates, revisions, and re-estimating; identifying resources and

Table 4.2. Sample Service Level Agreement

Step	Description of Activity	SLA for Project	Responsibility
1	Installation of new computer hardware Installation of communication equipment Installation of peripherals	1 day for small systems (desktops, printers) 1–2 days for large systems (servers) 1 week for routers, switches, communication controllers	SA
2	General troubleshooting and problem rectification of computer systems and peripherals in different projects	30 min–4 hr from request (if procurement, time is dependent on vendor)	SA
3	Operating system installation and troubleshooting	0.5–2 days	SA
4	PC/desktop printer allocation	1–3 days from requisition (subject to availability)	SA
5	Software/consumables issues	30–60 min (subject to availability)	SA
6	Software installation	2–4 hr	SA
7	Software problem/network troubleshooting/PC or printer	2–4 hr	SA
8	Mail server-related problems Proxy server-related problems	30–60 min	SA
9	Review and editing of proposals	25 pages/day	TW
10	Review and editing of documents (system and user documentation)	20 pages/day	SQAG
11	Conduct audit	1 day	SQAG
12	Prepare audit report	2 working days after audit complete	SQAG
13	Review project plans	2 days	SQAG
14	Conduct final inspection of deliveries	2–3 hr	SQAG
15	Conduct audit	0.5–2 days (depending on item)	SQAG
16	Conduct project closure	1–2 days	PMO
17	Conduct quality training	3 days	HR
18	Coordinate project-specific training	Within 2 weeks after receiving request (duration depends on type of training)	HR
19	Process waiver request	1 week	SEPG
20	Allocate skilled manpower to other projects	1–2 weeks required from date of request (provided necessary training requirement can be fulfilled)	HR

Legend: SA, systems administration; TW, technical writer; SQAG: software quality assurance group; PMO, project management office; HR, human resources; SEPG, software engineering process group.

raising requests for additional resources; preparing project plans; setting up the development environment; arranging for project-specific skill training; organizing the project team; training the team; conducting the project kickoff meeting; and arranging for a phase-end audit. The SPM takes ownership for all software project initiation (SPI) activities at the project level. As owner, the SPM either carries out the SPI activities or ensures that a designate performs them. Each of the typical activities of an SPM in SPI will now be considered in greater detail.

Ensuring that Project Specifications Are Complete

The SPM reviews all project specifications received from the client, even if the day-to-day responsibility for the project will be delegated to another manager. Project specifications can include:

- Technical specifications
- Delivery commitments
- Details of milestone events

As required, the SPM interacts with the PMO or the customer to fill in gaps in the specifications (if any). The SPM also reviews all other known aspects of the project. Based this review and assessment, the SPM gauges the work involved and the means for achieving the known aspects.

Reviewing Estimates and Revisions/Updates of Estimates

The SPM reviews all estimates and revised estimates. The best-case scenario is that the estimate prepared during the project acquisition phase is still valid. If no changes in specifications have been made, using the initial estimate is appropriate. However, a specification change that affects the scope of work requires the SPM to *revise and update* the acquisition estimate so that it reflects the current specifications:

- *New specification*: If an estimate is determined to be invalid, a newly added specification is generally the culprit. After the acquisition phase, the client (or management in the case of an internal project) may have added a new specification that affects the scope of work. Usually, the addition of a specification impacts the estimate that was prepared when the project was acquired.
- *Significant alteration*: An estimate can be rendered useless by significant alteration of project specifications. If the specifications have been significantly altered, the SPM needs to *re-estimate* the project using the current specifications. Re-estimation may require renegotiating the agreement with the client.

An important aspect to keep in mind while revising and re-estimating is that delivery commitments generally *cannot* be altered. Delivery commitments, without renegotiation, have usually already been made to the customer. Therefore, any change in delivery commitments can put the agreement at risk. If the estimated schedule for delivery overshoots the delivery commitments, the SPM must then use all of his or her skills to find a way to meet the schedule, including consultation with senior management and the PMO. The estimate review process will now be described.

Review the estimate prepared during the project acquisition stage. In this review, the SPM ensures that the existing estimate *matches* the current specifications. If there is variation between the existing estimate and the current specifications, the SPM:

- Determines the extent of variation
- Determines whether to use the existing estimate with or without modifications or to prepare a new estimate

Revise and update the acquisition estimate. If the SPM determines that the existing estimate *more or less* reflects the current specifications, albeit needing modification, the SPM revises the estimate so that it matches the current specifications. The SPM first updates the software size estimation by deleting obsolete entries, adding new entries, and modifying existing entries as necessary. Using the new software size estimate, and any other known attributes, the SPM then arrives at the effort required to execute the project at hand. Using the effort estimate, the SPM updates the schedule and cost estimates. Next, the SPM arranges for a peer review of the revised/updated estimates and implements the review feedback. The SPM considers all feedback and implements feedback that will improve the project. The SPM then arranges for a managerial review to obtain approval. All estimates should be reviewed and approved by management. These revised/approved estimates will then be used in execution of the project execution.

Re-estimate if needed. At times, re-estimation is needed. Many situations can require that a project be re-estimated, including:

- *No estimates* were made during the project acquisition stage. The project may have been acquired using an opportunity pricing model ("what we can get from this customer").
- *Ballpark estimates* that had little detail were used during the project acquisition stage. During the project execution stage, ballpark estimates *cannot* be used to manage a project.
- The *existing estimate* is unusable because specifications have changed significantly.

When re-estimating during the initiation phase, the process includes estimation of:

- The size of the software to be produced
- The effort needed to successfully execute the project as well as the skill sets necessary
- The schedule for project execution
- A new cost estimation for the project
- The known risks and issues

When feasible, the SPM (or a business analyst) usually estimates the size of the software product to be produced. (The SPM chooses an appropriate size measure for the software project based on the organization's standard and customer preference.) Next, the SPM converts the software size into effort in person days or hours, using applicable productivity figures or a parametric estimation model. (If for any reason, software size estimation for a project is not feasible, the SPM estimates the effort required to execute the project at hand using techniques such as task-based, Delphi, or analogy estimation.) The SPM then converts the estimated effort into a schedule for development and determines the cost of product development based on the estimated effort.

Note: Software estimation is vast topic in its own right and cannot be covered in this section in adequate detail. Readers are advised to refer to Chemuturi[1] and to interviews on estimation[2] for complete information on software estimation.

Following organizational processes, the SPM then submits the new estimates to the appropriate authority in the organization to obtain necessary appropriations and approval of the budget. The approvals and appropriations are then used to obtain the required resources for execution of the project.

Identifying Necessary Resources and Raising Requests

Based on the estimates and budgetary approvals, the SPM identifies the resources necessary to successfully execute the project. Based on the schedule, the SPM also determines the dates on which the resources are required. Generally, required resources include:

Human resources. Human resources may include:

- Programmers for each of the programming languages required by the project
- Database specialists to assist the programmers in designing an efficient database and to optimize data handling routines or to develop stored procedures (triggers) at the database level to reduce the programming effort of programmers

- Middleware specialists to program the middle tier software (if necessary)
- Testers to independently test the software to ensure that it is defect-free
- Graphics specialists to develop Web pages or other user interface components
- Any other human resources specifically required for the project at hand

Computer resources. Computer resources may include:
- Client machines, with the required configuration of RAM, hard disk, and system software
- Servers for the database, middle tier, and security
- The software development tool kit, including interactive development environment (IDE), testing tools, and personal Web servers
- Networking hardware, including routers, switches, and bandwidth

Physical logistics. Regardless of where the team is housed (or at how many locations), the SPM determines the number of seats that are required for the project team and ensures that they exist. When a co-located strategy is pursued, the SPM makes a judgment call about the team members who need to be co-located and the team members who can work from remote locations.

Networking and Internet services. The SPM determines the networking requirements of the project team and the amount of bandwidth needed for the team, as well as the timing of these requirements.

Miscellaneous resources. Miscellaneous resources include local transport facilities, travel arrangements for team members, petty cash for day-to-day project expenses (based on organizational standards and culture), etc.

Note: Although the level of formality for obtaining approvals for resource requests is driven by an organization's size and culture, the need for consideration of resources *always* exists.

Once identified, all required resources are then enumerated and estimated. Based on the estimates, requests are raised to the appropriate departments to obtain resources for the project when needed:

Human resources. Requests for human resources, including the necessary mix of skills, development platform experience, domain expertise and level, etc., are normally raised to the HR department. In larger organizations, having a resource group that is vested with the authority of allocating people to projects is common. If human resources need to be recruited (or acquired), this group interacts with HR.

Table 4.3. Sample Resource Request Form

Project ID: _____   Date: _____

Serial Number	Resource Requested	Resource Type	Quantity	Required by Date	Probable Release Date by Phase
1	Java programmers	Personnel	12	10-Oct-08	1. 5 by 20-Nov-08 2. 10 by 10-Dec-08 3. 5 by 1-Jan-09
2	Business analysts/ Finance	Personnel	2	1-Oct-08	1-Jan-09
3	PCs	Hardware	2	1-Oct-08	1-Jan-09
4	PCs	Hardware	12	10-Oct-08	1. 5 by 20-Nov-08 2. 10 by 10-Dec-08 3. 5 by 1-Jan-09
5	Oracle DBA	Personnel	1	1-Oct-08	10-Dec-08

Requested by/date: _____   Approved by/date: _____

Systems administration. Requests for *hardware resources* are raised to the systems administration department. Systems administration then allocates the necessary hardware for project execution. Systems administration is also charged with procuring any required special hardware and with making the special hardware available to the SPM. Requests for *software resources* are also raised to the systems administration department. Systems administration then allocates the necessary system software and development kits for project execution. As with hardware, the systems administration department procures any special software required for the project and makes the software available to the SPM. Requests for *connectivity requirements* (networking and Internet) are also raised to systems administration. Systems administration is responsible for providing the necessary interconnection for the project team and for security and Internet facilities.

Administration/facilities. Based on requests from the SPM or PMO, seating facilities are handled by the administration/facilities department. Administration/ facilities provides seating facilities for the project team to meet the needs of the project (ranging from co-location to distributed facilities).

Keeping the PMO in the information loop is critical to ensure that if conflicts arise, the PMO will be positioned to resolve them. A sample resource request form is shown in Table 4.3.

Preparing Project Plans

Project planning is a complex activity and a major factor leading to success or failure in the execution of a project. (Project planning is such a complex activity that it is addressed separately in Chapter 5.) In a nutshell, and depending on the size of the project and methodology followed, several plans are prepared:

- *Project management:* Details about the project's scope, milestones, and tools and techniques used in the project and how topics such as communication and issue-resolution mechanisms will be addressed
- *Configuration and change management:* Details about development configuration, development state promotion, change management procedures, and the naming conventions (and the tools to address these items) and the build strategies
- *Quality assurance:* Activities required to ensure that organizational processes are followed and that a quality product is delivered (includes topics such as proposed QA activities for the project, metrics to benchmark the project, and the QA roles and responsibilities for the project)
- *Project execution and delivery schedule:* A detailed work breakdown structure, typically expressed as a *schedule* listing all activities, assigned resources, and dates assigned for each of the activities and a *summary* of milestones, deliveries, and project completion dates for use in status documents and other communication vehicles
- *Product integration:* The proposed approach for integrating the product and integration testing, including the roles and the associated responsibilities for product integration
- *Deployment:* Details of hardware and software required for deploying the solution, the schedule of deployment, and who assumes roles and associated responsibilities for deployment
- *Induction training.* Details of topics to be covered when training new project team members (may also include information about course material, roles and associated responsibilities for conducting induction training, and how the induction training will be evaluated)
- *Handover:* Details of hardware and software components that will be handed over to the client's representatives, the acceptance mechanisms (including how the handover will be measured), and the roles and associated responsibilities for handover
- *Issue resolution:* Details about reporting issues, obtaining resolution, and roles and associated responsibilities required to support resolving issues

Setting Up the Development Environment

The development environment may involve co-locating the project team; ensuring that all of the developers have the necessary development tool kit; providing access to communication facilities; and ensuring that QA personnel have all of the necessary testing tools, as well as a separate test environment. Setting up a development environment includes several activities:

- *Seating:* Take possession of the seating resources provided by the administration/facilities department and allocate them to team members in such a way that each member is located in the most optimal configuration possible.
- *Hardware*: Provide necessary hardware resources to team members.
- *System software and development tool kit*: Ensure that all team members are provided with relevant and necessary software to perform their roles (may include, but is not limited to, system software, database management system, and a development tool kit, including editors, compilers, and debuggers).
- *Information sharing directories*: Organize information so the team can quickly and efficiently share knowledge. Directories may include user requirements, design documents, project plans, training materials, issue reporting formats, test plans, and all other formats and templates needed by the team. Setting up the information sharing directories includes providing access to all the team members and ensuring sufficient security (based on need).
- *Networking and Internet*: Ensure interconnection of all hardware of the project team.
- *Work allocation and execution mechanisms*: Deploy work registers at commonly accessible locations and inform team members of the communication protocols for making work allocations. Work allocation and execution mechanisms also include task/time accounting procedures and how task completion is reported.
- *Standards*: Identify appropriate standards and guidelines for coding, designing, testing, and reviewing. Identify the sources that are to assist in defining any standards or guidelines that are unavailable.

Arranging for Project-Specific Skill Training

In view of the ever-changing field of information technology, to enable successful project execution, team members often need specific training. As necessary, the SPM arranges for such training in coordination with the PMO and the HR/training department. Training can be classroom training, guided self-study training, or any other suitable training method. The goal of such training is equipping the team members to handle project tasks effectively and efficiently.

Organizing the Project Team

The SPM strategically organizes the project team into the various constituent teams that are required for the smooth execution of the project. A *functional approach* might leverage teams by role: module teams, QA and QC teams, database teams, etc., whereas an *integrated approach* might leverage cross-functional teams so that many roles within the organization interact continually.

If the project uses a functional or role-based approach, team breakdown may include:

- *Module teams*: A separate team for the development of each module of the software product
- *Database team*: All database specialists who will assist the project team in optimizing the data handling routines
- *Graphics team*: All graphics specialists who will assist the project team in developing the Web pages
- *Testing team*: All testing personnel who will carry out independent testing to uncover all defects and to ensure a defect-free delivery

If the project uses an integrated approach, the organizational structure of the team may use a cross-functional model. In a cross-functional team, personnel from the functional areas of the organization work together as a team to focus on objectives and to take responsibility for coordinating activities across the organization — particularly for problems that arise, but also for any issues that arise which are related to innovation. Functional areas represented on a cross-functional team may include research and development, engineering, marketing, finance, human resources, and operations.

Note: Although the choice of project methodology and the existing organizational culture of an organization do have significant impact on how an SPM organizes personnel to achieve any goal, there is no single *best* structure.

Training the Project Team on the Project Plans

The SPM informs team members of the contents of the project plans. Project plans training for team members includes:

- Details about the project
- Management methods
- Tools and techniques to be used
- Quality assurance and testing mechanisms

- Work allocation mechanisms
- Progress reporting mechanisms
- Configuration management to be used

Project plans training is conducted to ensure that the team members understand the team's organization, the roles and responsibilities of the personnel involved with the project, and the mechanisms for issue resolution. Project plans training typically takes a half day (or up to a full day for a large project). If a project is small or if a team has been in place for a long time, with few role changes, project plans training may be handled in a far more informal manner.

Conducting a Project Kickoff Meeting

A kickoff meeting is usually carried out with the help of the PMO, which arranges the meeting and invites all necessary department representatives/stakeholders. Typically, kickoff meetings include representatives from several departments: software quality assurance (SQA), systems administration, administration/facilities, networking, marketing, and customer relationship management (CRM). The project kickoff meeting is conducted by the SPM. During the kickoff meeting, the SPM presents the details of the project, including milestones and the support needed from those present as well as the SLAs needed. The goal of the SPM's presentation is to solicit/obtain the documented commitment of all present from the appropriate department in the organization: for any project requirements, for any project-specific SLAs, and for the mechanisms of issue resolution that these departments are to satisfy. (*Note*: Each organization has a different focus on being inclusive. Invite all areas of the organization that might need to know about the project.) The PMO formalizes the kickoff meeting by recording minutes of the meeting and circulating them to all stakeholders.

SLAs. Usually SLAs are worked out with support groups prior to the kickoff meeting; however, the kickoff meeting can provide a platform for final tweaking. During the kickoff meeting, a project support group should be formed. The project support group would consist of representatives from each support group that has committed to an SLA for the project. When services from any support group are needed, representatives from the support groups are to act as contact persons for the project team.

Arranging for a Phase-End Audit

A phase-end audit is the final activity of the project initiation phase. The phase-end audit for software project initiation is actually a QA activity. The audit ensures that all subactivities have been performed in conformance with the defined organizational process and also uncovers any activities or subactivities that were not performed in conformance with the defined process. Such deviations are termed as non-conformances (NCs).

The SPM invites the QA group or the internal auditor who has been designated for the project to audit the project for conformance with the defined project initiation process. Any NCs are reported to the SPM, who arranges for their rectification and then closes the NCs. When the phase-end audit is complete, the software project initiation phase is considered complete!

COMMON PITFALLS IN SOFTWARE PROJECT INITIALTION

Common pitfalls in SPI include selecting the wrong SPM, identifying inappropriate resources, and incurring delays in SPI activities.

Identifying the Wrong Software Project Manager

At times, an SPM is selected to lead a project just because he or she happens to be available at the time — not because this particular SPM is the most suitable leader for the project. For instance, the most suitable SPM might be unavailable due to a host of reasons: engaged in a different and equally important project, unwilling to take up the current project, etc. At other times, the selection of an SPM can become "political," particularly if prestige is associated with the project. When a prestigious project is involved, SPMs often vie with each other to manage the project.

Remember: Every effort must be made to select the *right* or the *best* SPM for the project. The goal is successful execution of the project. Try to minimize negative politics. If necessary, to ensure the success of a project, leverage the PMO to a greater degree by having the PMO serve as a mentor to an SPM who is not the first choice to lead the project.

Identifying Inappropriate Resources

In all software development projects, having the best-qualified human resources is crucial for success. Ideally, a project team should consist of resources who are proficient in the development platform and who have worked in similar domains. Practically, however, allocating the best resources to a project may be impossible. In this situation, one solution is to ensure that the project team has a balanced mix of expert and not-so-expert resources. Using a mix of expertise creates a scenario in which the more experienced team members can mentor the junior team members to ensure success of the project. A worst-case scenario is a situation in which all of the available experts are allocated to one project, while other projects are "starving" from a lack of needed expertise. Allocating the best mix of resources to a project is the best practice — the art, however, is finding that mix.

Incurring Delays in Software Project Initiation Activities

Sometimes, SPI activities simply experience unforeseen delays. Maybe the PMO takes extra time in identifying the SPM; or identification and allocation of the resources take longer than expected; or arriving at satisfactory SLAs in the project kickoff meeting consumes excess time. Delays such as these must be absorbed by project execution — which can cause a project to get off to a bad start. Sometimes a delay is even used as a "weapon" to get an SPM to accept the SLAs and resources that have been offered, even if they are suboptimal. Whatever the reasons are for delays, it is important to understand that *any* delay in initiation typically reduces the time available for completion of the remainder of the project — which increases pressure on project execution. The best practice is to consume only the minimum possible time allowed in the schedule for concluding SPI activities. (Additional best practices and pitfalls for SPI may be found in Chapter 12.)

REFERENCES

1. Murali Chemuturi. *Software Estimation: Best Practices, Tools & Techniques. A Complete Guide for Software Project Estimators* 2009. Ft. Lauderdale, FL: J. Ross Publishing.

2. *Software Process and Measurement Cast* (http://www.spamcast.net).

5

SOFTWARE PROJECT PLANNING

Nobody plans to fail –
they just fail to plan.
– Anonymous

If I were given six hours to fell a tree,
I would spend the first four hours sharpening the axe.
– Abraham Lincoln

INTRODUCTION

Most articles and books about achieving success (in any endeavor) begin by describing the necessity to plan and to plan well. In rare cases, success can be achieved without planning, but planning reduces the risk of failure and increases the chances of success. Better yet, planning coupled with control (control from the point of view of project discipline, including measuring progress and taking corrective actions) brings more predictability to the probable outcome of an endeavor.

An often-asked question is, "Can I plan in my head or should planning be documented on paper?" Although planning is a necessity, documenting the plan (or *planning on paper*) is not always a necessity. For instance, for a small, short-duration endeavor, mental planning may be adequate (Figure 5.1).

Few of us actually omit planning. Usually, we conduct the planning — it's just the degree of rigor with which we plan (including documenting the planning activities) that is open to discussion.

Figure 5.1. The planning dilemma.

Planning on paper has advantages. A documented plan can:

- Be *reviewed by others* to see if any important aspect has been over-looked, thereby improving the plan (or self-reviewed "after the dust has settled")
- Act as a *point of reference* for stakeholders concerned with or involved in the project
- Facilitate *control and performance evaluation* during execution
- Facilitate *validation of the planning parameters* by providing a baseline for comparison of the actual values generated during execution

Except for very small projects, written documentation of a plan is a good idea.

Once the decision has been made to document planning, the next question is usually, "What level of granularity should be used?" The granularity of planning (or the required detail) depends on:

- *Duration* of the endeavor
- *Number of resources* employed
- *Complexity* involved
- *Relationship* between the duration, number of resources, and complexity
- *Geography* of the project

Now consider some aspects of the duration of the endeavor, the number of resources employed, and the complexity involved in the project:

- The longer the *duration*, the greater the necessity for rigor. (If a project has no time constraints on completion, the level of rigor and granularity can be reduced. In the real world, however, it is *duration* that is often constrained, which increases the need for planning rigor.)
- As the *number of resources* employed in a project increases, the level of planning rigor increases.

- As *complexity* (of all varieties and above what is normal) for the team members increases, the greater is the need for greater planning rigor.
- Different combinations of *duration*, the *number of resources* employed, and *complexity* require different levels of rigor in planning.

Numerous other questions could be asked about project planning, but before proceeding with any further discussion on planning, let's define planning.

PLANNING DEFINED

Planning is defined as *the intelligent estimate of resources required to perform a predefined project successfully at a future date within a defined environment.* This definition of planning contains several key terms:

- *Estimate* indicates that planning is preceding performance and that it is based on organizational norms (also known as organization baselines). Simply, an estimate is a prediction of the future.
- *Resources* are the four M's of *men* (human resources, either male or female), *materials, methods,* and *machines* (equipment). Resources are always applied over a period of time (duration).
- *Project* indicates a specific scope of work that can be defined as a project (see Chapter 1).
- *At a future date* indicates that the dates for executing the project are in the future and are typically decided during the course of planning.
- *Within a defined environment* refers to the environment in which the work will be performed. The environment is either known or defined during the planning exercise. Any variation in the environment will have an effect on the plan. *Environment* may also refer to the technical environment, work logistics, workstation design, processes and methods of management, prevailing morale in the workplace, and the corporate culture to name a few.

The definition of planning also provides a framework for evaluating the process of planning.

In several aspects, the planning for software development projects is the same as the planning for many other types of projects. In software development planning, however, the planning process is tailored to suit the specific attributes of software development. So, what are the attributes that make software development projects unique?

- *Output is not physical*: The output from a software development project is not physical — in the sense that the primary deliverable is not an actual physical component. *Functionality* is the primary output of a software development project. (Physical and nonphysical resources are consumed, however, when a software product is created.)

- *Process inspection does not facilitate progress assessment*: In a manufacturing organization, the conversion of raw materials into work-in-progress and finally into finished goods is proof of progress. (Some say that progress may be assessed by the noise made by manufacturing equipment.) In a software development organization, however, visual inspection is not enough to ensure that work is being done and progress is being made. In a software project, *functional* software is the only true marker of progress.

- *Software engineering tools have limited predictability*: Although significant progress has been made in software engineering tools, these tools do not have nearly as much precision as engineering drawings and cannot produce the predictability that is seen in other engineering disciplines. Much of the energy expended in software development projects continues to be "sweat equity."

- *Professional associations in the software development field lack practice and behavior standards*: Organizations such as the Institute of Electrical and Electronic Engineers (IEEE) have defined some standards, but these standards do not rise to the levels of specificity and granularity that are found in other engineering fields.

- *Productivity and quality are dependent on human beings*: Significant improvement has been made in software development; however, for productivity and quality, the processes used continue to be largely dependent on human beings. Tools are available to support development and testing, but to meet the standards found in other engineering disciplines these tools need to evolve further. The goal must be shifting the onus for productivity and quality from human beings to tools in the hands of humans.

Because software development continues to rely primarily on human endeavors, the rigor of planning needed becomes even more significant than that required for engineering projects (an environment in which tools provide a major impetus to the process). For example, in some engineering projects, a simple schedule based on PERT/CPM will suffice, whereas software development projects (especially large ones) require increased rigor and planning. The plans typically required for a software development project are now described in subsequent sections, but first, let's review the general attributes of a software project:

- A project has a definite beginning and a definite end.
- The project deliverable is software and the related artifacts (e.g., documentation).

- The activities in a software project may include defining the user and software requirements, software design, software construction, software testing, acceptance testing, and software delivery, deployment, and handover.

Project selection, acquisition, and post-handover activities are not part of a software development project.

PLANS PREPARED IN SOFTWARE PROJECT MANAGEMENT

A common misunderstanding among members of the software development fraternity is that a *schedule* constitutes software project planning. This is categorically untrue. Software project planning goes far beyond scheduling. Several plans are typically prepared for a large software development project.

A project management plan. A PMP describes how a software project will be managed. In engineering projects, how a project will be managed is covered in the standard operating procedures/policies (or SOPs) of an organization's production environment or production facility. SOPs work well for engineering projects because all projects are managed similarly. Therefore, a completely new management plan for every project may be unnecessary. The SOPs also ensure that how a project is to be managed is well understood. The software project developmental environment, however, is much more dynamic. In software projects, the developmental environment is completely different for almost every project, which necessitates the need to plan and document how each project will be managed. Information contained in a PMP includes:

- Project demographic information
- A software estimate (software size, effort, cost, and schedule)
- Milestones and delivery schedules
- Delivery acceptance criteria
- Human resources requirements and a projected timeframe for when they will be required
- Management methods (including but not limited to work allocation and management, information and source code management, quality control, communication management, etc.)
- Tools to be used for the project (development tools, testing configuration tools, and project management tools, etc.)

The elements of a software PMP template are shown in Figure 5.2. IEEE Standard 1058 provides details for a PMP and a suggested template for documenting a plan.

Title: Software Project Management Plan
Name of Client:
Revision History:
Table of Contents

1.0 Project Overview	7.0 Support Process Plans
1.1 Project Summary	7.1 Software Configuration
1.2 Purpose, Scope, and Objectives	Management Plan
1.3 Deliverables	7.2 Software Quality Assurance Plan
1.4 Major Milestones	7.3 Process Improvement Plan
2.0 References	7.4 Induction Training Plan
3.0 Definitions and Acronyms	7.5 Schedule
4.0 Project Organization	7.6 Work Breakdown Structure
4.1 Project Team	7.7 Issue Resolution Plan
4.2 Client Interfaces	8.0 Any Additional Plans
4.3 Roles and Responsibilities	8.1 Deployment Plan
5.0 Managerial Process	8.2 Warranty Support Plan
5.1 Project Startup	8.3 Data Migration Plan
5.2 Project Execution	8.4 Any Other Plans
5.3 Project Control	9.0 Annexes
5.4 Risk Management	10.0 Waivers
5.5 Project Closure	
6.0 Technical Process	
6.1 Software Development Life Cycle	
6.2 Methods, Tools, and Techniques	
6.3 Product Acceptance Plan	

Figure 5.2. Software project management elements.

A configuration management plan. A CMP describes how code and noncode assets of a project will be managed. Information in a CMP includes:

- Naming conventions to be followed for project artifacts, including documents and code units of all types (including databases and tables); procedures for managing changes to configuration items
- Organization of project information to facilitate access by project teams when a reference is needed
- References to organizational standards and processes for use in the project
- Code and code library organization, check-in and check-out criteria, authorizations, and procedures for state changes of source code artifacts (from development to review/testing, to integration and delivery, etc.)

IEEE Standard 828 provides details of a CMP and a suggested CMP template.

A quality assurance plan. A QAP describes how a project will ensure that the deliverables meet the quality requirements for the project. Information in a QAP typically includes:

- Standards selected for use during the project (coding, design, and testing guidelines)
- Quality control activities proposed for the project (code walk-through, review of requirements and design, proposed tests including but not limited to unit testing, integration testing, functional testing, negative testing, end-to-end testing, system testing, and acceptance testing)
- Software metrics to be collected for the project and how they will be used
- Processes, procedures, and events that trigger the need for causal analysis, whether for failures, defects, or even successes
- Audits proposed for the project and who will perform them

IEEE Standard 730 gives details of preparing a QAP and a suggested QAP template.

A schedule. The schedule contains a work breakdown structure for the project, including the start and end dates and the resources required for each of the activities. The schedule document is used to plan and to monitor the progress of the project. Analysis techniques, such the Critical Path Method and the Program Evaluation and Review Technique (often referred to collectively as PERT/CPM), are useful to evaluate task flows and relationships. The CPM is a step-by-step project management planning technique that identifies the tasks in a project that are on a *critical path.* Tasks (activities from the start milestone to the end milestone and in between) that are on a *critical path* are those tasks that are critical in meeting the project's schedule and for the success of the project. The goal of identifying the critical tasks is to prevent time-related problems. Knowledge gained from the CMP is used to focus attention on the truly important tasks so that a project's overall completion date is not impacted. (*Note*: Because the critical path shifts over time as project execution progresses, the critical path should be monitored so that events do not suddenly become overwhelming.) PERT/CPM can also be used to assist in resource allocation. Through the use of probability theory, PERT helps a project manager to understand and mitigate the uncertainty that is inherent in working out a schedule. Knowledge of PERT/CPM techniques is essential to arriving at a credible schedule for a project. (Many resources describing how to perform PERT and CPM analyses are available on the Internet.)

An induction training plan. Also known as an *onboarding* plan (as well as an initiation or assimilation plan, etc.), an induction training plan contains the training requirements for new team members who join the project. Explicitly stated are the requirements for bringing a new team member up to par with other team members. Typically, the induction training plan focuses on processes and standards rather than on explicit technical requirements, which have a longer-term learning horizon). Topics also included are knowledge building about the project plans that are being leveraged on the project: the "how's" of executing and controlling the project; the quality assurance activities; the mechanisms for communication and issue resolution; project-specific tool/development platform training, etc.

A build plan. The strategy for building the code is included in a build plan. This plan details the build period (ranging from continuous to daily or some other period) and how the build will be tested and validated. Also included is the number of planned builds for delivery of the product to the client.

A deployment plan. Contained in a deployment plan is a description of the target location of the project's functionality, including deployment of the hardware, the system software, the middleware, and pilot runs.

A user training plan. A user training plan outlines the user training, the deployment strategy (classroom, online, etc.), and the duration and includes an anticipated schedule for the training.

A handover plan. Details included in a handover plan describe how the system will be handed over to the team that will operate the system. Also included in the plan are the handover timelines, the team or the person who will accept the application, the artifacts required at handover, acceptance test criteria, and any required signoffs.

A software maintenance plan. The mechanisms for identifying and prioritizing maintenance work requests, any required service levels for maintenance, and the support turnaround times necessary for maintaining the software are included in a software maintenance plan.

All of these plans may not be required as separate documents (depending on the methodology used, the content also may not be applicable). For instance, in a smaller project, the plans described above can easily be included in the PMP. In a medium-sized project, usually a PMP, CMP, QAP, and a schedule are prepared (any other plans are included in the PMP).

Next, how to carry out software project planning and the preparation of typical project planning deliverables are described in greater detail.

THE PROJECT MANAGEMENT PLAN

A PMP is the *top-level plan* that consolidates all of the relevant information about a project, from the purchase order to the initial estimates and requirements, into the plan. The PMP also incorporates the methods that will be used for managing the project, the project management tools to be used, the project milestones, the communication protocols, and the mechanisms for escalation and issue resolution.

Resources

A resource plan is typically a subsection of a PMP. Once a project has been estimated, a work schedule for execution of the project can be developed. The work schedule provides details of the resources required and the dates when the resources will be needed.[1] Attributes that influence the human resources aspects of estimation include:

- *Skill sets required for the project*: The initial, required skill sets are derived from the technical specifications of the project. (Over the life of a project, innovation may alter the skill sets needed.)
- *Size of software to be developed*: The size of the software is estimated using accepted software size measures, such as Function Point Analysis, The Netherlands Software Metrics Association (NESMA) Function Point Analysis, or Software Size Units (SSU).
- *Amount of effort required to deliver the project*: Effort is directly estimated using estimation techniques, such as parametric estimation, task-based estimation, analogy, or Delphi estimation. Effort also can be derived from the estimated software size. (Remember from an earlier discussion that effort and duration are not the same.)
- *Duration that resources will be required on the project*: Duration is estimated by allocating the resources and assigning calendar dates to the activities that have to be performed to execute the project — a process called *scheduling*. (Scheduling will be covered in greater detail in Chapter 9).
- *Likely dates for resources*: Based on estimated and compiled data, the dates on which the resources are likely to be needed by the project are derived. Estimates and schedules are fluid and can be adversely affected by events; therefore, monitoring is critical. A schedule is not a "fire and forget" task.

Skill Sets

Capers Jones, a leading authority in software estimating, has said that IT has more specialties than any other profession. In a large project, therefore, a wide range of different skill sets may be needed. In addition to a project leader/SPM, several roles are typical:

- *Programmers*: to write the necessary programs
- *Database administrator/database specialists*: for data modeling and to design the database, to develop stored procedures (programs written at the database end for data handling), and then to offer assistance to programmers in the efficient development of data handling routines (DBAs can also carry out data migration or assist the team in data migration activity as applicable.)
- *Team leaders*: to lead and manage teams of programmers, testers, and DBAs on a day-to-day basis
- *Software testers/testing specialists*: to prepare test plans and test cases, carry out software testing, and guide the team to ensure that testing is properly carried out and all defects are uncovered and rectified
- *Language smiths*: to assist in troubleshooting programming issues (Language smiths, also known as lead programmers or expert programmers, are experts in the programming languages used on a project. Language smiths use their expertise to assist in troubleshooting programming issues and are often requested on an "as required" basis.)
- *Software (solution) architects*: for process modeling to develop application architecture and to integrate the developed solution
- *Business (systems) analysts*: to interact with the customer(s) to understand requirements and to translate those needs/requirements into a form which can be understood and used by the software developers to produce the solution that meets the client requirements (In some cases, business analysts also act as a proxy for the customer within the project team.)
- *Configuration controller*: to ensure that the artifacts (both information and software) are available to various team members and to ensure that deliveries to the customer contain the correct versions of all deliverables (also known as a configuration manager)
- *Process coordinator*: to ensure that the organization's processes are implemented and that process-related information is made available on time to concerned functionaries of the organization

Other possible roles are process and product quality assurance analysts (PPQA), user interface designers (UI), usability testers, etc. The list could go on and on.

At times, some roles are handled on a part-time or as-needed basis. A project leader or project manager often takes on the roles of configuration controller, process coordinator, and software architect. Programmers may take on the role of testers. Once the required skill sets and the duration for which they are required are identified, resource requests can be placed with the department that allocates human resources to projects.

Computer Systems

Depending on the nature of the project, a project team needs various hardware items for execution of a project execution. Typical hardware and system software requirements for a project include:

- Special computers (based on project needs)
- Personal computers (with appropriate terminal emulation software, if necessary, to connect to the development machine/server or appropriate system software, a development tool kit, and any other necessary tools)
- Networking hardware and software
- Connectivity to customer machines (if the project is to be executed from a remote location)
- Bandwidth (if communication with a remote customer or testing of a Web application is involved)
- Special software (databases, programming languages, testing tools, configuration management tools, documentation tools, team collaboration tools, etc.)

Project Management Method

A number of methods may be used to manage a project. (*Note*: Methods are part of the *Project Management Body of Knowledge* that forms the basis of PMP© certification.[2]) Project management methods include work allocation, progress measurement and review, and communication.

Work allocation. In the work allocation method, work is allocated to the human resources to execute the *tasks*. Then progress reporting is done at the *task level*. Work allocation may use a variety of vehicles: an Excel sheet, Microsoft Project or Primavera scheduling tools, or PMPal, a work breakdown structure (WBS) collaboration tool. Work allocation may also be performed using a tool such as Microsoft Project Server, in a formal email, and by telephone or even in person. Reporting then leverages the same tool or method.

Progress measurement and review. In progress measurement and review, tools and methods are used to ensure that the status of a project is clearly understood. Progress measurement and review techniques include earned value analysis (EVA) and line of balance (LOB). A weekly status report is the most common progress reporting vehicle for projects. (*Note*: In agile projects, a daily stand-up meeting and monthly sprint reviews/planning sessions take the place of status reports.) In all cases, from EVA to stand-up meetings, the reporting process is used as a basis for progress review and for deciding on action points.

Communication. Meetings, emails, and telephone calls are the most frequently used mechanisms for communication within and outside a project team — albeit new tools, such as wikis, Twitter, and instant messaging, are in the process of supplementing email and telephone messaging systems due to their intimacy and immediacy. The communication plan in the PMP should cover several scenarios:

- Communicating within the project team
- Communicating work allocation and completion dates
- Progress reporting
- Communicating with the client
- Communicating with project support groups

Other considerations related to communication concern the environment and issue-resolution and escalation mechanisms:

- *Environment*: Ensure that the tools, techniques, hardware, system software, database, integrated (also interactive) development environment (IDE), testing tools, CM tools, and folder structures for artifacts in various states that are required for the project are clearly described.
- *Issue resolution*: Ensure that the process is described so that whenever there is ambiguity and clarifications are needed that an issue is raised and tracked to resolution. Description of the process must include the mechanism used to record all issues for the project, how the issue is communicated to the appropriate person, and how the issue is tracked to resolution. (Appendix E discusses issue-resolution mechanisms in greater detail.)
- *Escalation*: Ensure that the process to raise an issue to the next higher level is described. Include the levels to which an issue can be escalated, when to escalate an issue, and to whom the issue should be escalated.

Typically, issue-resolution and escalation mechanisms form part of a PMP.

THE CONFIGURATION MANAGEMENT PLAN

A software development project has several configurations:

Development. The development configuration is the arrangement of the hardware (the development machines: PCs, servers, and networks) and software (the development platform, including the programming language(s), database(s), IDE, and third-party software used in the project) to be used by the programmers for developing the software product. A development configuration plan typically has two distinct parts:

- *Code*: the source code being developed
- *Information/documentation*: information received from the client; developed for use in the project (requirement specifications, design, test plans, test cases, etc.); and generated by the project (test and review logs); all change requests

Review/testing. The review/testing configuration is the arrangement of the hardware and software to be used by the reviewers and testers. Generally, software does not change in the review/testing configuration. Programs enter the configuration and after testing:

- Are returned to the development configuration for rectification *or*
- Are promoted to the integration configuration for integration with other code units

Software is transient when in the review/testing configuration, i.e., the data portion of the development configuration is used for testing and to unearth any defects in the software.

Integration (build). The integration/build configuration is the arrangement of the hardware and software to be used by product integrators. Integration is the process that receives software components and integrates them into the build of the product. Software components enter this configuration only when they have been reviewed, tested, and all known defects have been satisfactorily rectified (or put on a backlog).

Delivery. The delivery configuration is the arrangement for delivery of the software components to the client. Typically the delivery configuration contains some combination of the following:

- The software build
- The source code components
- Third-party software
- Software libraries
- Artifacts received from client
- Images
- User documentation and training materials
- Installation guide, operations guide, and troubleshooting manual

---

Title: Software Configuration Management Plan

Name of Client:

Revision History:

Table of Contents

1.0 Introduction

2.0 References

3.0 Definitions and Acronyms

4.0 Organization of Configuration
Management
- Roles and Responsibilities
- Configuration Control Board Roles
  and Responsibilities

5.0 Tools, Techniques, and Methodology

6.0 Configuration Management Activities
- Identification of Configuration Items
- List of Configuration Items
- Naming Conventions
- Baseline Management
- Repositories
- Configuration Management Software

7.0 Change Management
- Change Control
- Change Requests and Change
  Register
- Release Management

8.0 Configuration Status and Accounting
- Storage and Release
- Reports
- Audits

9.0 Training

10.0 Subcontractor Configuration Control
Activities

Figure 5.3. Configuration management plan elements.

Deployment (target/production). The deployment configuration is the arrangement of the hardware and software components in the target system on which the developed software will be deployed and used.

All required configurations are determined and then documented in configuration management planning. Because different configurations are needed at different levels of granularity at various times in a project, plans will be modified as needed. As the level of knowledge changes, definitions should be also augmented. (The necessity to modify plans and to update the project definitions is why a plan is said to be "a living and breathing document.")

Daily configuration management activities generally revolve around two basic roles: moving components from one configuration to another and the processes required to ensure that the "right" versions of components (software and information artifacts) are assembled for delivery to the customer. Suggested template elements for a CMP are shown in Figure 5.3.

Obsolete artifacts. An important aspect of configuration management planning is the management of artifacts that are undergoing improvement and the management of obsolete artifacts that are created by every project. Obsolete artifacts are not destroyed — at least not until a project is complete. A mechanism is needed to ensure that concerned parties refer only to the appropriate set. (The word *appropriate* is used because at times previous baselines are needed as much as an unambiguous reference to the "current set.") A simple approach to managing artifacts is to create three folders:

- *Current*: all relevant, active artifacts that are complete and which will be referred to when needed
- *Archives*: all previous versions of artifacts
- *In process*: all artifacts that are being developed/revised

Ensure that a version of an artifact is in *only one* of the folders. No artifact of the same version is to be duplicated (except as a project backup).

Naming Conventions

Naming conventions are typically part of a CMP or part of an organizational standard referred in a CMP or PMP. Why are naming conventions needed? Naming conventions:

- Prevent duplicate names or bring clarity when similar names are used
- Easily recognize the contents of the artifact
- Easily identify a group of artifacts (such as all artifacts related to a specific module)
- Achieve uniformity in the naming of artifacts across teams in the same project and across different projects within the organization

In programming, naming conventions allow one type of variable to be distinguished from another type of variable (e.g., programming variables and table fields).

One approach to naming conventions is to use prefixes to distinguish between the various categories. Several prefixes can be combined to provide a rich layering of meaning. Typical naming conventions include:

- Document names
- Program/subprogram names
- Screens, reports
- Numeric variables
- Alphanumeric variables
- Flags
- Counters
- Database table names

- Database table field names
- Error messages
- Information messages
- Window
- Controls (combo box, text box, command buttons)

Change Management

Change is an inevitable occurrence in a software project (similar to death and taxes!). Identifying (or defining) the process required for change management typically occurs in a configuration management plan. (See Chapter 8 for more detailed information about change management.) Inclusion of the contents of the change management process in the CMP is not an absolute, but no matter where change management is documented, the contents of the process are important. Change management in software projects includes:

- *Receiving change requests*: designates a single point for receiving CRs (from all sources), for consolidating the CRs, and for maintaining a change register (also known as a change log)
- *Analyzing change requests*: specifies who is responsible for analyzing CRs (Analysis includes developing an understanding of the impact on schedule, effort, and cost.)
- *Establishing a change control board*: receives data from the CR analysis process and uses that data to make accept or reject decisions or to request more information about the CR. If the CR is accepted for implementation, the change control board:
  - Decides when to implement the CR (as and when received, in a later release, or to retrofit all CRs in the final release?)
  - Decides how to absorb the impact of the CR (internally or pass impact on to the customer?)
  - Obtains/accords approval for implementation of the CR
  - Implements the CR
  - Monitors quality control of CR implementation
  - Closes the CR
- *Reporting progress*: determines the mechanisms to be used to track all CRs received, to track all CRs to resolution, and to communicate the status of all CRs to all concerned parties on a periodic basis
- *Closing change requests*: closes CRs when no further attention is required (Authority for closing a CR rests with the change control board. When a CR is closed, the requesting party receives notification of the final disposition of the CR.)

THE QUALITY ASSURANCE PLAN

Quality assurance planning focuses on achieving the specified level of quality of the artifacts to be produced by a development team. A QAP usually contains:

- Standards to be used in the project:
  - Coding
  - Database design
  - GUI design
  - Test case design
  - Testing
  - Review
  - Organizational process reference
  - Other organization-specific standards
- Quality goals for the project:
  - Defect injection rate
  - Defect density
  - Productivity for the project's artifacts
  - Schedule variances
  - Other project-specific quality goals
- Quality assurance and control activities to be implemented in the project:
  - Code walk-through
  - Peer review
  - Managerial review
  - Types of tests to be carried out during project execution (At a minimum, testing should include unit, integration, system, and acceptance testing.)
- Measures and the processes for measurement (Cover the defined quality levels, the periodicity of testing, and the reporting mechanisms.)
- Causal analysis (process and schedule) for positive and negative variances
- Schedules for proposed project audits:
  - Periodic conformance
  - Phase-end
  - Criteria for investigative audits
  - Delivery
- Process improvement activities (if any)
- Progress reporting mechanisms for the status of quality assurance activities implemented in the project (for all concerned parties)

Title: Software Quality Assurance Plan	
Name of Client:	Proposed Reviews for Project:
Revision History:	Proposed Tests for Project:
Table of Contents	

1.0 Introduction	7.0 Metrics Proposed to Be Collected for
1.1 Scope	the Project
1.2 Objectives	
1.3 Overview	8.0 Tools, Techniques, and Methodologies
2.0 References	9.0 Causal Analysis Proposed
3.0 Definitions and Acronyms	
4.0 Roles and Responsibilities	10.0 Quality Assurance of Subcontracted/
5.0 Standards and Guidelines	Client-Supplied Products
6.0 Quality Assurance Activities	11.0 Training

Figure 5.4. Quality assurance plan elements.

A suggested template for a QAP is shown in Figure 5.4.

As with all other plans, each section of a QAP must be evaluated for its pertinence to the project. For example, the section on standards could contain a reference to existing organizational standards. (*Note*: The authors are firm believers in doing what is needed — not just approaching project quality management and control as a rote checklist.)

THE SCHEDULE PLAN

Scheduling planning is best achieved by using scheduling software (e.g., Microsoft Project or Primavera). All of the activities that are needed to execute a project are enumerated; their predecessor relationships are defined; the resources are allocated; and the dates are set for the activities. (Chapter 9 provides greater detail about scheduling a project.)

THE INDUCTION TRAINING PLAN

An induction training plan (also known as an *onboarding* plan) describes how personnel are to be brought up to speed to ensure the highest level of efficiency for the project throughout its entire life cycle. An induction training plan contains the training topics, duration of training, and the possible faculty for each topic needed by the personnel before beginning to work on the project. The plan should

Title: Induction Training Plan
Name of Client:
Revision History:
Table of Contents

1.0 Introduction	5.0 Training Approach
1.1 Scope	6.0 Training Resources
1.2 Objectives	7.0 Training Topics
1.3 Overview	8.0 Project-Specific Skill Training
2.0 References	9.0 Training Evaluation
3.0 Definitions and Acronyms	
4.0 Roles and Responsibilities	

Figure 5.5. Induction training plan elements.

also include a waiver process for the personnel who do not require training due to previous training or their level of experience. Training topics may include:

- Project plans
- Team communication methods
- Quality assurance activities
- Issue-resolution mechanisms
- Escalation procedures
- Development platform
- Training methods
- Availability of self-study materials
- Waiver process

Suggested template elements for an induction training plan are shown in Figure 5.5.

THE RISK MANAGEMENT PLAN

A risk management plan describes how risks will be identified, prioritized, and managed across the life of the project. Having a risk management plan helps to ensure that risks do not disrupt progress if at all possible. The risk management plan may be included as a part of a PMP or developed and documented as a stand-alone plan. Typical risk management activities include:

- Risk identification
- Risk quantification
- Risk prioritization

Title: Risk Management Plan
Name of Client:
Revision History:
Table of Contents

1.0 Introduction	4.0 Risk Management for the Project
1.1 Scope	4.1 Overview
1.2 Objectives	4.2 Risk Identification
1.3 Overview	4.3 Risk Mitigation
	4.4 Risk Monitoring Activities
2.0 References	4.5 Tools and Techniques
3.0 Definitions and Acronyms	5.0 Training

Figure 5.6. Risk management plan elements.

- Risk mitigation
- Risk monitoring and reporting

Suggested template elements for a risk management plan are illustrated in Figure 5.6.

THE BUILD PLAN

A build plan contains the strategy for building the software project's code and details the build period (ranging from continuous to daily or to some other period) and how the build will be tested. Details of the build plan include when and how functionality will be delivered to the client. A typical build plan contains:

- The approach for integration (i.e., top-down or bottom-up)
- Roles and responsibilities for preparing the builds
- Configuration of the integration environment
- Quality assurance activities before accepting components into the build environment
- Quality assurance activities after integrating each component, after integrating each module, and at completion of the build

THE DEPLOYMENT PLAN

A deployment plan contains a description of the target location of the project's functionality, including the deployment of hardware, system software, middleware, and pilot runs. A deployment plan typically contains:

- A schematic diagram of the deployment components, including hardware, software, networking, etc.

Title: Deployment Plan

Name of Client:	Proposed Reviews for Project:
Revision History:	Proposed Tests for Project:
Table of Contents	

1.0 Introduction   6.0 Resources Required for Deployment

    1.1 Scope   7.0 Facilities

    1.2 Objectives   8.0 Hardware

    1.3 Overview   9.0 Deployment Unit

2.0 References   10.0 Support Necessary for Deployment

3.0 Definitions and Acronyms   11.0 Training

4.0 Roles and Responsibilities

5.0 Schedule of Deployment

Figure 5.7. Deployment plan elements.

- Floor plans for deployment of hardware and networking (if necessary)
- A bill of materials (lists all components being deployed along with the technical specifications of each of the components)
- Quality assurance activities planned for deployment
- Technical methods for deploying the configuration (if necessary)

Suggested template elements for a deployment plan are shown in Figure 5.7.

THE USER TRAINING PLAN

A user training plan describes how users of the system will be taught to use the functionality being delivered. A user training plan minimally contains:

- A delineation of the types of users to be trained and the topics for each type of user
- Details of each of the training topics
- Course material for each course (including, but not limited to, training slides, teaching notes, lesson plans, session breakdown, and participant handouts)
- A schedule of the courses to be conducted
- Details of the facilities needed for conducting the training

THE HANDOVER PLAN

A handover plan describes how the functionality will be delivered to the client or support organization. A typical handover plan contains:

- A bill of materials (all components to be handed over to the client)
- The mode of handover/takeover
- The required sign-off details
- A schedule for the handover

THE SOFTWARE MAINTENANCE PLAN

A software maintenance plan is typically driven by contractual requirements. At a minimum, however, a software maintenance plan describes the activities, roles, and processes for the usual warranty period (sometimes, longer warranty periods may be requested; if so, a separate software maintenance project is usually spawned). A software maintenance plan may contain:

- The process for raising requests for software maintenance
- Formats and templates for raising software maintenance requests
- Service level agreements (including turnaround times for software maintenance requests)
- The procedure for classifying software maintenance requests and prioritizing them
- Issue-resolution mechanisms and escalation mechanisms during maintenance
- The environment for software maintenance

THE DOCUMENTATION PLAN

Documenting of software project plans differs significantly from standard business writing. Software project plans are documents that are used by many individuals as a reference for guiding human efforts and for incurring expenditures. Therefore, approach the writing of a software project plan document as if it were an engineering drawing. Attributes of an engineering drawing include:

- *Unambiguous representation*: The same inference would be drawn from the document irrespective of the person who is interpreting it.
- *One fact — one location*: A fact is presented at one *and only one* location and is never repeated. Presentation of information at multiple locations may cause conflict or create a maintenance nightmare.

- *Specific language*: No free-flowing language is used in writing project plans. Project plans are *not* literature.

Therefore, using the analogy of an engineering drawing, a project plan should:

- Adhere to the documentation guidelines of the organization
- Avoid duplication of information at multiple locations
- Avoid ambiguity

Keeping in mind that multiple individuals are likely to prepare plan documents, uniformity can be achieved in an organization through the use of templates and reviews. Every organization, therefore, should define its templates. One suggestion is to start by using templates from industry associations, standards organizations (e.g., IEEE), or a consulting group.

ROLES IN PLANNING

Collaboration between various groups within an organization is critical in achieving effective project planning. At least two entities in an organization impact project planning: the organization that provides the infrastructure and the individual who carries out the project planning.

The Organization

To plot a project's future, an organization needs project planning. Therefore, to facilitate process planning, the organization provides an infrastructure that facilitates and enables effective project planning:

- Development, establishment, implementation, and continuous improvement of the project planning process in the organization (procedures, templates, formats, and quality assurance for plans)
- Implementation guidelines and standards (documentation guidelines, checklists for the preparation and review of plans, and estimation guidelines and productivity figures for various technologies used in the organization)
- Establishment of a PMO (or similar) that takes charge of all project plans and assists all concerned individuals in preparing project plans and that also acts a lightening rod to receive feedback and to ensure that feedback is analyzed, acted upon, and incorporated into processes, standards, and guidelines
- Arranging for peer and managerial reviews of all plans at the preparation stage and, upon completion of a project, conducting a variance analysis to capture the best and worst practices and to measure the efficacy of the project plans

- Development and population of a knowledge repository for project planning that acts as the corporate "memory" of past estimates and project plans (a repository) so information can be used as reference for project planning
- Providing structured training for planning projects
- Recognizing that project planning is a specialist activity and subjecting it to the rigors of process improvement
- Rewarding individuals who excel at project planning

The Software Project Manager

Individuals can "make or break" project planning. An individual who is vested with the responsibility of project planning should be a person who strives to excel at project planning. In addition to making the best use of the available infrastructure, an SPM who is well versed in project planning can achieve effective planning for the projects. A good project planner can add value to the organizational project planning process through:

- Diligently planning the project and preparing plan documents so that they adhere to organizational processes, standards, and guidelines
- Recognizing that project planning is important. It is not just preparing documents — it is *planning the project*. The documents are an offshoot of the planning process that are to be used for the purposes of review, improvement, and reference by all concerned groups in the organization
- Assisting the organization in developing, establishing, implementing, and continuously improving the project planning process
- Adhering to organizational processes, standards, and guidelines in "letter and spirit"
- Giving feedback to concerned parties
- Participating in process improvement activities wholeheartedly
- Carrying out the project planning activity to the best of one's ability as diligently as possible

Individuals who are poorly suited for project planning usually whine about the planning process. They generally cause more effort to be spent on the process than needed. Vesting the exercise of project planning in an SPM or a team member who is unsuited for project planning is just one of many potential pitfalls in software project planning, the subject of the next section.

PITFALLS IN SOFTWARE PROJECT PLANNING

Briefly, some common pitfalls in project planning in organizations include:

Preparing only documents. As discussed earlier, creating documents is *not* the same as project planning. (*Remember*: Documentation is done to *organize* thoughts and information about a project's plans and to *allow* information from the plans to be used as a reference for project stakeholders.) Many organizations, however, treat the project planning process as nothing more than the preparation of documents. Sometimes, with little or no thought, a past plan is converted to the plan for a new project. This lack of thought causes the focus on the planning aspects of a project to be reduced. Each aspect of a plan must be well considered and thought out *before* a plan is documented. The bottom line is that a plan must be implementable.

Best practice: Shift the focus from treating planning as documentation to using documentation as a tool to organize a project.

Inadequate time for planning. Often, when an organization is in a hurry to begin a project, the start of the project will be rushed and inadequate time will be allotted to planning. Planning, however, is a crucial activity. Failing to allow enough time to permit adequate planning causes the plans to be less likely to be effective. Execution is also more likely to require deviations from the plan and a greater frequency of midcourse corrections. An organization is well served to remember the wise counsel of Abraham Lincoln about felling a tree, which is quoted at the beginning of this chapter.

Best practice: Allow adequate time for planning activities — plan for planning.

No training or the wrong training. Project planning training for computer science students by educational institutions, if done at all, is rare. Even more unlikely is training for these students in the art and science of project planning. Therefore, when promoting or recruiting a programmer to become a project manager, training in the art and science of planning will be needed. (*Note*: Most individuals learn to use Microsoft Project from their peers or from senior members in the organization. Few are formally trained in Microsoft Project — and many of those confuse scheduling and planning. Individuals who do receive training in Microsoft Project rarely receive training about the theory and practice of PERT/CPM, the basis of actually using the tool. Not uncommon is seeing Microsoft Project plans with hanging nodes and no resource constraints. Needless to say, these schedules are obviously in error and not being used to their full value.)

Best practice: Provide formal training in PERT/CPM and other project management tools to individuals who are vested with the responsibility of planning.

Skipping reviews. Two types of reviews are essential for quality control: a peer review and a managerial review. A peer review is conducted by a person (or persons) who has similar experience in a similar role. A *peer* review looks very closely at the details, whereas a *managerial* review looks at the "big picture." Both of these reviews have a significant value. Cutting either one short (but more frequently the peer review) would be compromising. Because planning is the initial stage of a project, errors that are undetected in the planning review process will likely have costly consequences for the project.

Best practice: Conduct peer and managerial reviews.

Lacking a PMO or having an ineffective PMO. Because a PMO is a cost center that needs costly senior and human resources, many organizations have a PMO in name only. In this scenario, the "non-PMO" is more project administration than project management. This type of PMO does not assist SPMs, but instead actually causes a greater expenditure of resources. By demanding all sorts of data and analyses, this type of PMO typically becomes a hindrance for SPMs. (*Remember*: The PMO should collect data from the SPMs to carry out analyses in the most nonintrusive manner possible. These analyses are then supplied to SPMs and senior management to facilitate the corrective actions needed to keep the project on course.)

Best practice: Establish a robust and effective PMO based on a well-defined and well-implemented process framework.

Lacking a knowledge repository or having a poorly organized knowledge repository. Many organizations fail to take the development and maintenance of a knowledge repository seriously. The knowledge repository becomes a "dumping ground" for records from completed projects. To have a proper knowledge repository, resources (hardware, software, and human resources) need to be dedicated to the vital activity of maintaining a knowledge repository. Not only does a well-structured knowledge repository assist in ensuring project success, but it also provides a springboard for taking an organization to the next higher level of increased effectiveness.

Best practice: Have a well-structured knowledge repository.

BEST PRACTICES IN SOFTWARE PROJECT PLANNING

In addition to the best practices already described, a few additional best practices include:

Process-driven planning. A process-driven planning approach facilitates uniformity among SPMs in the project planning community of an organization. By providing templates to ensure that no important aspect is forgotten or overlooked, process-driven planning also facilitates more comprehensive planning. Defining the process planning process and then subjecting it to continuous improvement will hone organizational project planning skills and progressively improve planning to a stage in which the variances between planned and actual achievements are narrowed down to a minimum.

Best practice: Have a process-driven planning approach.

Balanced planning. When planning each project, strike a balance between "what is needed" and "what is mandated." Although having a PMP is a "bare minimum" planning requirement, a PMP will be inadequate for many projects. A better option (unless a project is very small) is to prepare a minimum of three plans: a PMP, a CMP, and a QAP. Include other pertinent aspects as needed in these three documents. Based on the complexity, duration, and the person-month effort required to execute the project, the preparation of more detailed (or additional) plans may be needed. For example, as additional human resources are employed, the complexity of management increases. Having three plans (a PMP, CMP, and QAP) may be adequate if the number of teams in a project is one (one team consists of six to ten people), but if the number of teams increases beyond one, the number and rigor of these plans must increase.

Best practice: Create a balanced set of plans based on the type of project, the effort required to execute the project, the expected duration, and the number of teams working on the project. Refer to the organizational norms for the recommended set of plan documents.

Norms for planning. For the estimation component of planning to be realistic, norms, especially for software estimation, resource estimation, and other software engineering activities, must be made available to project planners. Obviously these norms should form a part of the organization's knowledge repository. Derivation of norms based on studies and periodic adjustment, taking into consideration actual achievements, goes a long way in ensuring effective planning.

Best practice: Use organizational norms from the knowledge repository for the estimation component of planning.

Variance analysis. Once a project is completed, an analysis of the variances from estimates to actual achievements needs to be carried out. A variance analysis includes comparing the original plan to the actual achievements, eliminating abnormal achievements with assignable causes that are specific to the project, drawing the correct inferences from the data, and updating the organizational norms. Subjecting a completed project to variance analysis and then adding updates to the knowledge repository ensure that the knowledge repository contains reliable and credible information. Although variance analysis is an important step in the postmortem process, in many organizations, conducting a variance analysis is more often an exception rather than the rule.

Best practice: Conduct a variance analysis during project postmortems and update the knowledge repository.

REFERENCES

1. Chemuturi, Murali. *Software Estimation Best Practices, Tools & Techniques: a Complete Guide for Software Project Estimators* 2009. Ft. Lauderdale, FL: J. Ross Publishing.

2. PMI. *A Guide to the Project Management Body of Knowledge, Fourth Edition (PMBOK® Guide)* 2009 January. Chicago: The Project Management Institute.

6

SOFTWARE PROJECT EXECUTION

INTRODUCTION

Software process execution is where "the rubber hits the road" — it is the crux of software project management. In project execution, the art and science aspects of management are implemented and results are obtained; the efficacy of the planning is put to the test; and the deliverables are constructed, tested, and delivered to the customer. Software project execution is typically composed of several management activities:

- Work
- Configuration
- Quality
- Team morale
- Productivity
- Stakeholder expectations
  - Customers
  - The organization and management
  - Project teams
- Product integration
- Control

Software project execution activities are illustrated in Figure 6.1. Appendix A also covers the broad subject of management in greater detail. (*Note*: Because of the

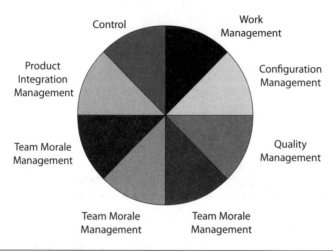

Figure 6.1. Software project management execution.

importance of control management, Chapter 7 is devoted entirely to the subject of project control.)

WORK MANAGEMENT

Work management in software projects has no specific definition, but in software projects, work is managed by executing it in a stepwise process:

1. Allocating the work for execution
2. Assuring that completed work is under configuration management and that it is subjected to appropriate QA activities
3. De-allocating human resources so that they can take up other task
4. Promoting an artifact to the next level of activity

These four steps are iterated until all work is completed.

Before work can be managed using this stepwise process, the work needs to be broken down into components for allocation. In other types of projects, *work* consists of performing tasks. In software development, however, because components are constructed, changed, or repaired, it is *functionality* that needs to be broken down into constituent modules. Then these modules are broken into submodules, and so on, until no further breakdown is feasible or until any further breakdown will yield no additional advantage in work allocation. The work "package" should be a stand-alone piece, i.e., it can be allocated to one person for construction.

But how large should a work package be for allocation to one person? Whenever possible, when allocating work to an individual, consider the following guidelines:

- A work package should consist of a single component. (Allocating more than two or three components at the same time is possible, but not ideal. Instead, components of the same module should be allocated to the same person serially.)
- The component should be amenable for independent testing.
- The allocation should have independent functionality. (If functionality is divided into more than one component, all components should be allocated to one individual or to members of the same team.)
- A work allocation should occupy an individual for at least a full day or for multiples of a day thereafter. (Allocating work multiple times in a day is cumbersome for the individual as well as the SPM/project leader. Also possible is that fractions of a day will simply be lost if the individual does not remember to report completion of the work allocation an hour before the close of the day and ask for the next allocation. Completion of work is expected to be reported immediately, to the minute, but in reality many individuals take a break before they report completion of work.)
- A work allocation should be no longer than a week.

So, how is work allocated? Two approaches are common: an ad hoc approach and a process-driven approach:

Ad hoc. In an ad hoc approach, work is allocated by:

- Sitting with the person in a one-on-one meeting
- Explaining the functionality
- Bargaining and setting a completion target
- Getting the individual to carry out the work

Process driven. In a process-driven approach, work is allocated by:

- Maintaining a work register that is available to all project team members (e.g., using an Excel sheet or a software tool such as Microsoft Project or PMPal)
- Entering work allocations in the work register

At the beginning of each workday, a team member checks the work register for his/her work allocation (as well as to determine the next work allocation when the work allocation is completed). Then the team member:

- Collects the appropriate support information (e.g., the design document from the common information repository)

Table 6.1. An Activity-Based Work Register: Construction Activity

Component Name	Attribute	Estimated Size	Actual Size	Allocated to	Scheduled Start	Actual Start	Scheduled Completion	Actual Completion
XYZ	C	200 LOC		ABC	10 Oct 09		11-Oct-09	

- Notes the effort estimate and targets from the work register (and if necessary bargains with the SPM/PL for correction of the effort estimate or the completion target until agreement is reached)
- Starts the work

Work Registers

A work register consists of multiple columns. A work register may be maintained as a single register or by using multiple registers (one for each phase). When multiple registers are maintained, a separate register is used for each development activity: requirements, software design, construction, review/walk-through, unit testing, integration, integration testing, build preparation, and system testing.

An activity-based work register. In an activity-based register, the *Attribute* column states the size measure and the size. Actual values for the *Actual Size* column are captured from the individual who completes the work. (*Note*: The size of a work allocation might not be given if the size does not lend itself to measurement, but this situation does not indicate that recording project-level size data should be abandoned.) A work register based on a development activity is illustrated in Table 6.1.

A single register. A single register tracks the work allocation against the components. In a single register, product integration and build preparation, as well as their associated QA activities, are treated as components. Each row depicts allocation information for all of the activities for a single component. Advantages of a single work register include:

- All components are tracked in a single place: finding out if every component has been included is easy.
- All information pertaining to a component is in one row: finding out if a specific activity has been carried out is easy.
- Because all components are tracked, determining project status is easy.
- Metrics computation is easy.
- Automating register maintenance and data collection is easy.

Each row in a single register is very long, however, which makes using the register a bit tedious when maintained manually. A single work register is shown in Table 6.2.

Table 6.2. A Single Work Register

Component	
Module name	
Attribute	
Estimated size	
Actual size	
Allocated for construction to	
Scheduled start of construction	
Actual start of construction	
Scheduled finish of construction	
Actual finish of construction	
Allocated for review to	
Scheduled start of review	
Actual start of review	
Scheduled finish of review	
Actual finish of review	
Number of defects uncovered in review	
Allocated for unit testing to	
Scheduled start of unit testing	
Actual start of unit testing	
Scheduled finish of unit testing	
Actual finish of unit testing	
Number of defects uncovered in unit testing	

Multiple registers. Similarly to maintaining a single work register, multiple registers maintain several registers — one for *each* phase-level activity. Some advantages of maintaining multiple registers include:

- The information in each register is homogenous: register maintenance is easy.
- Work is tracked based on type of activity: finding out if a component has been completed in a certain activity is easy.

Some disadvantages of multiple registers include:

- As the number of moving parts increases and overhead levels become higher, a single activity becomes more likely to "fall through the cracks" and be overlooked (e.g., overlooking a quality assurance activity for a component is possible).

- Determining project status requires referring to multiple registers.
- Metrics computation requires compilation of data from multiple registers.
- Duplication of data is possible in some registers (if not all).

De-allocation

The term *de-allocated* sounds harsh, but *de-allocated* merely refers to the assignment of an individual to another task. De-allocation is a stepwise process in which an individual completes an allocated work; the results of the work are promoted; and the individual is reassigned to other work:

1. The individual to whom the work has been allocated completes the work.
2. The individual informs the SPM/PL that the work is complete.
3. The SPM/PL takes possession of the completed artifact and does a cursory inspection to ensure that the work is indeed complete.
4. The SPM/PL obtains the completion information and the actual size of the product constructed for construction allocations. (For QA allocations, the number of discovered defects is obtained.)
5. The SPM/PL updates information in the work register.
6. The SPM/PL uses the data collected to determine the level of productivity achieved by the individual on the component. (Depending on the level of productivity achieved, the SPM/PL provides any mentoring needed to the individual.)
7. The individual is de-allocated from the current allocation, which makes the individual available for the next allocation.
8. The SPM/PL promotes the artifact to the next step in the artifact's development life cycle.

This process of allocation and de-allocation is leveraged until all components are constructed, integrated, and tested; the final build is prepared, tested, delivered to the customer; and all resources are released. The de-allocation process is illustrated in Figure 6.2.

But, why go to all this trouble? The answer: using work registers and de-allocation is effective in work management. They ensure that:

- All construction work and all related activities are tracked so that they will be completed on time.
- All QA activities are performed and defects are fixed.
- Wait time between work allocations is eliminated or minimized.
- Re-work due to lack of coordination is minimized.
- No work allocation is duplicated (i.e., no component is built twice).

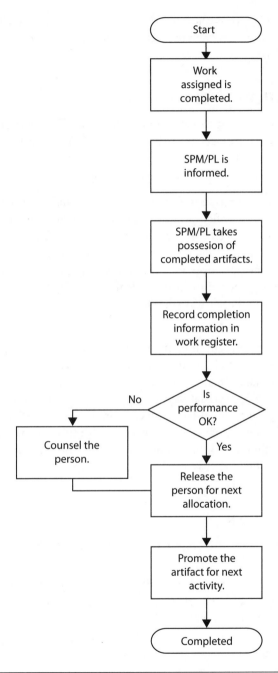

Figure 6.2. The work de-allocation process.

- The "right" work is allocated to the "right" person (the right person for every assignment and the right assignment for every person — pun intended!).

CONFIGURATION MANAGEMENT

Configuration management in software development deals with *safekeeping the integrity* of all project artifacts and with *controlling the changes* that need to be effected on the artifacts. Configuration management covers system configurations of two types: production configuration and development configuration.

Note: Production configuration is established in the actual environment in which the software will run. Configuration management in production configuration deals with the maintenance of the artifacts through a system of checks and balances and a series of approvals to ensure that end-users are using the right software. This book does not cover management of the production configuration. Configuration management in this book deals with the *development configuration*: the time frame in the software development life cycle (SDLC) when software is being developed.

In development configuration management, each software project should have a configuration control board (CCB). The CCB oversees implementation of the configuration management process in a project. A CCB typically consists of one or more persons. The actual day-to-day work of configuration management is carried out by an individual (sometimes more than one individual), who has been designated as the configuration controller (CC; this role may be referred to by other titles, including configuration manager). Configuration management in development configuration is applicable to two types of artifacts: information artifacts and code artifacts.

Information Artifacts

Information artifacts are the *project-specific* documents. Project-specific documents include:

- Project initiation records (the PIN, RFP, feasibility report, proposal, order, and approvals)
- Requirements documents
- Design documents
- Project plans
- Test plans, test cases, and test logs
- Review records
- Work registers

- Change requests and the change register
- Customer interface communications (approvals, commendations, and complaints)
- Progress reports
- Meeting minutes
- Any other related documents

Information generated within a project may be maintained in three macro-states:

- *Under preparation set*: Documents remain in "under preparation" while they are being prepared and until they are either approved or discarded.
- *Current set*: Documents to be used by the project team in carrying out work on other deliverables are kept in "current set."
- *Archive set*: Documents are kept in "archive set" when they have been superseded. They are maintained for the duration specified in the configuration management plan.

Information received from a client or from another department, however, has only one state: *current state*. Configuration management ensures that for that any given document, a given version is available at *only one* place.

Replacing a document in the current set. Steps in a recommended process for replacing an existing document in the *current state* with an updated document include:

1. The originator of a proposed replacement requests that the CCB process the change. (The actual communication may be through email or via a wide variety of methods. More and more often, software configuration tools are replacing the need for external communication methods.)
2. The CCB verifies the new artifact to ensure that it is complete that that it has received the required approvals.
3. If complete and the required approvals have been accorded, the CCB instructs the CC to effect the change. The CC then copies the existing artifact from *current set* to *archive set* and deletes it from *current set*.
4. The CC then copies the new artifact from the *under preparation set* to *current set* and deletes it from *under preparation set*.
5. The configuration controller then arranges for a peer review of the change and informs the CCB.
6. The CCB informs the originator of the request that the process is complete.

The document replacement process is depicted in Figure 6.3. Most current change management tools or scripts automate these steps through some form of work flow, creating records of the change process and obtaining approvals (as required) for auditing and security reasons.

Code Artifacts

Code artifacts are the second, and the more important, set of artifacts managed in configuration management. Code artifacts typically include:

- The program code that is being developed by the project
- Components supplied by the customer
- Components obtained from a subcontractor
- Reusable components from the organization's code repository:
  - Components that can be used without any modification
  - Components that can be used with modification
- Code libraries obtained from a third party (e.g., a COTS product)
- Software components obtained from a third party (e.g., a COTS product or a component)
- Database table scripts
- Test data

Of these code artifacts, four have multiple states — the program code, components that can be used with modification, database table scripts, and test data:

1. Initial coding
2. Review
3. Unit testing
4. Rectification
5. Integration
6. Integration testing
7. Build preparation
8. System testing
9. Acceptance testing
10. Delivery

Code integrity. Usually, developing code for a component takes multiple days. Performing the quality assurance (QA) activities designed for the component also takes multiple days. Therefore, until the component has been completed in all respects, including QA, the integrity of the code must be ensured. (*Note:* Code integrity means that the right version of code is promoted to the next stage of development work.) Configuration management of code artifacts ensures the

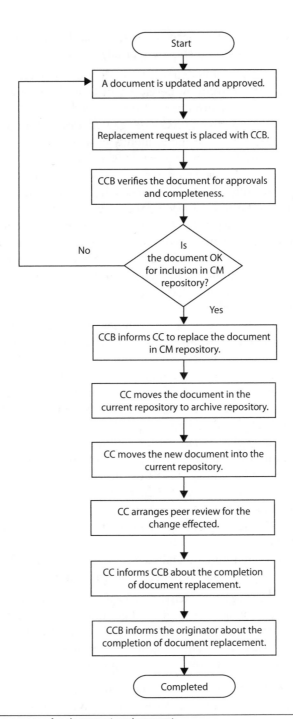

Figure 6.3. The process for document replacement.

integrity of the code being developed. To ensure that the integrity of the code is protected, code library environments are typically leveraged:

- *Development*: The foundation of the development environment is comprised of the software development tool kit. Programmers use the development environment to develop code and to conduct self-testing. Each programmer has a designated area and the appropriate access rights to the code and to modify programs. Code in the development environment undergoes frequent changes.

- *Testing*: The testing environment consists of the testing tools, the test data, and any other components necessary to carry out testing of the code that has been developed by the programmers. (Usually, no system testing is carried out in the testing environment: system testing is carried out in the actual environment or in a simulation of the actual environment.) No changes should be made to code in the testing environment. To effect this recommendation, allow no access rights to the code. Testers should only have access to execute the code and modify test data as needed.

- *Integration*: The integration environment is similar to the development environment. Access rights in the integration environment are limited to only the programmers who are charged with integration of the individual units and building them into the designed software product. In larger projects that consist of multiple modules, each module could have an environment for integration and an environment designated to final build preparation.

- *Systems testing*: The systems testing environment consists of the target configurations in which the developed software product is expected to function in "real life." No changes to code should be made in the systems testing environment. Testers only have access to execute the code and modify test data as necessary.

- *Delivery*: The delivery environment is a repository where all components to be delivered are collated. No changes to code are allowed in the delivery environment. Only the configuration controller/configuration manager has access rights in this environment.

Configuration management activity is heavily focused on controlling the movement of code. Most of the work in configuration management is carried out by managing the state transition of code (i.e., from one state to another) to ensure that only the right version of code is ultimately delivered to the customer. The movement of code typically follows a stepwise process:

1. The code begins in the development environment.
2. The code moves from the development environment to the testing environment for code review.

3. If any defects are uncovered in code review, the code goes from the testing environment back to the development environment for rectification.

4. After the defects are fixed, the code again moves from the development environment to the testing environment for re-review (as appropriate).

Steps 3 and 4 are iterated until all defects are fixed or a threshold level has been triggered (based on thresholds in the organizational review process).

5. Upon certification of integration by the reviewer that the code is free of defects, the code is retained in the testing environment for unit testing.

6. If any defects are uncovered in unit testing, the code moves from the testing environment back to the development environment for rectification of the defects that have been unearthed in unit testing.

7. After fixing the defects, the code again moves from the development environment to testing environment for regression testing.

Steps 6 and 7 are iterated until all defects are fixed.

8. Once testing certifies the code as defect-free, the code moves from the testing environment to the integration environment for integration.

9. Once integration of the product (or a module) is completed, self-reviewed, and self-tested, the code is moved from the integration environment to the testing environment for integration testing.

10. If any defects are uncovered during integration testing, the code moves from the testing environment back to the integration environment to rectify the defects that have been unearthed in integration testing.

11. After fixing the defects, the code again moves from the integration environment to the testing environment for regression testing.

Steps 10 and 11 are iterated until all defects are fixed.

12. Once testing certifies the code as defect-free, the code moves from the testing environment to the system testing environment for system testing.

13. System testing and any other related tests planned for the software product are conducted in the system testing environment. If any defects are uncovered by these tests, the code would be moved back to the integration/development environment for rectification of the defects.

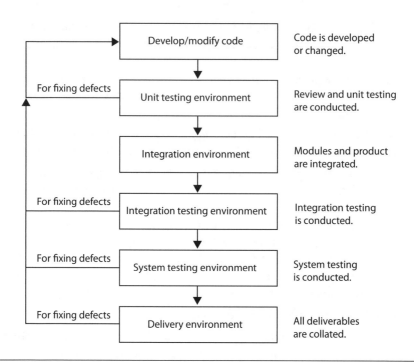

Figure 6.4. State transition of code in configuration management.

14. After fixing the defects, the code is moved from the integration environment to the system testing environment for regression testing.

Steps 13 and 14 are iterated until all defects uncovered by system testing are fixed.

15. Once the testers certify the code as defect-free, the code would be moved to the delivery environment for delivery to the customer.

16. If any change requests are received for the code in any environment, the code is moved to the development environment for implementation of the change request. Once a change is completed, it follows the same procedure as described above.

The state transition of code artifacts is illustrated in Figure 6.4.

All software development organizations might not use all of these environments individually. Instead, a combination of environments could be used, e.g., combining the testing environment and the system testing environment to become a single testing environment. Similarly, the development environment and integration environment could be combined into a single development environment. Another possibility is that an organization with specialized needs might create additional environments to meet a specific need.

Code maintenance. In software maintenance projects, typical code maintenance environments are production, development, testing, and delivery:

- *Production*: contains all code and the data being used
- *Development*: a replica of the production environment that is used to make software modifications
- *Testing*: for carrying out the testing of software fixes
- *Delivery*: for staging changes before they are promoted to the production environment

In the maintenance environment, code movement follows a stepwise process:

1. When a maintenance work request (MWR) is received, the affected code is copied from the production environment to the development environment to implement the changes described in the MWR.
2. After implementing the changes described in the MWR and self-testing, the code is moved to the testing environment for regression testing.
3. If any defects are uncovered during regression testing, the code is moved back to the development environment for repair.

Steps 2 and 3 are iterated until all defects are fixed.

4. Once the code is certified as defect-free, the code is moved to the delivery environment.
5. The code is moved from the delivery environment to the production environment.

Note: Movement into the production environment (as well as movement into and out of all environments) must conform to change management procedures. Approvals are typically part of change management procedures. Movement into production also occurs according to an organizational norm: weekly, monthly, need-based, or in some other interval that meets the organization's business needs.

Configuration Registers

The goal of this section is not to identify a particular format, but to give the reader an understanding of the configuration register and to emphasize the necessity of monitoring and tracking the movement of configuration items. The number of columns used in a manual configuration register is based on organizational needs. The number of columns used is also based on the configuration management process used. Almost all current configuration management tools can track and provide register-like reporting. In many of the more popular tools, code and information artifacts are tracked, versioned, and maintained side-by-side virtually,

Table 6.3. Format for a Manual Configuration Register

Name of Artifact	Current Version	Location (References Location of the Artifact)	Date of First Check-In to Configuration Register	Date of Approval for Current Version	Checked in By	Baseline Purpose

capabilities that have caused many organizations to replace manual registers with configuration management tools.

A configuration register (also known as configuration records) is maintained by a configuration controller under the guidance of the CCB. A configuration register contains a list of all project artifacts: the *information artifacts* and the *code artifacts*. A configuration register also maintains a version number for each type of artifact: an artifact with a version number *less than* the number in the configuration register is considered to be obsolete; an artifact with a version number *greater than* the number in the configuration register is understood to not yet be approved for use:

- *Information artifacts*: Version numbers are maintained as part of the document, normally in a table referred to as the revision history or the approval record.
- *Code artifacts*: The version number is maintained in the revision history inside the code.

Maintaining two registers for a project is customary: one for information artifacts and another for code artifacts. A format for a manual configuration register is shown in Table 6.3. Entries in the cells in Table 6.3 contain the following information:

- *Name of Artifact*: the name of the artifact (e.g., the document file name or the program file name)
- *Current Version*: the current version number of the approved artifact
- *Location*: the directory/folder/library where the artifact resides (with the current version number)
- *Date of First Check-In to Configuration Register*: the date on which the artifact is entered in the configuration register
- *Date of Approval for Current Version*: the date on which the artifact is approved (with the current version number)
- *Checked In By*: the name of the person who checked the current version into its current location (usually the configuration controller)
- *Baseline Purpose*: the purpose of the current baseline and its intended use (testing, integration, delivery, etc.)

Table 6.4. Alternate Format for a Configuration Register

Name of Artifact	Development Baseline		Testing Baseline		Integration Baseline		Delivery Baseline	
	Date	Version	Date	Version	Date	Version	Date	Version

When making delivery to a customer, the configuration register is checked for the purpose for which the artifact is baselined. Only when the baseline purpose for an artifact has been flagged as "delivery" does an artifact qualify for delivery.

Another format for a manual configuration register is shown in Table 6.4. In this register, entries in the cells contain baseline information:

- *Name of Artifact*: the name of the artifact (e.g., document file name or the program file name)
- *Development Baseline Date*: the date on which development is completed and approved
- *Development Baseline Version*: the version number of the artifact that has been completed and approved
- *Testing Baseline Date*: the date on which testing is completed and all defects uncovered have been fixed and approved
- *Testing Baseline Version*: the version number of the artifact that has been tested and all uncovered defects have been fixed and approved
- *Integration Baseline Date*: the date on which integration is completed and integration testing is completed for the artifact and approved
- *Integration Baseline Version*: the version number of the artifact that has had integration completed in all respects and has been approved
- *Delivery Baseline Date*: the date on which the artifact is approved for delivery to a customer
- *Delivery Baseline Version*: the version number of the artifact that is ready for delivery to a customer

The two *Delivery Baseline* columns must be completed for all relevant artifacts before delivery to a customer can occur.

When delivery to a customer is completed, delivery inspection is carried out to ensure that the version number on each artifact matches the corresponding version number for the artifact in the configuration register. Any deviation is reported as a defect. Rectification must be carried out before the artifact is "passed" for delivery.

Baselining an artifact. Baselining an artifact refers to updating the version number for an artifact and entering the information in a configuration register.

Although variations of the baseline procedure exist in organizations, baselining typically follows several steps:

1. An artifact is allocated to an individual for construction.
2. When construction of the artifact is completed and approved for promotion to testing, the first baseline for the artifact is established.
3. Whenever any modification is carried out on the artifact, for any reason, the version number is incremented according to the version numbering guidelines for the project.
4. When testing of the artifact (review in the case of an information artifact) is completed and all defects uncovered have been fixed, the testing baseline is established using the version number and the date on which the artifact was approved for the next stage.
5. When the artifact is integrated into its module or product, the integration testing is completed, and all defects uncovered during integration testing have been fixed, the integration baseline is established using the version number and the date on which approval for the next stage was received.
6. When all activities on the artifact are completed and the artifact is approved for delivery to a client, the delivery baseline is established using the version number and the date on which approval for the next stage was received. The delivery baseline is the final baseline.

Note: Should a change request be received for any artifact after it has been baselined, the artifact's status is returned to development baseline. Once development is completed, the artifact reenters the process at the beginning of testing.

Obtaining approval for baselines. A typical approach for obtaining approval to baseline an artifact includes:

- A request to baseline an artifact is made by the SPM/PL to the CCB.
- The CCB considers the request and inspects the pertinent reports to ensure that the prerequisite activities for baselining have indeed been completed.
- If appropriate, the CCB instructs the configuration controller to baseline the artifact.
- The configuration controller enters/updates the information in the configuration register and physically moves the artifact to the next stage.

Managing all of these activities constitutes configuration management during software development. At times, an SPM takes on the configuration management roles, particularly when a project is small in size and in duration; however, a formal definition of the various configuration roles is typically done in large development and software maintenance projects.

Configuration Management Tools

A plethora of configuration management tools are available. Although using a configuration management tool is not mandatory, these tools do provide a separate security system over and above an operating system's security layer. (If you are willing to expend the effort, you can achieve the same results by using the operating system's directory/library/folder structures and its security cover as can be achieved by using a configuration management tool.) Configuration management tools can provide:

- Controlled check-in and check-out of artifacts
- Retrieval of any earlier versions without having to keep manual backups of every version (enables the selection of one version for a particular project/customer and another version for another project)
- Maintenance of a version number within an artifact itself, automatically updating the version number every time the artifact is checked in (eliminates the necessity of manual modification and automates revision history maintenance)
- Facilitation of final build preparation (Configuration management tools have facilities for automatic build preparation or to provide an interface to build preparation utilities: once a list of artifacts with their version numbers is provided, the majority of the build process is managed by the tool.)

Note: The ability to retrieve an earlier version without having to keep manual backups of every version is especially useful for COTS developers who maintain products that are being used by different environments/customers. As the complexity caused by the number of configurations increases, a tool-based configuration register assumes its true significance and importance. Perhaps this version retrieval ability is the greatest advantage of using a configuration management tool. Life without a configuration management tool for COTS product developers would be very difficult.

Configuration management tools provide excellent facilities. Older tools, however, focus more on *production* configuration management than on software *development* configuration. Once a software product is in production, the artifacts do not change daily. During development, however, artifacts can undergo daily change until the final build is ready.

Note: If configuration management tools are used without the proper guidelines, some "interesting" situations can occur. In one situation, we observed 20 as being the version of a program — and the final build was not even prepared! This situation happened because the programmer checked in every evening and checked out every morning. By the time the program passed unit testing, its version had already shot up to 10! The point of this story is that a program must be complete before it is checked back in.

When a configuration management tool is used, the following are helpful check-in guidelines:

- *Initial check-in*: Do not check-in a program unit/screen/report, etc. to a configuration management tool until it has passed through independent unit testing. One approach for an information artifact is to not check-in until the artifact has received its first approval. (This piece of advice is found on the introduction page of the Help file of more than one configuration management tool, but who reads Help files these days?)
- *Recheck-in*: Only allow recheck-in after due approval has been obtained. For a code artifact, passing regression testing could be a criterion when using a configuration management tool. For an information artifact, approval by a competent person could be a criterion.
- *When under development*: The configuration management tool should not be used as an online backup device. While under coding/preparation/rectification, an artifact should not be checked into the tool.
- *Limited check-in access*: Allow only one person to check-in artifacts (if not for the entire project, at least for each module). Enforce check-in security strictly.

Adhering to all of these precautions is a *sine qua non* (absolutely indispensable) in the production environment. Based on the development process being used, this type of discipline should also be inculcated in the development environment.

Any tool or process is similar to a knife: a knife can be used to cause injury or be put to some productive purpose. Similarly, configuration management tools can cause problems or they can greatly assist in ensuring the integrity of software artifacts. To use configuration management tools effectively, first learn how to properly use them; next define the guidelines, including the best practices for using the tool; and then diligently follow the guidelines when using the tool.

So, if using a configuration management tool can sometimes cause problems, what would be the negative impact associated with not using a tool? Without a configuration management tool, ensuring the integrity of an artifact becomes a manual task. Maintenance that would have to be done manually includes:

- The creation of directory/library/folder structures, the configuration register, check-in and check-out (with more diligence), and security enforcement
- The artifact revision history

- Backups of all versions for historical purposes and for retrieval of older versions
- Retrieval of artifacts for builds

Each scenario needs careful evaluation to facilitate selecting the right configuration management tool. For example, for a small, less complicated project, the "right" tool might be no tool at all.

The perils of poor configuration management. Poor CM practices can result in delivery of the wrong version of software and information artifacts to a customer. If a wrong version is delivered, the artifacts may contain defects that were actually fixed during a subsequent development activity. Suggested best practices for better CM include:

- Training all members of the project management team, the CCB, and the configuration controller on the concepts of CM (Knowledge goes a long way toward improving performance.)
- Having formal training for the project team on how to use the configuration management tool (if appropriate)
- Setting up appropriate security for check-in and check-out procedures in the configuration management plan of the project and then enforcing them diligently.
- Maintaining a body of knowledge on CM in the organizational knowledge repository.
- Conducting CM audits periodically and diligently
- Analyzing the CM practices used during project execution and sharing the best practices and pitfalls with the organization during the project postmortem process (knowledge is a terrible thing to waste)

QUALITY MANAGEMENT

Because software quality assurance is a major topic that merits an entire book, this section will only provide an overview of quality management activities. *Quality management* refers to all of the activities performed to ensure that quality is built into the project deliveries. But before describing quality management activities, let's first define the term *quality*.

Quality is generally defined as a *fitness for use*. The words *fitness* and *use* apply to separate scenarios:

- *Fitness* refers to the robustness of the software product and the use limits to which it can be put.
- *Use* defines how the product will be used.

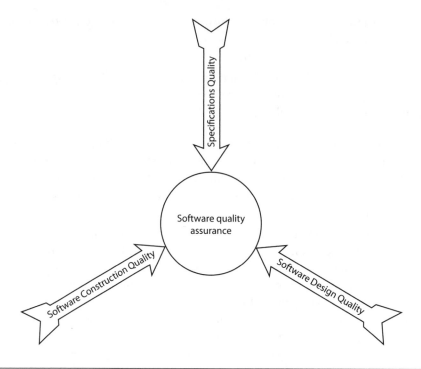

Figure 6.5. Elements of software quality assurance.

So, for every product, *fitness* and *use* need to be interpreted in the product specifications for every product and in the project scenario. *Simply put*: Fitness and use are user requirements that influence software design.

In a project scenario, quality management can be defined as the *need to ensure quality* for:

- Specifications (all requirements)
- Software design
- Software construction

These elements are illustrated in Figure 6.5. Quality assurance tools and the techniques appropriate for each of the project artifacts are shown in Table 6.5.

Two sets of tools and techniques are used to ensure conformance to quality:

- *Verification*: code walk-through, peer review, expert review, and managerial review
- *Validation*: several types of software testing

Table 6.5. Quality Assurance Tools and Techniques for Project Artifacts

Artifact	Quality Assurance Techniques
Source code	Code walk-through and inspection
Executable code	Software testing: at a minimum, unit, integration, system, and acceptance testing
User requirements document	Peer review, expert review, and managerial review
Software design documents	Usability testing, peer review, expert review, and managerial review
Test plans	Peer review and managerial review
Test results	Managerial review

Verification Techniques

Included in verification techniques are code walk-through, peer review, and managerial review:

Code walk-through. A code walk-through is a process in which peers (one or more who have similar experience and knowledge) go through every line of code, assessing its usefulness, necessity, and compliance to standards. A code walk-through may be assisted or unassisted. In an unassisted walk-through, the code is given to a peer who walks through each line of code and makes a report detailing any defects uncovered (the least formal approach). In an assisted walk-through, the author of the code presents the code to one or more peers and notes any improvement suggestions (a more formal approach). A code walk-through is a very valuable tool for ensuring code quality; code walk-throughs should never be skipped. Typical objectives of a code walk-through include:

- Ensuring fulfillment of a designated functionality
- Enforcing conformance to code formatting guidelines and standards
- Pressuring teams to conform to guidelines: efficiency of execution, defect prevention, naming conventions, and resource usage
- Detecting trash code which increases complexity without improving functionality (Examples of trash code are the existence of unused variables; statements inserted for debugging, but left lying in the code; unnecessary loops; etc. Removal of trash code is sometimes called refactoring/retrofitting.)
- Removing of malicious code such as time bombs (unwanted functionality triggered by system clock), trigger bombs (unwanted functionality triggered by an event), and any other unwanted or potentially harmful functionality
- Enforcing the use of the right constructs or frameworks in the code

Peer review. Peer review is similar to code walk-through except that peer reviews are used for information artifacts. Formal inspections are the most rigorous form of inspection (and are also known as Fagan inspections). They are a structured process that tries to find defects in the deliverables (code and noncode). Most formal inspections include the use of moderators and other formal roles. Statistically, formal reviews have been shown to be very effective in uncovering and removing defects.

Managerial review. Managerial review is an approval step that is performed by a person (or persons) who has been designated as the management approver for the project plan. Generally, a managerial review does not deal with minute details. Instead, based on the approver's knowledge of the environment and the circumstances, the approver makes a judgment call about the level of review required: the viewpoint is from an overall perspective of the contents of the artifact. The approver also ensures that peer review has been conducted on the artifact and that all defects uncovered in the peer review have been fixed. The hurdle associated with a managerial review is answering the question: can the artifact be implemented in the project with no concerns? (*Note*: On occasion, fixing all of the defects is unnecessary due to business decisions or some prearranged criteria).

Validation Techniques

The primary validation technique is testing. Two well-known macro-level testing techniques are commonly used: white box and black box testing.

White box testing. The white box technique uses an *internal* perspective that focuses on using the tester's knowledge of the software to uncover defects that are lurking (i.e., are concealed, but can be discovered). White box testing assumes that a tester understands the underlying code. Typically, white box testing involves exercising as much of the code and branch as feasible. Also critical for a tester is knowledge of the software's programming language and structure of the program. (*Note*: In recent years, white box testing has been strengthened by the use of automated testing tools, which make possible the evaluation of more code and branches than is typically possible using manual brute force techniques.)

Black box testing. The black box technique uses an *external* perspective in which the tester has little or no knowledge of the software's internal structure. A set of inputs is fed to the software and the resultant outputs from the software are compared to expected outputs. The black box technique is most effectively executed, however, when the tester is familiar with the required functionality of the system.

When software is developed as a product for delivery to a single client or for use at a single location, the product undergoes the following tests:

- *Unit*: Unit testing is the responsibility of the person who wrote the code. In most circumstances, unit testing is replicated by an independent peer using the white box testing technique. There are two schools of thought, however, on leveraging independent testers for unit testing. The first is that unit testing is the responsibility of the programmer who developed the code: who else would know when the work has been completed? So, in this school of thought, no independent unit testing is necessary. The second school says that only through independent unit testing can an organization be assured that an artifact is without defects. This school of thought believes that humans in general are blind to their own defects and therefore cannot uncover all of the defects that are lurking in their own code. Both schools of thought exist in the industry.

- *Integration*: Integration testing is carried out as a *one-off* (when all integration is completed) or *incrementally* (whenever one unit of the software is integrated and until all units are integrated; also known as continual testing). Black box testing is typically used for one-off integration testing. When leveraging continual integration, white box testing and black box testing are used.

- *System*: System testing is carried out to ensure that the software works in all intended target systems.

- *User acceptance*: User acceptance testing (also known as UAT) is carried out with the customer or only by the customer. The goal of user acceptance testing is to obtain a sign-off so that the software can be delivered and payment will be received from the customer.

Numerous other tests may be conducted at the request of the customer, because of a specific project/product need, or based on an organization's methodology.

Product Testing

Product testing is a specialized form of testing: a product is first developed as a project and then it undergoes all of the typical tests for a project (e.g., unit, integration, and system testing). Then, in the systems testing component, testing is more rigorous than in the unit testing and integration testing components. Testing is also on *all systems* that the product is likely to target. Some of the more rigorous tests carried out include:

- *Load testing*: Load testing may be accomplished in Web or multiuser applications by having a large number of users log on to the application and use the software in a random manner as well as in typical patterns. Load testing reveals issues that are connected with bandwidth, database, and sufficiency of RAM and storage. The objective of load testing is to see if the software can manage multiple requests and accurately provide results.

- *Volume testing*: Volume testing subjects the software to a high volume of data or transactions to determine if performance meets the standards set for the application as the amount of data grows.
- *Functional testing*: Functional testing ensures that all functions of the software are working as specified.
- *End-to-end testing*: End-to-end testing tracks an entity from beginning to end as the entity traverses an application. For example, in a payroll application, an employee joins the organization, is promoted, and then demoted. As a result, salary increases and decreases are made, kept in abeyance, or transferred. Then the employee may quit, be terminated, or retire. The goal of end-to-end testing is to ensure that the state transitions occur as designed.
- *Parallel testing*: Parallel testing is conducted on software that is designed to handle a number of users who are performing the same function at the same time (e.g., call center software). Parallel testing assesses the ability of the system to handle multiple requests that are given at the same time and to preserve data integrity.
- *Concurrent testing*: Concurrent testing is similar to parallel testing. Concurrent testing is conducted to reveal issues that occur when two or more users use the same functions, at the same time, to retrieve, update, or modify the same data, but with different values. For example, in a ticket reservation scenario in which only one seat is available, the seat would be shown as being available to more than one user. If two of the users confirm purchase of the seat at the same time, the system should accept *only* one request and reject the other. At other times, seat allocation occurs first and then a credit card transaction must take place. If payment does not go through, the seat allocation must be reversed. The goal of concurrent testing is to unearth any issues that occur when two or more users use the same functions to retrieve, update, or modify the same data with different values at the same time.
- *Stress testing*: Stress testing seeks to determine what happens when an application exceeds the planned/expected resources. Stress testing can include causing deadlock scenarios to determine if resources are released to ensure that the software has routines built in to handle such stress. Other scenarios in stress testing are events such as machine reset, Internet disconnection, and server timeouts.

- *Positive testing*: Positive testing involves using the software *as designed* to ensure that all defined functions perform as expected when properly used. Positive testing is typically performed during customer/end-user acceptance testing.

- *Negative testing*: Negative testing involves using the software in a manner for which it is not designed or using it in an unexpected way to thereby reveal all hidden defects. Negative testing is conducted to ensure that even malicious usage will not affect the software or data integrity.

- *User manual testing*: User manual testing involves using the software as it is documented in the user manual. User manual testing ensures that the manual and the software are in sync with each other.

- *Deployment testing*: Deployment testing executes the software in the target environment to ensure that the deployment specified is appropriate.

- *Regression testing*: Regression testing is best carried out after defects unearthed in an earlier test have been fixed. The goal of regression testing is to determine if changes made to an application have affected unchanged portions.

- *Security testing*: Security testing is conducted to expose vulnerability to hacking, viruses, and spyware threats.

- *Performance testing*: Performance testing determines if an application performs within an acceptable range. Test results are gauged against response time requirements, standards, and service level agreements.

- *Usability testing*: Usability testing determines if a software product is fit for use. Usability testing includes determining if the software is fit for its intended purpose as well as if the software meets legal access standards (e.g., usability testing must be performed if the software is to be used by persons with disabilities).

- *Install/uninstall testing*: Install/uninstall testing is typically the most important for shrink-wrapped software (retail or available over the counter in stores). Install/uninstall testing ensures that the install and uninstall operations can be satisfactorily performed on all target platforms without affecting the existing software performance.

- *Comparison testing*: Comparison testing (also known as benchmarking) involves determining how a software product performs against a competing product(s). Comparison testing contrasts the differences between competing products to determine the relative market position of the product.

- *Intuitive testing*: Intuitive testing is conducted to determine if the product can be used with little or no reference to a user guide.

- *Sanity testing*: Sanity testing ensures that the components of the software package are complete and that they represent the appropriate versions. Sanity testing is typically the *final* test carried out before delivery to a customer or before compiling a software build.

Although product testing often includes several of these tests, rarely are all of them (or even a majority of them) carried out for every project executed in an organization. (Some organizations might conduct additional types of testing, but only on an "if time and budget are available" or an "if essential" basis.) Often some combination of tests is conducted. Most organizations, however, conduct at least these four types of testing:

- *Functional*: to ensure that all functionalities allocated to the software are working and that when used properly, there are no inaccuracies
- *Integration*: to ensure that there is coupling between various software modules
- *Positive testing acceptance testing*: to ensure user acceptance of the software
- *Load testing*: to ensure that a system does not crash when heavy loads occur

Allocation of Quality Assurance Activities

Maintaining a common work register makes tracking the QA activities performed for every component easier. If a separate work register is used for executing QA activities, however, manual monitoring of all components and recording whether each component has undergone QA activities are required (separate actions and more "moving parts"). A separate work register as shown in Table 6.1 may be used for the allocation and performance of QA activities. Alternatively, Table 6.2, the same work register used for the construction of software, may be used for the allocation and performance of QA activities.

But *How Much* Quality Assurance?

A frequently asked question is, "How much quality assurance activity makes sense, especially for code walk-through and independent unit testing?" The next question is often, "Should we carry out a 100% code walk-through or can we use a sample and then draw conclusions based on the results of the sample?"

In manufacturing, sampling is typically used for QA if:

- The process is predominantly carried out by machines and the role of human resources is limited (roles that would affect the quality of the output).

- The operations process is stable and variances are known to be within an acceptable limit.
- The operations are identical and the output is homogenous, i.e., the same component or product is produced.

If software development were compared to these manufacturing scenarios, the differences would be notable:

- Human resources are critical to achieving quality in software output. Machines have a limited role in achieving quality.
- It cannot be said that the software process is stable or that variances are known. No software project is identical to another.
- The output is not identical at all!

Sampling should be used sparingly at best. The best practice is to perform code walk-throughs and independent unit testing on 100% of the components. Although more rigorous and invasive techniques, such as inspections, are often approached by using sampling techniques, these invasive techniques are *in addition to* walk-throughs and unit testing.

Testing Tools

Many testing tools have the facility to "record and play back." In the record-and-play-back technique, a test is done once manually and then the tool will automatically execute the test. *A **word of caution***: Products with elaborate functionality may need programming to conduct testing automatically. To ensure that the tools integrate into the project processes, project planning must include how tools will be used. Tools are widely used to conduct tests such as load testing (to simulate use by a number of users) and parallel and concurrent testing (in which functions are replicated accurately only by a tool).

For a first-time use, testing tools place the tool programming overhead on the project team or on the testing department. Although subsequent testing will accrue potential savings of a huge amount of effort, each organization must evaluate if investment in the tool, programming of the testing tool, and in maintenance of the test scripts provides a significant advantage. In general, the need for a tool needs to be assessed on a case-by-case basis and appropriate decisions made.

The bottom line is that *quality assurance* for the individual components of a project is the responsibility of the individual team members who built them and *quality management* is the primary responsibility of an SPM, including ensuring a fully functional product and defect-free delivery, while minimizing the effort spent on confirming quality and minimizing rework.

MORALE MANAGEMENT

Team morale is the confidence team members have in their combined capability to achieve the objective of a project. Morale includes the self-esteem of the team and the pride that the team takes in its work. Morale is also the "spirit" of the team. Morale can be positive, neutral, or negative. A team with negative morale will underperform a team with somewhat better morale, whereas a team with positive morale generally outperforms a team with poor morale.

Role of an SPM. Team morale is the most important area of focus for an SPM. If an SPM can achieve and sustain positive morale in a project team, the team will act as one and achieve wonders (if not near miracles!). An SPM who can achieve positive morale and sustain it throughout project completion is always in high demand.

Note: A technically competent SPM is easier to find than an SPM who is technically competent *and* a strong team morale builder. Finding the proper balance required is always difficult, but we suggest that when "push comes to shove" and compromise is needed, usually the correct tradeoff is to accept lower technical capabilities if an SPM has strong morale-building skills.

Team morale is primarily achieved through *motivation*. SPMs are first and foremost technical people. Very few SPMs are trained to understand the psychological needs of project team members and then treat or coach them individually to higher levels of performance. (*Note*: Although generally not practical, many organizations are beginning to leverage coaches that have specific training for a motivational role.) An SPM, however, should have at least a rudimentary understanding of how to motivate people. Team members are not just pairs of hands — they are human beings with skills, aspirations, and likes and dislikes that affect how they interact and work with other team members.

Motivation

Although numerous theories apply to motivation in the workplace, our discussion will deal with only three of the practical aspects of motivation: the work itself, treatment in the workplace, and workplace expectations. A complete survey of the various motivational theories, however, is beyond the scope of this book.

The work. The work itself can be a great motivator. Does this statement sound strange? If so, consider this example. Surely you have observed checkout clerks in a mall during after-Thanksgiving sales. The checkout clerks are constantly busy. Many customers are waiting in long lines. But the checkout clerks do their jobs even if the pay is low. Perhaps they are even temporary hires. Have you ever wondered what could possibly motivate them? The answer: the work that needs to be done — the work itself is demanding their constant attention. This example may seem a bit simplistic, but apply it to the challenge of an important project (with the *challenge* being a critical motivational factor) and the example might seem less farfetched. Why? No one wants to be the person on a team who blocks progress toward reaching an important goal. Therefore, everyone "stretches" to reach the finish line. Remember that the stretch must be possible — unattainable goals are strong de-motivators. (*Note*: Sometimes the monotony of repetitive work causes complaints. Most work-related complaints, however, stem from having *inadequate* work to fill the available time. But in projects, the question of repetitive work does not arise. So, if there are complaints, they must be due to a lack of adequate work.) Ensuring the right quantity and quality of work requires forethought. Consider some best practices for work loading:

- The work load needs to be commensurate with the abilities and skills of the team member.
- The team member must be able to carry out the work. (Nothing is more frustrating than to be responsible for work in which failure is a foregone conclusion. No one likes to fail.)
- The work must be achievable and at the same time test and stretch the capabilities of the team member charged with performing the task. (The possibilities of learning and growth are important components of motivation.)
- The work allocation must be perceived as being fair; the workload allocation ought to be comparable to that of the other team members. (If an individual perceives that he or she is overloaded unfairly, morale will be affected.)
- Team members do not like to admit that they do not have enough work to do or to ask for more work. (The sense of self-esteem and value of team members depends on the quality and quantity of work in hand. If no work is planned for the next day, team members may leave for the day thinking that there will be nothing to do the next day or that a layoff is coming.) When possible, allocate workloads so that team members do not have to continually ask for more work. Just-in-time allocation is the best practice.
- Conversely, very few team members prefer to receive multiple work allocations on a single day, especially professionals such as software engineers. When allocating work that takes more than a day, an effective practice is to allocate tasks that take a calendar week. Select Mondays or Fridays to allocate work for the week. (Multiple daily work allocations appear to be micromanagement.)

- Use a formal mechanism to allocate work and communicate how the mechanism will be used. (Formal mechanisms are efficient. A shared Excel sheet, a work register tool, or stand-up meetings are excellent tools.)
- Set project targets tightly — just slightly tighter than the organizational norms. Tight project targets give an impression that the work is important and therefore urgent. Take care when dealing with urgency, however, because an artificial sense of urgency can be very debilitating.

Treatment in the workplace. Everyone wants to be treated fairly and well. Well-known industrial experiments by Elton Mayo at the Western Electric Hawthorne plant examined the impact of working conditions in employee productivity. (Numerous publications and Internet sources describe the Hawthorne effect in detail.) These early experiments, also known as the Hawthorne Studies, examined the physical and environmental influences of the workplace (e.g., the lighting and humidity) on productivity, but they later addressed the psychological aspects of the workplace and how they affected productivity (e.g., group dynamics, work hours, number of breaks, managerial involvement, etc.). *Fair treatment* today is translated by team members as having:

- Fair allocations of work (based on the best practices of work allocation previously described)
- Fair recognition of the results achieved
- A voice in matters of concern
- Access to information about matters of concern

Note: According to stimulus-response theory, a response to a stimulus will be proportional to the stimulus. The theory works when a positive stimulus gets a positive response and a negative stimulus gets a negative response. But this association gets a bit messy in the workplace if a team member suppresses his or her immediate, natural response based on the prevailing situation. Even if a response is not immediately expressed, the response is still there — lurking just below the surface, but waiting until later to be expressed. An SPM should carefully consider positive and negative stimuli to ensure that the stimulus used generates the most positive response possible.

Workplace expectations. Everyone comes to the workplace with a certain set of expectations. One of those expectations is to earn wages in return for performing the work that is assigned. Another expectation is that team members (or an SPM) should expect to expend a fair amount of effort coupled with the skills that he or she possesses to do a job. (A familiar maxim is "a fair day's work for a fair day's pay.") Another expectation is extra compensation for extra effort (but not less compensation for less effort; and *extra compensation* can mean any number of things). Because most people have an innate need for recognition, to satisfy that need, they may put in extra effort, bring additional skills to a project, show creativity, or come up with innovative ideas. All of these things can be viewed as being a higher level of performance. Having an awareness of the innate need for recognition is mandatory for an SPM. Individuals translate their need for recognition into action for many reasons:

- To receive higher monetary compensation
- To receive a reward
- To receive recognition (either public or private)
- To receive a promotion
- To be treated as being superior to others
- To just please you, if you are the leader

No matter what an expectation concerns, realize that the degree of expectation will likely be different for each team member. Sometimes, just the pursuit of the project's goal will not generate motivation, particularly if expectations are not met. When one team member's expectations are not met, for example, he or she might be likely to become frustrated and then become negative. More often than not, frustration does arise if high expectations are set or there is an implication that the expectations cannot be met. Maybe there is an understanding gap about the expectations. Although meeting team members' expectations does not guarantee that the team members will be better motivated for even higher performance levels, avoid frustration by establishing realistic expectations at the beginning of a project. Setting realistic expectations involves rewarding performance: positive rewards for positive performance and negative rewards for negative performance. Defining what team members can expect for higher levels of performance should to be fair and commensurate with performance.

Team members also expect negative "rewards" to be received for negative performance. Failing to give negative rewards can be very detrimental to team morale. If a team member deserves a negative reward, but does not receive it, other team members receive the message that negative performance is acceptable.

Motivation is one thing — developing a cohesive team is quite another. Numerous books on motivation are available. The three aspects discussed in this section are practical approaches to motivation. Motivation is merely a tool to create a team of highly motivated individuals — because a highly motivated team performs better than a team with little motivation.

But what causes low morale in a team that has highly motivated members? The answer is *conflict*. Conflict can damage team morale. The probability of conflict occurring is directly proportional to the stress levels of the members of the team. Higher levels of stress increase the probability for conflict (and vice versa).

To achieve successful performance results, teams depend on other teams. One team's output is the input for another team. When working on a team, however, sometimes the paths of various team members cross in a negative sense. Sometimes the success of one team seems to be at cross-purposes with that of another team. For example, the effectiveness of QA is directly measured by the quantity of defects found, but the effectiveness of software construction is measured by productivity and the defect injection rate (i.e., the number of errors made that introduce defects into the product). So, if the QA function uncovers more defects, the programmers may be viewed negatively; if the QA function finds fewer defects, QA may be seen as being ineffective. So, some amount of stress and potential conflict is unavoidable — it is inherent in an organization. Stress and conflict in the workplace lead to the topic of "conflict management."

Conflict

An SPM must recognize that conflict is part of life and then manage it. Although a high level of conflict may indicate low morale, no conflict may also mean a team has low morale. (*Note*: This section provides conflict management information that is only relevant to an SPM. A comprehensive discussion of conflict management is beyond the scope of this book.) Reflecting on successful IT organizations, some practical tips for managing conflict and individual competition and keeping it at a healthy level include:

- Conflict and competition are closely related. If not managed well, competition will result in conflict. *Tip*: Promote competition and manage conflict.
- Competition and one-upmanship are also closely related. Their aim is to get ahead of others. Although both competition and one-upmanship cause conflict, competition is somewhat better because competition focuses on self-excellence as the route to get ahead — one-upmanship is just unhealthy. One-upmanship blocks the path of others trying to get ahead by putting hurdles in their way (sometimes referred to as "politics"). *Tip*: Discourage one-upmanship with a gentle but firm hand ("use an iron fist inside a velvet glove") and promote competition.
- Encourage QA to uncover as many defects as possible. After all, detecting defects while a project is in hand is better than learning about them after the product reaches a customer. *Tip*: Discourage listing frivolous defects by the testing group just to run up the statistics.

- Encourage programmers to accept the defects found by the QA team with grace. Ensure that programmers draw lessons from a reported defect to avoid its repetition (it is human to err; but it is foolish to repeat a mistake). *Tip*: Conduct benchmarking. Know if a team is improving and if the processes being used are effective. Record and compare defect injection rates to other teams (or team members) to help a team determine if its defect injection rates are comparable to the organization and if the trend of defect injection rates is decreasing.
- Ensure transparency in reward criteria. Let's face it, as soon as one person hears that the reward criteria are secret, everyone else will hear about it. Transparency in the reward criteria will go a long way in keeping morale at a high level. *Tip*: Base rewards on objective data, not subjective considerations. If rewards are given based on subjective considerations, the team gets the message that performance is not being measured. To avoid sending a message that there is a team "favorite," do not give a reward to the same team member repetitively. *Bottom line:* Be scrupulously fair in rewards and ensure everyone knows you are fair.

Motivation and conflict management are tools used to create a team with high morale. Although each team or organizational culture may have different levels of acceptable conflict, specific techniques may be required to managing motivation, competition, and conflict. An SPM who works daily on these areas is more likely to create and maintain high team morale.

PRODUCTIVITY MANAGEMENT

Completing allocated work is the responsibility of team members. Ensuring that only the right amount of effort is spent on completing the work is the responsibility of an SPM. Productivity management is a major focus area for an SPM.

In a production process, *productivity* is the measure of output from input (i.e., from converting an input into an output). *Efficiency* is one dimension of a team's effectiveness. *Productivity* is also the achievements of an endeavor — a reflection of what was done during the project. Productivity measurement is also used to benchmark the performance of one team member against another as well as to benchmark the performance of the team against other teams. An SPM's knowledge of productivity is used to estimate and set equitable targets for a team. (Productivity concepts are discussed in greater detail in Appendix D.)

One approach to setting equitable targets for an entire project is to set productivity and defect injection rate targets for each separate activity at the beginning of the project at a level that is meaningful for the project and team. Publish the goals in a way that ensures that they are available to all team members. Team members need to know exactly what has to be achieved to reach an acceptable level of performance.

In many organizations, performance norms are obtained by an SPM from the organizational knowledge repository, the software engineering process group (SEPG), the PMO, or the quality department. If organizational norms are not available, an SPM should brainstorm with the team members to arrive at the norms through a consensus (*groupthink*). Types of norms include:

- Coding, with an acceptable defect injection rate for each programming language
- Documentation, with an acceptable defect injection rate
- Code walk-through
- Unit testing
- Integration testing
- System testing

Ensure that the norms cover all of the activities that are to be carried out in the project (including QA activities).

The crux of productivity measurement is defining size. Some guidelines to selecting the unit of measure for measuring software size include:

- Once selected, apply a size measure consistently.
- For software coding, use a software size measure such as Function Point Analysis (FPA) or Software Size Units (SSU).
- For documentation, use the number of pages (physical or logical).
- For software testing, use the number of test cases or a software size measure (FPA or SSU).
- For all other activities, measure the output in the form that is to be delivered and divide that quantity by the effort spent to achieve the output.

When measuring the productivity of all work allocations, look for large deviations from the norms. If a variance is large, find the root cause of the variance. Finding the root cause of a variance determines if there are any assignable causes (e.g., unforeseen issues, delays in receiving approvals, malfunction of a software tool, or the genesis of a new best practice). If a variance is negative, carry out a critical examination to arrive at the reasons for the variance and take corrective and preventive actions so that a recurrence can be prevented. In summary, productivity management:

- Determines and sets appropriate productivity norms for a project during the project planning stage
- Uses norms to set targets during the work allocation process

- Measures productivity for each work allocation after the assignment is complete (*Note*: Determine the applicable level of granularity. Only measure at the level you will manage.).
- Conducts variance analysis between targeted and achieved productivity and takes corrective and preventive actions as needed

STAKEHOLDER EXPECTATIONS MANAGEMENT

Expectations are typically implicit performance assumptions that are requirements for a project. (Although performance assumptions are implicit, we suggest that an SPM makes performance expectations explicit and then documents them). Common expectations that may be used as the basis for translating expectations into requirements are provided in Table 6.6 and Figure 6.6.

All stakeholders have expectations: the customer, the organization, management, and the team. Not all expectations are reasonable, but neither are they always unreasonable. For example, a customer expects courtesy, lucid communications, and accommodation of change requests. The organization and the team expect to accommodate change requests if the requests are reasonable and can be done in terms of cost and schedule. All of these expectations are reasonable. But what about expectations that are unreasonable? Unreasonable expectations can translate into *requirements* if they are not confronted and discussed. The best way to manage expectations is identify them as early as possible and then openly discuss those expectations so they are set correctly. But what expectations are reasonable and what ones are not? Unfortunately, there is no standard formula for *reasonable*: being reasonable depends on the circumstances of the project.

Customer expectations. Remember that customers pay the expenses of projects:

- Be professional. Show the courtesies that are due to the customer.
- Ensure that all communications are lucid and timely.
- Extend cooperation in all matters.
- Come to an understanding about the impact of change requests. Create a set of rules to evaluate each change request so that specific project needs and organizational culture norms are met. For example:
  - A change request that consumes less than 8 person hours *will be* absorbed *if* it does not impact the project schedule or its cost. Set a limit on the number of such absorbable requests.
  - A change request that consumes more than 8 person hours, but less than 24 person hours, *will be* absorbed *if* the schedule impact is acceptable.

Table 6.6. Stakeholder Expectations

Artifact	Requirements	Expectations
Customer	Software product that meets specified functionality	The team will use its expertise to bridge any gaps in specifications
	Defect-free delivery	Cooperation: to accommodate change requests without impacting price, schedule, or quality
	Timely delivery	Lucid communications
	Professionalism	Extend all courtesies due to customer, including polite interaction
	Customer service	Show patience if payments are delayed
	Customer service	Never escalate issues to a higher level
Organizational management	Execute project successfully	Avoid complaints from customer
	Deliver on time	Deliver a referable customer and obtain a commendation letter from the customer
	Control change	Use a price-escalation clause to get a client to pay extra for each change request received from the customer
	Ensure defect-free delivery	Test software against stated and unstated requirements
	Follow up and obtain payments from the customer	Ensure you follow up with the client; shepherd invoices through any of the client's accounting processes
	Good internal teamwork	Release resources if they are required in another project or for any other use willingly, without complaining and without impacting your project
	Be a communicator	Be a channel of communication between management and the project team, especially when conveying bad news
	Be a leader	All deserving persons cannot be rewarded, so find a way to maintain team morale even if some injustices occur
Project team	Fair allocation of work	"Allocation of work ought to consider my likes and dislikes."
	Fair assessment of work completed	"Fairness ought to be tempered with an understanding of human frailties."
	Fair performance appraisals	"Fairness ought to be tilted toward the employee."
	Fair rewards	"Fairness ought to be tilted toward the employee."
	Fair treatment	"We have the right to criticize you, but you ought to be realistic before criticizing a team member. Leaders should never be insensitive."
		"Project urgencies and deadlines are the usual, but my need for leave is rare. So you should grant me a leave of absence when I require one, not just when you can spare me."
		"Your norms are too unrealistic."

Customer Management
- Functionality expectations
- Quality expectations
- Schedule expectations
- Professionalism expectations
- Service expectations
- Cooperation expectations

Organizational Management
- Success expectations
- Schedule expectations
- Quality expectations
- Change control expectations
- Team building expectations
- Monetary expectations
- Communication expectations
- Leadership expectations

Expectation Management

Project Management
- Fairness expectations
- Reward expectations
- Treatment expectations
- Accommodation expectations

Figure 6.6. Stakeholder expectations.

- A change request that consumes more than 24 person hours impacts the cost and the schedule and therefore *will not be* undertaken unless additional time and budget are provided.
- Strive to bridge specification gaps; raise issues for clarification only after the "homework" has been done.
- Escalate issues to a higher level only as a last resort. Do not resort to escalation unless absolutely necessary.

Note: A "cumulative test" must be applied to *absorbable* change requests. If a project continually receives small change requests, and they are absorbed, the cumulative effect can be significant. One of us participated in supporting litigation for a project that had continually received small change requests that were absorbed.

These change requests cumulatively had a huge impact — so much so, that the multimillion-dollar project failed.)

Organizational and management expectations. Organizational management expects a project team to:

- Plan time adequately to support organizational initiatives. Organizational initiatives enhance capabilities for everyone in an organization.
- Negotiate the release of resources to other projects when required to reach win-win solutions.
- Base price escalations on fact. Based on a project's circumstances, create a set of criteria that provides guidelines for price escalations.
- Communicate with management. A project manager is a channel of communication between management and a project team. Use this channel wisely.
- Keep organizational imperatives in mind when demanding promotions and rewards for your team members (as well as yourself).

Project team expectations. A project team has expectations of its own, so:

- Consider the personal aspects of individual team members as well as their skill sets when allocating work to team members. (*Note*: In "real life," allocating work to a team member that is not to his or her liking often becomes necessary. When this situation occurs, present the assignment in such a way that the work becomes a personal challenge or learning opportunity. Sometimes the only choice is to just make the assignment and tell the team member that you have no other choice. So, for the team to succeed, he or she needs to succeed.)
- Ensure that performance appraisals are based on objective criteria, meticulous record keeping, and benchmarking between the team members so there can be no concerns from the team members about fairness.
- Recognize that team members are "juniors" and hence are likely to be less mature when handling criticism — giving or receiving. Encourage team members to give constructive criticism and to develop tactful ways to make suggestions. (If you are competent and also fair, the view that you are negatively criticizing a team member will only come about because of a communication gap.)
- Involve team members in target setting and be transparent in setting norms to reduce the team's resistance to setting tight targets. Regular communication will mitigate resistance when an urgent need arises. Communicate well and regularly.

The key to managing stakeholders' expectations. The word *communicate* appears frequently in the descriptions of the classes of project stakeholders. Why? The answer: communication is an essential aspect of expectation management. *Excellent communication*, defined as providing information that is right for the receiver and is timely and lucid, bridges many communication gaps and solves many issues. Diligently work to have excellent communication. In particular, communicate progress. Remember that all stakeholders want to know "what's happening." They want first-hand, official, and accurate information. Progress reports and stand-up meetings are convenient vehicles for communicating with customers:

- *Progress reports*: Send progress reports regularly to a customer, preferably every week, on Monday (or the first workday of the week if Monday is a holiday), and at the beginning of the day. By the time customer stakeholders come to their workstations on the first workday of the week, the progress report should be available (as output or as an email). Depending on the progress of the project, early availability provides necessary information and allows activity planning. Action items are also noted so required actions may be taken. (Not having information about a project's status or having to ask for information about the progress of the project and the action points can be very frustrating for a customer.)
- *Daily stand-up meetings*: If feasible, hold daily stand-up meetings (an agile practice) in which customers also participate in updates of a project's status, any problems, and the possible solutions. (Typically, everyone attending the meeting stands up in a circle to keep discussions short.)

Similarly, regular progress reporting to the organization's management stakeholders is a necessity and should follow the same pattern as that is used for customers. (*Note*: Often many of the issues and topics reported within an organization are not appropriate for communicating to customers. Purely internal action points for organizational management stakeholders should be kept "in the family.")

The goal of any type of project meeting is to get the project team "on the same page" as project management and get the team members involved in the project in a more committed manner. Although holding daily stand-up meetings is a best practice, at the very least, project team members should hold a weekly project meeting in which the overall progress of the project is reported. These project meetings should also be used as a platform for bringing issues faced by the team members to the surface for resolution.

In summary, three classes of stakeholder expectations are managed in a project: customer expectations, organizational management expectations, and project team expectations. Managing these stakeholder expectations can be accomplished by:

- Listening to stakeholders and understanding that there will be expectations
- Meeting and fulfilling all reasonable expectations
- Setting the *right* expectations in case of remaining expectations
- Communicating clearly, with the *right* communication and in a timely manner

PRODUCT INTEGRATION MANAGEMENT

Building components that are defect-free is the responsibility of the entire project team, but *integrating* all of the individual components into a fully functional, defect-free product is ultimately the responsibility of an SPM (and still another measure of success). Although software construction and assembly (of the software and the software modules) are mainly software engineering activities, the SPM acts the "conductor," ensuring that all of the pieces come together at the right place and at the right time. Product integration involves several steps:

1. Decide the integration approach. (Many integration approaches may be used: two popular approaches are top down and bottom up.)
2. Develop all of the shared components first, test them, and make them available to the module integrators (said by some to be "where the miracles happen").
3a. If the approach is top down:
    - Assign one person to integrate each module.
    - Ensure that the component(s) that acts as the framework for other components to link into has been developed and tested. (The authors strongly suggest that the framework standards be developed and published *before* design and coding.)
    - As components are finished (coded and tested) have the integrator add each component to the assembly and then put the component through QA and testing activities.
    - Iterate the second and third steps of this approach until integration is complete.
3b. If the approach is bottom up:
    - Collect all components into the assigned code library as their construction and testing activities are completed.

Table 6.7. Components List for Module XYZ

Component Name	Type of Component	Nature of Component	Location
ABC	Screen/report/stored procedure/ middleware routine/table graphic, etc.	Shared/dedicated to this module	Library

- When all of the modules are completed (or at preassigned time points in the CM plan), assign a person(s) to integrate them into the macro components and then into the product.
- Once integration is completed, carry out all testing activities and arrange to fix all relevant defects uncovered.

4. Plan and execute integration testing of all modules.
5. Assign a person(s) to prepare the product build and hand over all of the integrated modules.
6. Once the product is built, arrange for QA activities (review and testing) to be carried out.
7. Arrange for all relevant defects uncovered during QA activities to be fixed and complete the product build.
8. Arrange for system testing (as required by the quality plan) and arrange for all relevant defects uncovered in system testing to be fixed.
9. Prepare the product for acceptance testing (if required) and delivery. (This is where you spike the ball!)

Configuration management assumes a significant role during the project integration process in ensuring defect-free integration and preparation of the product build. Because careful attention should be given to product integration management, the SPM should personally oversee this function. To achieve flawless integration, the SPM needs to maintain a register for each module. This register is made available to the integrator for ensuring that all components are integrated into the module. A sample register is shown in Table 6.7.

Note: We suggest integrating location and status into the work register. Microsoft Excel, for example, can filter information to easily present the data needed. PMPal can also efficiently manage a work register. If configuration management tools are used, however, separate registers do not need to be maintained for product integration. Configuration management tools can facilitate module integration and build preparation without the necessity of maintaining separate registers.

PITFALLS AND BEST PRACTICES

Nonconformance to the plan. Frequently, significant time and effort are spent on planning a project, but once the plan is approved, it is relegated to the project's records. The project team then fails to conform to the plan and project execution is undertaken intuitively. Failing to conform to the project's plan can be detrimental to successful execution of the project. Intuition tends to rely on luck.

Best practice: Plan a project diligently and then comply with the plan during execution, revising the plan as necessary.

Informal work allocation. In an informal scenario, work is allocated informally without using a formal work register. Informal work allocation can result in duplication of some components and the possibility of overlooking other components. Informal work allocation can also create an imbalance of work allocation to team members.

Best practice: Allocate work using a formal work register.

Bulk work allocation. Bulk allocation is the assignment of work to a team of three or four people that allows those team members to distribute the work among themselves. Although this type of informal allocation might reduce the work burden of an SPM, informal allocation often tends to result in delays. (The 90/10 rule says that 90% of the activities may be reported as being accomplished, but it is the remaining 10% that will be the most time consuming.) Work allocation is the responsibility of an SPM and should be done by following a formal process. (In large projects, however, work allocation may be delegated one level downward to a lead team member.) An SPM who allows team members to allocate work in an informal manner is simply shirking an important responsibility.

Best practice: Allocate work to team members using formal methods.

Nonconformance to productivity and quality norms. Arbitrarily setting target norms can be detrimental to team morale. Appropriate norms for a project should be set at the project planning stage. Then, during work allocation, the productivity and quality targets should be set based on these norms. Targets based on appropriate norms encourage team members to think that performance appraisals will be based on objective criteria, which motivates them to achieve higher levels of performance.

Best practice: Set performance targets that are based on appropriate norms that have been set at the beginning of a project.

Failing to measure. Appropriate measurements, such as capturing the actual size of a completed artifact and the actual effort expended and conducting a variance analysis, should be routinely carried out. Unless data at completion is captured and variance analysis is performed, assessing performance and the efficacy of target setting cannot be validated.

Best practice: Capture data for an actual achievement and then conduct a variance analysis to eliminate any variances due to assignable causes and to provide validated data for future use.

Some words of caution about using configuration management tools: When tools are used for configuration management of code artifacts, the guidelines for using these tools may be neglected. Neglect, however, negates the benefits of using a configuration management tool. The best practice is to define tool usage guidelines before a configuration management tool is used in a project and then to train team members in the correct usage of the configuration management tool as well. Another pitfall is that an artifact is checked in during its initial preparation, but the artifact has not gone through testing. Configuration management tools can provide a great advantage for configuration management during state transition and for preparing the final build, but configuration management tools need to be used in a disciplined manner: a code artifact should be checked in only after it passed through unit testing; an information artifact should be checked in only after it has been approved.

Best practice: Control check-in and check-out procedures in accordance with the configuration management plan.

Assuming multiple roles. Often an SPM takes on the role of configuration control board and configuration controller (particularly in small-to-medium-sized projects). The roles of approval and implementation should be kept separate. If both of these roles are played by one person, the checks and balances of the approval process are negated.

Best practice: Keep the roles of CCB and CC separate. If an SPM must take on one of these roles, it should be the role of the CCB rather than the CC.

Skipping quality assurance activities. The most frequently skipped QA activities are peer review and independent unit testing. Often peer review is supplanted by managerial review. Managerial review, however, does not delve into the minute details. Only peer review looks at an artifact with a magnifying lens. At times, peer review is arranged for only a sample of the programs (perhaps because these programs are considered to be more complex in the opinion of the module leader or the PL). Although peer review of a sample of the programs is better than nothing, peer review should be done for all software artifacts.

Best practice: Conduct peer review of all programs. Skipping peer reviews is risky (i.e., your own personal risk!).

Omitting white box testing. White box testing is *only* practical for unit testing. It is impractical for all other types of software testing. Never miss an opportunity to conduct white box testing. Independent unit testing is a best practice that is often foregone. All developed code should be unit tested, period.

Best practice: In all cases carry out independent unit testing. Always conduct white box testing.

Failing to conduct independent system testing. Although independent system testing is often conducted by a member of the project team (albeit by a team member who did not code the artifact), system testing that ensures that the software product works without issues in the field should be done by an independent testing team. (*Note*: The number of permutations and combinations possible in software, especially in Web applications, is mind-boggling. When considering, for example, the office suites, anti-virus software, anti-spyware software, operating systems and browsers, and other free utilities that are present in the field, the number of permutations becomes more understandable. Many organizations recognize that testing is complex, so they focus on using tools and independent testing teams.)

Best practice: Leverage independent testing.

Setting unrealistic expectations. Although unrealistic expectations are rarely set by explicit statements, sometimes they are implied. For example, by promising team members a bonus, or promotions, or higher wages, an SPM might easily raise the expectations of the team to an unrealistic level. Ensure that there is no reason for team members to have unrealistic expectations. Unrealistic expectations can also be set for an organization's management when issues (or potential issues) are not revealed until they become hurdles. Management thus does not become involved with an issue(s) until a much later stage. Sometimes, SPMs avoid reporting issues because they want to resolve the issues themselves. SPMs also fear that management will take a dim view of them if issues are raised. Late involvement of management in a problem scenario, however, does not solve a problem, it only compounds it. One way to make management aware of potential problems is to include a section in progress reports that lists potential issues. Management can them intervene when they deem intervention is appropriate. Management that is involved early can often derive a satisfactory resolution before an issue becomes a problem.

Best practice: Leave no room for unrealistic expectations by a project team and inform management early if a project encounters a problem.

7

SOFTWARE PROJECT
EXECUTION CONTROL

INTRODUCTION

The term *control* has many connotations, some good and some less so. In some organizations, the term control is frequently followed by the word *freak*, which describes a person who unfairly manipulates the people around him/her. So, in those organizations, *control* has a negative connotation. But in software project management, *control* has a totally different connotation (or at least it should).

In software project management, *control* is defined as the *corrective action that is taken periodically during project execution that stems from measuring the progress on various aspects of the project and comparing and contrasting the actual achievements against the desired achievements.* Let's look at some key terms in this definition:

- *Project execution*: As used in this book, the definition focuses on project control during the project execution phase and excludes the phases of planning and post-delivery (these phases are outside of the scope of this chapter).
- *Measuring the progress*: Progress is determined by periodically measuring the aspects of a project, with *measure* signifying quantitative versus qualitative measurement.
- *Comparing and contrasting*: Two aspects receive focus:
  - *Desired achievements*: The desired achievements are the targets that have been set and accepted through estimation, planning, and

scheduling: what is desired and who desires it. These targets are set by project management in concurrence with the project's stakeholders (the customer, organizational management, and the project team).

- *Actual achievements*: Knowing what is desired and the actual performance achieved is valuable only if the actual values achieved are compared with the desired values. The process of comparison can reveal gaps in achievement. A situation in which no gap exists (i.e., there is no difference between the actual achievement and the desired progress) indicates conformance of performance with the desired value. A positive gap is when achievement is better than desired. A negative gap occurs when achievement is worse than the desired progress.

- *Corrective action*: When a negative gap is revealed during comparing and contrasting activities, taking action becomes necessary to bridge the negative gap. Corrective action may be of many forms, including pumping more resources into the project so that the negative gap will disappear by the time the next measurement takes place or correcting the expectations.

- *That is taken periodically*: Measurement, comparing and contrasting, and taking corrective actions take place regularly during project execution. Although spot audits may be conducted, typically measurement, comparing/contrasting, and taking corrective action activities occur at preset time intervals.

- *Various aspects of the project*: Many areas of a project require periodic oversight and measurement (and correction if necessary). Typical aspects that are measured include:
  - Scope
  - Cost
  - Schedule
  - Quality
  - Effort
  - Productivity

Levels of control in software project management are depicted in Figure 7.1.

ASPECTS OF CONTROL IN PROJECT EXECUTION

Who is actually responsible for taking corrective action in the various aspects of a project? The answer: it depends on what needs to be done. Usually, however,

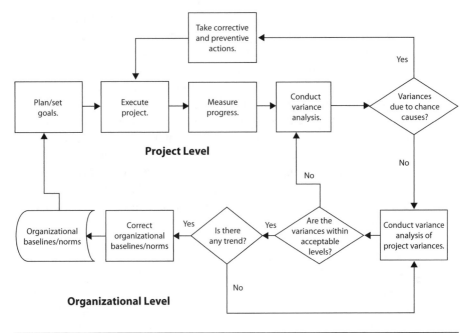

Figure 7.1. Control in software project management.

corrective actions are the responsibility of the project team and other relevant stakeholders. So, let's discuss each of the typical aspects of control.

Scope Control

The term *scope* refers to the amount of work required to deliver the requirements of a project. Scope is typically determined during project acquisition or start-up and with agreement between the stakeholders. Scope, however, can increase or decrease (rarely) during the project execution phase. By the end of the project, a significant gap may be found to exist between what was originally agreed upon and what was finally delivered. This increase or decrease in scope is often referred to as *scope creep* (also scope churn). Many scenarios can modify the original scope, ranging from approved changes to phasing the deliveries. More often than not, however, more work is delivered than was originally agreed to (or possibly was agreed to subsequently). If not properly addressed during project acquisition, technology requirements can also result in scope creep. Scope creep occurs mainly due to:

- *User requirements*: Insufficient/improper understanding of user requirements can occur at the project acquisition stage. During the project acquisition stage, in an eagerness to acquire a project, marketing (or the area negotiating the technical aspects) may make overcommitments without making proportionate increases in the cost, effort, and schedule estimates. This situation may occur as a conscious or an unconscious choice.

- *Scope statement implications*: Making ambitious scope commitments, without fully realizing their implications, is inherent in writing scope statements. At other times, when a project is accepted, and the scope of the work is stated by using high-level statements, the implications of the scope statement are not recognized. As the project evolves, however, the scope implications are realized, e.g., during the requirements analysis or in software design, the scope implications became known, but it is now too late to renegotiate the impact of the implications on the schedule, cost, and effort.

- *Business analysts*: When business analysts are improperly or inadequately trained, they may not visualize the full scope of work when conducting the business analysis of a project, which can lead to scope creep during project execution. Business analysts must be competent so that they realize the implications contained in scope statements.

- *Change requests*: Change requests are an integral part of project execution. Lack of a proper change management process or nonconformance to an existing change management process can cause scope creep. Adhering to an appropriate change management process helps ensure that increases in scope also have concomitant adjustments of cost, schedule, and effort.

- *Standards*: Using a defined process, templates, and checklists for requirements gathering, scope commitment, and review helps ensure that the scope of a project is understood and that commitments are carefully made. Checklists, standards, and guidelines also assist negotiators in "right sizing" the scope of the work.

Remember that scope creep affects all project parameters: cost, schedule, and effort. Diligently control the scope of work during project execution.

Cost Control

Effort is the major cost component in a software development project. Effort is impacted by:

- Poor productivity, which could result from:
  - Poor supervision
  - Lack of proper software development tools
  - Lack of proper infrastructure (which results in wasted time due to low-quality hardware and software, inadequate power supply

or power outages, lack of the right common facilities, inadequate lighting, ventilation, environmental control, etc.)
- Human resources practices (which results in low levels of morale or a lack of motivation in the organization)
  - Poor processes
- Scope creep
- Change requests

Ensure that productivity is maintained at the levels needed (or at better levels) and that all costs are closely monitored and controlled to meet the commitments made during project acquisition.

Schedule/Progress Control

A schedule can go "haywire" for any number of reasons. Common issues that cause schedule problems include:

- Laxity in conforming to the original schedule by project management (*Remember*: Having a schedule is essentially immaterial if the schedule is not used.)
- An improperly developed original schedule (e.g., when tasks are not granular enough to be properly tracked)
- Not getting timely approvals for deliverables from identified persons
- Allowing most of the tasks to be slightly elastic and then stretching them during execution (Even if the effect on the schedule for each task is minor, the cumulative effect can be significant. In simple terms: failing to studiously take care of the cents can lead to the loss of dollars, a scenario that arises from poor project management.)
- Scope creep
- Uncontrolled acceptance of change requests
- Poor monitoring by superiors (If the schedule is not important to management, it probably will not be important to anyone else either.)

Quality Control

The importance of quality in project execution cannot be overemphasized. Suffice it to say: "Quality has to be built in — it is not an addendum." Poor-quality work causes re-work. Productivity of re-work is very low, and re-work causes loss of motivation:

- Control quality in all phases and in all deliverables by using standards, guidelines, specifications, and peer review and testing by peers in these dimensions:
  - Specifications quality

- • Design quality
- • Construction quality
- ▪ Confirm quality through an appropriate organizational quality assurance process, tools, and managerial support.
- ▪ Ensure that organizational motivation and morale are at levels that will achieve high quality.

Any and all effort spent on quality assurance pays rich dividends.

Effort Control

As already discussed, effort is a major component of cost that has a major impact on the schedule. Every increase in effort results in proportionate increases in the cost of a project and in the schedule. Effort increases due to:

- • Scope creep
- • Low productivity
- • Poor-quality work that results in re-work
- • Uncontrolled change requests
- • Poor levels of motivation or morale in the organization that result in low productivity

Closely monitor the effort being spent on a project.

Productivity Monitoring

Low productivity results in increased effort and inefficient use of other resources in a project, which leads to cost escalation. Reasons for lower productivity include:

- • Poor working environment
- • Poor supervision
- • Lack of the proper tools (e.g., tools that would increase productivity)
- • Lack of a software process, a poor definition of the process, or laxity in conforming to a defined process
- • A poor quality assurance process or quality assurance practices that result in re-work and reduced productivity
- • Low motivation or morale in the organization

Productivity improvement is a continuous process. Pay close attention to monitoring productivity levels in software projects. Humans are often capable of delivering much higher productivity levels. We must therefore focus close attention on monitoring productivity levels in our software projects.

CONTROL MECHANISMS

So, how do we ensure that proper control is exercised in software projects? What tools and mechanisms are available to provide assistance? Projects that leverage project tracking and monitoring processes, audits, metrics, software verification and validation processes, checklists, standards, guidelines, and assessments are likely to keep project execution controlled and closely aligned with the project plans.

A well-defined software process. Having a well-defined software process goes a long way in exercising control on project execution (assuming the plan is followed). Behavioral and performance norms are a particularly important component of an organizational process definition. Norms are defined for productivity and permissible variances in schedule, effort, productivity, and cost. These norms help support the definitions of what is important to measure and analyze to support project execution and control.

Progress reporting and monitoring meetings are important tools that can be used as control mechanisms. They provide excellent assistance to project stakeholders for exercising control over a project's activities:

Progress reports. Typically, progress reports are generated on a periodic basis (weekly usually) by the project manager and distributed to all project stakeholders. Progress reports allow all stakeholders to assess the progress of a project and then to determine if corrective intervention is needed. Progress reports also allow stakeholders to determine if any resolution issues are pending on their docket and then to take the necessary action to resolve these issues. Suggested elements of a progress report template are illustrated in Figure 7.2. This template can be customized to meet specific project needs. A progress report usually contains:

- Project status and the project plans
- Metrics that give quantitative measures for quality, productivity, effort, and schedule
- Issues that could impact the project execution and their status
- Other aspects as defined in the project management plan

Progress monitoring meetings. These meetings are conducted as adjuncts to project progress reports. Monitoring meetings can occur in a face-to-face manner, as teleconferences, or as videoconferences (whether by telephone or Internet, the manner in which a meeting is held is less important than that the meeting actually occurs). Usually, progress monitoring meetings are conducted a day or two after the progress report has been communicated to all stakeholders. In monitoring meetings, all stakeholders analyze the project's progress, using the project's plans and progress reports as the basis of comparison. The meeting generally begins with an explanation of the project's status by the SPM as well a description of any

---

Project Information:
  1.1   Name of Project
  1.2   Name of Project Manager
  1.3   Reporting Period

Executive Summary:

Status of Project:
  • Overall Status
  • Tasks Completed During the Period
  • Tasks Planned for the Next Period
  • Any Tasks that Are Outside Project Work

Resource Position:

Issue-Resolution Status:

Project Metrics:

Significant Events During Period:

Customer Interface:
  • Commendations Received
  • Complaints Received

Issues Needing Management Attention:
  • Project Support Group Issues
  • Employee Grievances
  • Any Interface Issues

Best Practices/Pitfalls to Share with Organization:

Process Improvement Suggestions:

Figure 7.2. Elements for a weekly project progress report.

issues that need resolution. Then the stakeholders discuss the progress as well as the issues needing resolution. Action points are then assigned to an appropriate person who is participating in the meeting. These action points are recorded in the meeting minutes and distributed to all stakeholders. The action points thus captured are tracked to closure. This record is used as a reference for monitoring further progress. During the meeting, stakeholders also agree on any corrective action that needs to be implemented. A suggested format for recording the minutes of progress monitoring meetings is illustrated in Figure 7.3. Multiple types of progress monitoring meetings may be conducted:

  • The SPM and the project team
  • The SPM, the project team, and organizational management
  • The SPM and the customer
  • The SPM, organizational management, and the customer

Item Number	Action Item	Date of Origination	Scheduled Date of Completion	Person Responsible	Status (Open/Closed)
1					
2					
3					

Figure 7.3. A format for recording meeting minutes of project progress monitoring meetings.

Many formats and structures are available for progress meetings, ranging from stand-up meetings (e.g., as used in scrum) to very formal presentations to boards of directors. Implement progress meetings in a manner that meets the needs and corporate culture of each project.

Audits. Two types of audits are normally conducted in organizations: organization-level and project-level audits. Organizational audits are conducted on a periodic basis, whereas project-level audits are conducted upon completion of a project phase. Let's take a closer look at each type of audit.

Organization-level audits. Organizational audits are normally conducted on a *periodic* basis (e.g., once a quarter, semiannually, or annually). Organizational audits mainly look for evidence of implementation of project plan and organizational processes; hence, organizational audits are often referred to as conformance audits. The quality assurance department (or another department vested with this responsibility) organizes organizational audits. At times, during an organizational audit, all aspects of all projects are audited. When all aspects are audited, the audit is referred to as a *vertical* audit. At other times, only one aspect is audited in greater detail in all projects, e.g., configuration management or the project planning processes. When one aspect is audited, the audit is referred to as a *horizontal* audit. A common practice, however, is to conduct a combination of these two audits to provide the data needed to analyze process implementation and to unearth any opportunities for process improvements across the organization. Organization-level audits also assist management in identifying slippages and initiating corrective action as early as possible to get a project(s) back on track. Audit findings for all projects are consolidated and analyzed to detect patterns or trends. The audit findings are then presented to all SPMs and organizational management so that any process improvement opportunities can be discovered and implemented.

The purpose of an organizational audit is to ensure that:

- All projects are adhering to the defined software process of the organization

- All projects are being executed in conformance with their project plans
- All QA activities planned for projects are being diligently implemented.

If an audit finds any evidence of nonconformance in any aspect of a project, a nonconformance report (NCR) is raised on the project. NCRs require that corrective action be taken and that preventive action plans be developed to avoid nonconformance in the future.

Project-level audits. Project-level audits are not period based, but rather are tied to an *execution phase.* The purpose of a project-level audit is to identify, as early as possible, any lack of diligence that could cause serious issues in the later stages of project execution and also to ensure that the project is ready for the next stage. Project-level audits are conducted upon completion of project phases and deliverables:

1. Project initiation
2. Project planning
3. Completion of construction of a module
4. Integration of a module
5. Preparation of the product build
6. Completion of testing
7. Ready for delivery
8. Project closure

Customarily, at a minimum, three audits are conducted for every project: one after project initiation; one in the middle of project execution; and then a final audit following project closure, particularly for short-duration projects. For longer-duration projects (e.g., 12 calendar months or longer), we recommend combining some of the phases and conducting an audit every 2 months (i.e., using a periodic audit process).

Metrics. Metrics facilitate close control of a project and assist in the quantitative assessment of the project's health. Analysis of the variances in a project provides an objective view of the efficiency of project execution and also facilitates taking the corrective action necessary to bring a project back on track with the project plan. Project progress reports or a dashboard (a large chart) that is maintained on daily basis are useful tools for distributing metrics. Six classes of metrics are typically collated, computed, and distributed to project stakeholders:

- *Quality*: the defect injection rate of a deliverable and the code development; the defect removal efficiency of each QA activity
- *Schedule*: schedule variances, such as occurrences of meeting the schedule (expressed as a percentage) or not meeting the schedule (expressed as a percentage); the occurrence of replanning the schedules

- *Productivity*: the productivity of each software engineering activity and any variances from plan
- *Cost*: actual expenditure; the budged expenditure; and variance analysis
- *Change*: the number of change requests received; the impact of change requests on effort, schedule, and cost
- *Effort*: actual effort expended; the planned effort; and variance analysis

Computation of a project's metrics can consume a significant amount of time and effort for an SPM. A tool such as PMPal is of great assistance in reducing the overhead associated with computing project metrics.

PROGRESS ASSESSMENT: EARNED VALUE ANALYSIS

Because project execution has so many facets, obtaining an accurate assessment of a project's progress is difficult. Projects do not come with a GPS! But earned value analysis (EVA), a popular measurement technique, can be used to assess a project's progress. In simple terms, EVA (also referred to as BCWP or the budgeted cost of work performed) indicates how much of the budget should have been spent when compared to the amount of work that has actually been completed. EVA is particularly useful in large projects with longer duration. Although EVA is extensively used in large construction projects and in U.S. defense projects, in commercial software development, use of EVA is more the exception than the rule.

EVA measures a project's performance using financial terms. Measuring the progress of a large project by simply tracking a large number of activities, which are in various stages of completion, is tedious. Keeping track of the money spent on the project is much easier. Comparing the amount of money actually spent on the project with the amount budgeted allows the progress of the project to be expressed with a single number. In simple words: "We should have spent $5000, and we actually completed $4000 of work; therefore, we have completed about 80% of the planned work."

The three primary values. EVA uses three primary values for each task:

- *BCWS (the budgeted cost of work scheduled)*: BCWS is the portion of the cost that is planned to be spent on a task (or project) between the task's start date and the status date. For example, the total planned budget for a 4-day task is $100. The task starts on a Monday. If the status date is set for the following Wednesday, the BCWS is $75.
- *ACWP (the actual cost of work performed)*: ACWP is the total actual cost incurred while work is performed on a task (or project) during a given period. For example, if the 4-day task actually incurs a total cost of $35 during each of the first 2 days, the ACWP for this period is $70.

- *BCWP (the budgeted cost of work performed)*: BCWP is the percentage of the budget that should have been spent for a given percentage of work performed on a task (or project). For example, if after 2 days, 60% of the work on a task has been completed, 60% of the total task budget is expected to have been spent or $60.

Other key values are determined from these three primary values. The most common and useful ones are cost variance, schedule variance, the cost performance index, and the schedule performance index. To better understand these key values, let's continue with the example of a 4-day task, with BCWS of $100, an ACWP of $70, and BCWP of $60.

Cost variance (CV) is the difference between a task's estimated cost and its actual cost:

$$CV = BCWP - ACWP$$
$$CV = 60 - 70$$
$$CV = (-)\ 10$$

As can easily be seen, we budgeted $60, but we spent $70. We have overspent by $10! We may need to make cuts in the future or allocate more funds to complete the task.

Schedule variance (SV) is the difference between the current progress and the scheduled progress of a task in terms of cost.

$$SV = BCWP - BCWS$$
$$SV = 60 - 75$$
$$SV = (-)\ 15$$

This computation indicates that we are behind schedule. Against a budgeted expenditure of $75, we have spent only $60. Some might say that we have saved budget funds. Possibly, we did. If so, the savings will be reflected in the cost performance index and the schedule performance index. If CPI and SPI are more than 1, then we can infer that we have saved budget funds.

The cost performance index (CPI) is the ratio of budgeted costs to actual costs:

$$CPI = BCWP/ACWP$$
$$CPI = 60/70$$
$$CPI = 0.86$$

The CPI is 0.86, so we have overspent the budget for the task. A CPI of less than 1 indicates overspending; a CPI of more than 1 indicates saving.

The schedule performance index (SPI) is the ratio of work performed to work scheduled:

$$SPI = BCWP/BCWS$$
$$SPI = 60/75$$
$$SPI = 0.8$$

The SPI is 0.80, so we have completed 80% of the work. An SPI of less than 1 indicates that we are behind schedule; an SPI more than 1 indicates that we are ahead of schedule.

An interpretation. EVA results can be interpreted in multiple ways:

- Earned value indicators that are variances, such as cost variance, can be positive or negative:
  - A positive variance indicates that a task or project is ahead of schedule or under budget. A positive variance might enable reallocation of money and resources from tasks or projects with positive variances to tasks or projects with negative variances.
  - A negative variance indicates that a task or project is behind schedule or over budget and action needs to be taken. If a task or project has a negative cost variance (CV), the budget might have to be increased or reduced profit margins may have to be accepted.
- Earned value indicators that are ratios, such as the cost performance index (CPI) and the schedule performance index (SPI), can be greater than 1 or less than 1:
  - A value that is greater than 1 indicates that the task or project is ahead of schedule or under budget. An SPI of 1.5 means that only 67% of the planned time to complete a portion of a task in a given time period has been used.
  - A value that is less than 1 indicates that a task or project is behind schedule or over budget. A CPI of 0.8 means that 25% more has been spent on a task than was planned for a given time period.

Some benefits of earned value analysis. In summary, performing EVA has certain benefits:

- Earned value *analysis* provides reliable answers to key questions:
  - Is there enough money left in the budget to complete the project?
  - Is there enough time left in the schedule to finish the project on time?
- Earned value *indicators* express a project's progress in terms of cost and schedule:
  - Will the money run out before the project is completed?
  - Will there be a surplus when the project is completed?

Earned value analysis is especially useful in large projects that have longer durations.

8

CHANGE MANAGEMENT IN SOFTWARE DEVELOPMENT PROJECTS

INTRODUCTION

The Greek Philosopher Heraclitus said, "There is nothing permanent except change." A reflection of these words is particularly evident in software development projects. To say that rarely is any software development project completed without some change(s) being necessary during the execution phase is not far-fetched. (*Note*: In one of the author's experience, only two projects did not change; both of them had a legally mandated scope and both of them ended in litigation.) Even though change is inevitable and expected, rarely is receiving a change request (CR) a welcome event for a project team.

Change management during a project is a primary (majority) activity that is especially critical during initial software development. As discussed in Chapters 5 and 6, change management is part of configuration management (CM). While software is still in the development phase, however, configuration management deals mostly with the *state transition* of software artifacts. (*Note*: Change management is also part of configuration management when software is in production. When in the production environment, change management deals with changing out artifacts with updated artifacts.) To deal with change, software process specialists have provided the software development industry with a change management process for handling CRs with equanimity and to do so effectively.

In its simplest form, *change* is basically a requirement from a stakeholder in a software project that is specified "after the event." *After the event* means that the new requirement is specified after completion of the phase in which it should have been specified. For example, if a new user requirement is specified after the user requirement specification document has been approved and the next activity is being carried out, then the new requirement is a change. A screen modification that is requested from the development team after a screen has been coded and unit tested is another example of change, e.g., the addition of another control to the screen, the deletion of a control from a screen, or a rearrangement of controls on a screen. Other examples of change include:

- A change in specifications for a software product or a new specification after specifications have been approved
- A change in user requirements or a new user requirement after the user requirements have been approved
- A change in the software design of the product or an addition to the existing design after the design has been finalized and approved
- A change in the source code or an addition or deletion of existing code after the unit has been coded and tested

Changes necessitate the retracing of steps already taken or the modifying of artifacts so that the required changes can be implemented. Changes cause disruption to the flow of project execution, regardless of whether the flow is on a smooth or chaotic path.

Rarely does a CR impact an artifact that is incomplete. Instead, the timing of the CR usually impacts a completed artifact and tends to be severe. If the CR impacts only a current artifact, however, the impact tends to be less severe. Regardless of the scenario, artifacts such as requirements documents, design documents, etc. will have to be reviewed and perhaps revised, which will certainly impact the flow of project execution. The phase of development in which a CR is received also determines the severity of the impact. For example, a CR that is received just after the requirements phase is completed tends to cause the least severe impact as compared to a CR for the same item that is received when the project is in the system testing phase. The severity of the impact of CRs on project execution flow is shown in Table 8.1.

ORIGINS OF CHANGE

CRs may originate from various stakeholders:

Customers. Customer representatives may raise CRs that affect the overall project. Sometimes, a security specification is changed when a new security threat

Table 8.1. Severity of Impact Caused by Change Requests

Phase in which Change Request Received	Severity of Impact Caused by Change Request Based on Type			
	Specification CR	User Requirement CR	Design CR	Construction CR
Specification	Nil	Nil	Nil	Nil
User requirements	Medium severity	Nil	Nil	Nil
Design	High severity	Medium severity	Nil	Nil
Construction	High severity	High severity	High severity	• Medium if component is already constructed • Low if component is not yet constructed

is reported; the middleware that a customer plans to use releases a new version; additional management reports are needed; or a new governmental regulation may be enacted that necessitates making changes in a project. Any number of other reasons, including the dynamic nature of the world, can cause customer representatives to raise CRs.

End users. Similarly, end users may raise CRs if they are aware of the project and participating in overall project execution, e.g., if they realize an error was introduced during the user requirements gathering phase. End users raise CRs in other scenarios that are as simple as needing an additional report or because an internal procedural change necessitates the modification of a screen or report.

A project team. Although rare, project team members can raise a CR. Sometimes, the design may not be practical, especially while packing controls on the screen or in a report. Practicality issues necessitate seeking a design concession from the designers of the project: perhaps to split the screen into two screens, to create two tabs, or to use a popup facility. Sometimes, team members suggest a better method of achieving functionality, such as reducing the number of screens by a better combination of controls or developing a shared component instead of replicating similar functionality in multiple modules, etc. Often when team members request a change, they are either seeking a concession or are attempting to improve the product's technical performance.

A testing team. A testing team may find opportunities for improvement while carrying out testing. Although these opportunities are raised as CRs, in practical terms these changes often are initially confused with problem reports. Testing

---

Project Name:

Date:

Change Request Reference:

Initiator Information:

Details of Change Requested:

Implementation Information:

Figure 8.1. Elements of a change request.

---

teams, however, do find opportunities for improvement and raise CRs to pursue those changes. The frequency of opportunity improvement-related CRs is driven by how integrated the testing team is with the development team.

The organizational standards group. The organizational standards group may change an existing standard or bring out a new one, which impacts projects that are in progress. In such cases, the organizational standards group raises a CR to retrofit the standard into the project deliverables. Unless the change addresses a critical issue, however, the organizational standards group generally identifies a migration path for the change and identifies pertinent grandfathering situations.

Changes are communicated to the SPM using a CR form. The CR would contain details of the project, the module, and the component(s) that are likely to be affected by the CR. The CR should also include reasons for the CR. Suggested CR form elements are illustrated in Figure 8.1. Remember that scope creep occurs when changes are made without a CR.

THE CHANGE REQUEST REGISTER

A CR register is used to record all CRs received from any source and to track each CR to closure. The CR register is the main tool for monitoring all CRs to resolution. When a CR is received, the first activity is to record it in the CR register. Usually, a CR register is maintained electronically (also known as soft copy). The actual format of CR register can be an Excel Worksheet or a tool-based register such as PMPal that facilitates the functionality of the register. A CR register usually contains:

CR Reference	CR Date	Approved By	Approval Date	Analyzed By	Analysis Start Date	Analysis End Date	Implemented By	Implementation Start Date	Implementation End Date	Reviewed By	Review Start Date	Review End Date	Tested By	Testing Start Date	Testing End Date	Status	Close Date

Figure 8.2. Format of a change register

- The CR reference number
- Date on which the CR is received
- Allocation details for analysis, including to whom the CR is allocated and the completion date
- Allocation details for approval of the CR, including to whom it is allocated and the completion date
- Allocation details for resolution of the CR, including to whom it is allocated and the completion date
- Allocation details for peer review, including to whom it is allocated and the completion date
- Allocation details for regression testing, including to whom it is allocated and completion date
- Status: open, closed, or under analysis/approval/resolution/peer review/regression testing
- Date on which the CR is closed

A suggested CR register format is illustrated in Figure 8.2.

Table 8.2. Artifacts Impacted and Change Request Implementation Strategy Based on Phase When Change Request Received

Phase in which Change Request Received	Artifacts Impacted	Suitable Strategies for Implementation
Specifications/user requirements phase	Specifications and user requirements documents	As/when received or when convenient, but before design is started
Design phase	Specifications document, user requirements documents, and design documents	As/when received or when convenient, but before design is completed
Construction phase	Specifications document, user requirements documents, design documents, and source code	As/when received or retrofitted or situational implementation

CHANGE REQUEST RESOLUTION

Resolution of a change request can range from rejection to acceptance and implementation. In larger projects, after a CR has been logged into the CR register, the CR is analyzed by the configuration control board (CCB). In small projects, the CR is analyzed by the SPM or some other designated person. In either case, the analysis determines:

- If implementation of the CR is feasible (When a CR is raised by internal sources, such as a project team or testing team, in addition to feasibility, the analysis also determines if implementation is desirable from a user point of view.)
- The amount of effort and calendar time it will take to implement the CR
- The impact of the CR on the overall project: if it is accepted (especially in terms of effort, schedule, and cost) or if it is rejected (fit for use)

Once the analysis is completed, the impact analysis is submitted to the CCB or to the project's SPM, who approves or rejects the CR. If rejected, the decision and the reasons why the CR has been rejected are communicated to the originator of the CR. The CR is then closed in the CR register. If approved, the CR is implemented in accordance with the implementation strategy determined for the CR and then recorded in the software configuration management plan (SCMP). (*Note*: Whether rejected or accepted, all CRs received should be recorded and tracked to closure.)

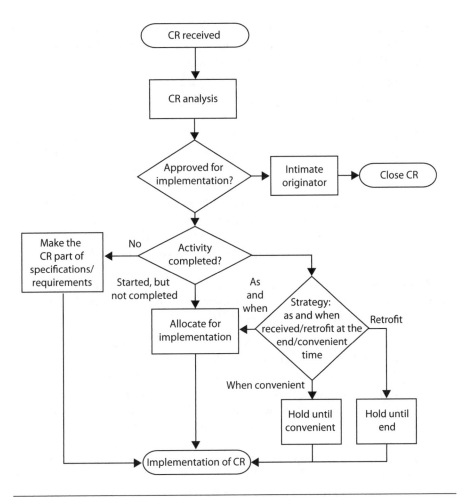

Figure 8.3. Determining the strategy for change request implementation.

Change Request Implementation Strategy

The timing of a CR can influence the implementation of the CR and the implementation strategy chosen. The impact on a set of typical artifacts, based on the phase during which a CR is received and the possible strategies for implementing the CR, are shown in Table 8.2. Typical approaches include the situational approach, consolidating/retrofitting at a specific time, and the as/when received approach. CR implementation strategy is illustrated in Figure 8.3. Initiating change implementation always assumes that the CR has been accepted.

Situational approach. First, let's look at the most typical strategy for change implementation: the situational approach. The steps generally followed for CR implementation in a situational strategy include:

1. If work on the activity is not complete (or not yet started), incorporate the CR into the specifications, requirements, and design (as required).
2. If work on the impacted component has started, but is not complete, hand the CR over for implementation to the team member who is carrying out the work. The CR is then incorporated into the required deliverables.
3. If work on the component impacted by the CR is complete, the CR is kept pending, either to be implemented at the end of the project or at a convenient time, such as when other resources become free or if part of the team is idle and waiting for an approval, clarification, etc.

Consolidating/retrofitting at a specific time. If a project is following a strategy of holding CRs and then retrofitting them at a specific point in time, the following steps are followed to implement CRs:

1. Each CR is further analyzed to determine the components and deliverables that will be impacted.
2. At the completion of analysis, CR implementation activities are consolidated into packages (perhaps by component).
3. Work allocation is made so that all CRs pertaining to one component or to one set of related components are given to the same team member(s).
4. The allocated team members complete the CR implementation activities.
5. The modifications are subjected to standard QA activities, such as peer and managerial reviews and regression testing.
6. All defects uncovered during reviews and testing are rectified by the appropriate team member(s).
7. When all CRs are implemented, a managerial review of CR implementation is carried out by the SPM or by a person designated by the SPM to ensure that all CRs are satisfactorily resolved and that they have passed through QA activities. The CRs would then be closed.
8. The software is promoted to the next stage.

This process is very similar the steps required for a software release after the initial implementation. The process for retrofitting CRs at the end of a project is illustrated in Figure 8.4.

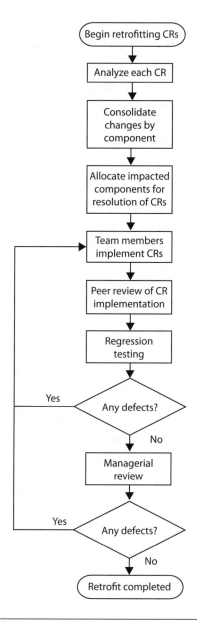

Figure 8.4. Retrofitting change requests at the end of a project.

As received/when convenient. If a CR is implemented when received or when convenient, the following steps are taken to resolve the CR:

1. The CR is allocated for resolution to the appropriate team member(s).
2. If the CR impacts an information artifact:
   - The information artifact is copied to an in-process folder.
   - The information artifact is modified as necessary.
   - The information artifact is subjected to QA activities, e.g., peer review and managerial review.
   - Any defects uncovered during QA are rectified by the concerned team member(s).
   - After all defects are rectified, the artifact receives appropriate approvals.
   - The artifact in the current artifacts folder is then moved to the archived artifacts folder and the updated artifact is moved to the current artifacts folder.
   - All concerned team members would be informed of the change in the artifact.
   - If CR implementation includes modifying the code artifacts, in addition to information artifacts, the CR is then passed on to the team members who are allocated the work of implementing the CR in the code artifacts along with reference to the updated information artifact.
3. If the CR impacts a code artifact, either independently or after an information artifact has been updated, the following steps are followed to implement the CR in code artifacts:
   - The SPM allocates the CR for resolution to an appropriate team member(s) for implementation along with references to any updated information artifacts.
   - The allocated team members carry out the necessary coding. (Coding activity is governed by coding guidelines for the project.)
   - The CR is then allocated for peer review. Peer review personnel review the code to ensure that:
     - Implementation fulfills the requirements of the CR.
     - The implementation conforms to the project guidelines and other software engineering standards of the organization.
     - No trash or malicious code is left in the software.
     - The changed code ensures efficiency of execution and response times.

- Once the CR is passed through peer review, it is submitted for regression testing.
  - The testing team carries out regression testing to ensure that all functionalities requested in the CR are correctly working and that the original functionality is unaffected by implementation of the CR.
  - Once regression testing is complete and all defects pointed out either in peer review or regression testing are resolved and closed, the CR is closed in the CR register. The artifact is then promoted to the next stage.

The process of CR implementation is illustrated in Figure 8.5.

THE VALUE OF METRICS DERIVED FROM A CHANGE REQUEST REGISTER

A CR is usually viewed as a change in requirements received from a customer. Yet, when a CR is not raised by a customer/user, but instead is raised by a team member or a QA person, can the change still be termed a "requirement" change? Of course, because the request is still a requirement — it is just not a user/customer requirement. For example, a team member may raise a change request because some requirement of the team has not been met. A QA person may raise a CR because a quality requirement has not been met. Sometimes conforming to a specific design item or a user requirement is determined to be impractical. In cases such as this, a CR is raised to amend the requirement itself — therefore making it a requirements change. (*Note*: A defect report is not a CR.)

The number of CRs can reflect the stability of the requirements. (*Note*: One argument is that if requirements analysis has been diligently carried out and all necessary QA activities have been applied, then CRs will not be present. When referring to requirements analysis, ensure that analysis activities include not only the user/customer requirements, but also other ancillary requirements, including the feasibility to achieve the user requirements, the security requirements, the usability requirements, the maintenance requirements, etc.) Therefore, the CR register becomes a source of information for measuring the stability of requirements: metrics which are normally referred to as change or CR metrics. The following formula is used to compute requirements stability (expressed as a percentage):

(Total number of requirements − number of change requests) ÷ total number of requirements

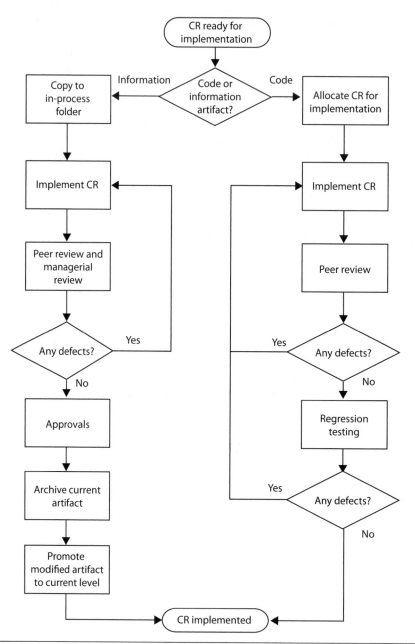

Figure 8.5. Implementation of a change request.

Another metric normally derived is the amount of relative effort spent on resolving CRs (expressed as a percentage):

(Total effort spent on resolving change requests ÷ total effort spent on project) × 100

Analysis that is carried out to segment the changes into various categories identifies the origin of changes and allows inferences to be developed to determine if any trend is emerging or if action is needed. Suppose the bulk of CRs:

- *Result from coding*: The organization is alerted that training for coders is necessary.
- *Indicate an unsatisfactory understanding of customer requirements*: The organization is alerted to the need of more training for the business analysts in effective processing of requirements solicitation/ elicitation/development.
- *Are due to defective design*: The organization is alerted to the need for software designers/architects improvement.

Status of CR implementation, the progress of CR resolution, and the CR metrics are usually reported as components of a weekly status reports to concerned executives. This report serves the purpose of providing historical records and alerting senior management to the need for intervention as necessary. In the opinion of the authors, however, most categories of CRs can be alleviated by adopting one or more of the following suggestions:

- Impart training to improve the skills of personnel.
- Develop better software development processes and procedures.
- Set higher standards and have strong guidelines for coding, design, architecture, and review.
- Rigorously implement conformance and investigative audits.

9

SCHEDULING

INTRODUCTION

Scheduling is a very important activity in software project management. To say that project planning in many organizations consists of only the scheduling activity would not be an exaggeration. In these organizations, project planning refers only to preparation of a schedule. A schedule during the project planning stage, however, is actually a *calendar* through which the project is envisaged for execution. This practice of schedule-based project planning/managing is apparently seductively simple, but a schedule is only one component of project planning. The schedule is but one of the tools that is available to a software project manager for project monitoring.

Scheduling in its simplest form is the sequencing and setting of calendar dates for the project activities that have been envisaged to accomplish the goals of a project. Yet, scheduling is not merely a rote activity. Good scheduling requires human creativity and ingenuity. When scheduling a project, having an understanding of the aspects of a project is essential:

- A project consists of a number of activities (tasks). Performing these activities/tasks results in execution of the project.
- A project has a number of milestones. Reaching the milestones signifies completion of a certain group of activities.
- A project has a starting point, which is the project's first milestone or *start* milestone.
- A project has an ending point, which is the project's last milestone or *end* milestone.

- All activities of a project must be performed between the start and the end milestones.
- Some activities of a project can be performed concurrently with (parallel to) each other.
- Some activities must be performed sequentially (one after the other).
- Some activities can use multiple resources and some activities cannot.
- There is a limit to the number of resources that can be deployed for any given activity.

Let's now schedule a project using a sample project.

THE INITIAL WORK BREAKDOWN STRUCTURE

The list of activities/tasks and milestones needed to execute and complete a project is commonly known as a work breakdown structure or WBS. The first item in a WBS is the *start* milestone, which signifies the beginning of the project. The last item in a WBS is the *end* milestone, which signifies completion of the project. The project "happens" between these two milestones.

So, the first step in scheduling a project is to prepare a WBS that contains all of the tasks that are to be scheduled. A simple initial WBS for a materials management software development project is illustrated in Table 9.1, where all activities are embedded between the *start* and *end* milestones. Of course, a real-life project would have many more activities.

A WORK BREAKDOWN STRUCTURE WITH PREDECESSORS DEFINED

Having prepared the initial WBS, the next step is to determine the sequence of the execution of the tasks listed in the WBS in Table 9.1. This is achieved by adding a *Predecessor* column to Table 9.1 (as shown in Table 9.2). Some organizations use *predecessors* and *successors* (what must come next) as a tool to define sequence. By definition, the *start* milestone does not have any predecessors (even though we know from earlier discussions that significant activities may have taken place to acquire the project before its start). The other project activities, however, should have at least one predecessor (some activities may have more). By definition, the *end* milestone has no successors.

Defining the predecessors consists of a process that includes considering each activity and then answering the question, "What activities should have already been completed before this activity can begin?" The answer is recorded in the *Predecessor* column. The *Predecessor* column indicates all of the activities that

Table 9.1. Initial Work Breakdown Structure

Task ID	Task Description	Effort in Person-Days
1	Start	0
2	Project initiation	2
3	Project planning	5
4	Requirements analysis	10
5	Software requirements specification	4
6	Design	12
7	Construction of warehouse module	15
8	Construction of purchase module	12
9	Construction of inventory control module	10
10	Construction of payables module	6
11	Integration	5
12	Integration testing and fixing defects	3
13	System testing	3
14	User acceptance testing	2
15	User documentation	5
16	User training	3
17	Software installation and master data creation	10
18	Pilot run	2
19	Handover and customer sign-off	1
20	End	0

need to be completed before the next activity can begin. The scheduler walks through the WBS, iterating the process of asking and answering this "order question" for each activity in the WBS, to ensure that predecessors are identified and recorded for all activities. Some activities will have only one predecessor, while others may have multiple activities as predecessors.

A task can also have multiple predecessors or multiple successors. In Table 9.2, the predecessor and the successor for each task are shown. For Task 2, the predecessor is Task 1 and the successor is Task 3 (and Task 2 is the predecessor for Task 3). For Task 5, the predecessor is Task 4 and the successor is Task 6. Notice that Task 6 is a predecessor for five tasks: five tasks can start once Task 6 is completed. Notice also that Task 11 has five predecessors: Task 11 cannot start until these five tasks have been completed (think of this as web converging to a single point). (*Note*: Predecessors and successors for each task may also be mapped in a Gantt/PERT chart, which will be briefly described at the end of this chapter.) In summary:

Table 9.2. Work Breakdown Structure with Predecessors

Task ID	Task Description	Effort in Person-Days	Predecessor
1	Start	0	
2	Project initiation	2	1
3	Project planning	5	2
4	Requirements analysis	10	3
5	Software requirements specification	4	4
6	Design	12	5
7	Construction of warehouse module	15	6
8	Construction of purchase module	12	6
9	Construction of inventory control module	10	6
10	Construction of payables module	6	6
11	Integration	5	6, 7, 8, 9, 10
12	Integration testing and fixing defects	3	11
13	System testing	3	12
14	User acceptance testing	2	13
15	User documentation	5	12
16	User training	3	14, 15
17	Software installation and master data creation	10	14
18	Pilot run	2	17
19	Handover and customer sign-off	1	18
20	End	0	19

- The number of milestones that can be documented between the *start* and *end* milestones have no limit: milestones enhance a schedule's clarity and understanding.
- Except for the *start* milestone of a schedule, which has no predecessor, and the *end* milestone, which has no successor, every task must have one or more predecessors and one or more successors.

Note: There may be multiple tasks as successors to the *start* milestone which are beyond the scope of the present project. Similarly, the *end* milestone may have multiple predecessors which are again beyond the scope of the present project.

Returning to Table 9.2, notice that no task lists Task 16 as a predecessor. But doesn't Task 16 have a successor? This is an anomaly that has to be rectified before we can have a complete schedule. Conversely, if we cannot perceive that another task or activity is a successor to an activity, its successor by definition is the *end milestone.*

Also notice in Table 9.2, that an analysis of the schedule will raise questions about the predecessor relationships. Look at Tasks 2 and 3. Task 3 (project planning) cannot be started unless Task 2 (project initiation) has been completed. This relationship is called a *finish-to-start relationship*: Task 2 must be finished before Task 3 can be started. Task 11 (integration) can start once Task 6 (design) has been completed, and other modules can be integrated when any module is completed. Therefore, there is a *finish-to-start relationship* between Task 6 and Task 11. So, in our example, Task 11 can start when Task 6 is finished, but Task 11 cannot be completed until Tasks 7, 8, 9, and 10 are completed. The relationship between Task 11 and Tasks 7, 8, 9, and 10 is called *finish-to-finish relationship*.

Now, look at Task 11 (integration) and Task 12 (integration testing and fixing defects). Should Task 12 wait until all four of the modules are integrated? It could, but waiting is not necessary because when a module is integrated, its integration can be tested. The relationship between Task 11 and Task 12 therefore is a called a *start-to-start relationship*. Task 12 can be started after Task 11 starts, but with the time lag that is necessary to allow finishing the integration of the first module.

To account for all of the possible relationships, one more relationship needs to be defined: the start-to-finish relationship. In the start-to-finish relationship, Task "n" must be started to finish Task "m." The start-to-finish relationship, however, is atypical in software development and is described here only for the sake of completeness.

Summarizing, there are four types of predecessor relationships:

- Finish (predecessor)-to-start (successor) or **FS-n** (with "n" being the days the successor must wait after finishing the predecessor; if "n" is not mentioned, n = 0)
- Start (predecessor)-to-start (successor) or **SS-n** (with "n" being the days the successor must wait after starting the predecessor; if "n" is not mentioned, n = 0)
- Finish (predecessor)-to-finish (successor) or **FF-n** (with "n" being the days the successor must wait after finishing the predecessor; if "n" is not mentioned, n = 0)
- Start (successor)-to-finish (predecessor) or **SF-n** (with "n" being the days the successor must wait after starting the predecessor to finish successor; if "n" is not mentioned, n = 0)

For each of these relationships, a *lag* (waiting time) may be specified before the successor is started:

- Task 3 can be started 1 day after finishing Task 2. This is depicted as **FS-1:** the relationship of Task 3 to predecessor Task 2 is **f**inish-to-**s**tart with a lag of **1** day.
- Task 12 can be started after 2 days of starting Task 11. This is depicted as **SS-2:** the relationship of Task 12 to Task 11 is **s**tart-to-**s**tart with a lag of **2** days.

A WORK BREAKDOWN SCHEDULE WITH INITIAL DATES

Once the structure of the WBS has been completed by defining the predecessors and the predecessor relationships, and by ensuring that all tasks have predecessors and successors, the next step is to start assigning dates to the tasks. Note the following points from the schedule depicted in Table 9.3:

- The start date for the *start* milestone is the project's starting date.
- The end date for the *end* milestone is the project's completion date.
- Weekends (Saturday and Sunday) are not counted as working days. (Also exclude holidays, e.g., notice that July 4, which is Independence Day in the United States, is excluded in Task 18.)
- Task 3 starts April 3 and Task 2 is completed on April 2 (the day before). Why? Because when a task is to be completed on April 2, typically the task will be completed by the end of the working day on April 2. Therefore, the successor can only start the next day.
- Task 11 (with five predecessors) starts on May 16, the day after the completion of Task 6. Task 11 has a finish-to-start (FS) relationship with Task 6. Task 11 also has a finish-to-finish with 2 days lag (FF-2) relationship with the rest of its predecessors. Therefore, Task 11 completes on June 9, 2 working days after the completion of Task 7. Task 7 is the predecessor that finishes last (on June 5) of all the predecessors of Task 11. Because the lag is 2 days, Task 11 completes on June 9, which is 2 working days after the completion of its last predecessor.
- No relationship for Task 16 is given. When no relationship is explicitly given, the relationship is a finish-to-start relationship (FS) with no lag. Task 16 has two predecessors: Task 14 (completes on June 19) and Task 15 (completes on June 26). Therefore, Task 16 can start 1 day after Task 15, which is the last of Task 16's predecessors.
- Look at the *end* milestone, which has two predecessors. Both of these predecessors must be completed for the end milestone to be reached. Therefore, the start date (as well as the end date) is July 7, the day on which Task 19 (the last task) is completed.

Table 9.3. Work Breakdown Structure with Initial Dates

Task ID	Task Description	Effort in Person-Days	Predecessor	Start Date	Finish Date
1	Start	0		1-Apr-08	1-Apr-08
2	Project initiation	2	1	1-Apr-08	2-Apr-08
3	Project planning	5	2	3-Apr-08	9-Apr-08
4	Requirements analysis	10	3	10-Apr-08	23-Apr-08
5	Software requirements specification	4	4	24-Apr-08	29-Apr-08
6	Design	12	5	30-Apr-08	15-May-08
7	Construction of warehouse module	15	6	16-May-08	5-Jun-08
8	Construction of purchase module	12	6	16-May-08	2-Jun-08
9	Construction of inventory control module	10	6	16-May-08	29-May-08
10	Construction of payables module	6	6	16-May-08	23-May-08
11	Integration	5	6 (FS), 7 (FF-2), 8 (FF-2), 9 (FF-2), 10 (FF-2)	16-May-08	9-Jun-08
12	Integration testing and fixing defects	3	11	10-Jun-08	12-Jun-08
13	System testing	3	12	13-Jun-08	17-Jun-08
14	User acceptance testing	2	13	18-Jun-08	19-Jun-08
15	User documentation	5	12	20-Jun-08	26-Jun-08
16	User training	3	14, 15	27-Jun-08	1-Jul-08
17	Software installation and master data creation	10	14	19-Jun-08	2-Jul-08
18	Pilot run	2	17	3-Jul-08	7-Jul-08
19	Handover and customer sign-off	1	18	8-Jul-08	8-Jul-08
20	End	0	19	8-Jul-08	8-Jul-08

Some inferences for future use may be drawn from this description of the relationships:

- The *start* date of an activity depends on its relationship with its predecessors:
  - In a finish-to-start relationship, the start date depends on the predecessor that finishes last.
  - In a start-to-start relationship, the start date depends on the predecessor that starts first.
  - Other relationships have no impact.
- The *end* date of an activity depends on its duration *and* on the relationship with its predecessors:
  - In a finish-to-finish relationship, the end date depends on its predecessor finishing last.
  - Other relationships have no impact.

A WORK BREAKDOWN STRUCTURE WITH RESOURCE ALLOCATION

In Table 9.3, the term *effort* is used synonymously for *duration*. In our example, this synonymous use of the term allows us to assume that only one resource has been allocated to the project. In most real-life projects, however, multiple resources are allocated to a project and the resources have different skill sets. Naturally, multiple resources and the various skill sets of these resources result in differences between the effort and the duration for specific activities.

For example, say that coding takes 100 person-days to complete. So, if one programmer is allocated to the task, the duration will be 100 workdays; if two programmers are allocated, the duration will be 50 workdays; and if four programmers are allocated, the duration will be 25 workdays (assuming that all programmers are equal). So, to get a realistic schedule, we need to add a *Resource Allocated* column and a *Duration* column to Table 9.3 and adjust duration.

Now, look at Table 9.4. Notice that *Duration* (effort ÷ number of resources) has been adjusted for each task by taking into consideration the number of resources allocated for each task. Duration depends on the effort in person-days and the number of resources allocated for the activity. The dates in the schedule have been set based on the duration and predecessor relationships. Table 9.4 now reflects all of the components needed to develop a useable schedule.

Table 9.4. Work Breakdown Structure with Resource Allocation

Task ID	Task Description	Effort in Person-Days	Resources Allocated	Duration	Predecessor	Start Date	Finish Date
1	Start	0	0	0		1-Apr-08	1-Apr-08
2	Project initiation	2	1	2	1	1-Apr-08	2-Apr-08
3	Project planning	5	1	5	2	3-Apr-08	9-Apr-08
4	Requirements analysis	10	2	5	3	10-Apr-08	23-Apr-08
5	Software requirements specification	4	1	4	4	24-Apr-08	29-Apr-08
6	Design	12	4	3	5	30-Apr-08	15-May-08
7	Construction of warehouse module	15	3	5	6	16-May-08	5-Jun-08
8	Construction of purchase module	12	4	3	6	16-May-08	2-Jun-08
9	Construction of inventory control module	10	2	5	6	16-May-08	29-May-08
10	Construction of payables module	6	3	2	6	16-May-08	23-May-08
11	Integration	5	1	5	6 (FS), 7 (FF-2), 8 (FF-2), 9 (FF-2), 10 (FF-2)	16-May-08	9-Jun-08
12	Integration testing and fixing defects	3	1	3	11	10-Jun-08	12-Jun-08
13	System testing	3	1	3	12	13-Jun-08	17-Jun-08
14	User acceptance testing	2	1	2	13	18-Jun-08	19-Jun-08
15	User documentation	5	1	5	12	20-Jun-08	26-Jun-08
16	User training	3	1	3	14, 15	27-Jun-08	1-Jul-08
17	Software installation and master data creation	10	2	5	14	19-Jun-08	2-Jul-08
18	Pilot run	2	1	2	17	3-Jul-08	7-Jul-08
19	Handover and customer sign-off	1	1	1	18	8-Jul-08	8-Jul-08
20	End	0	0	0	19	8-Jul-08	8-Jul-08

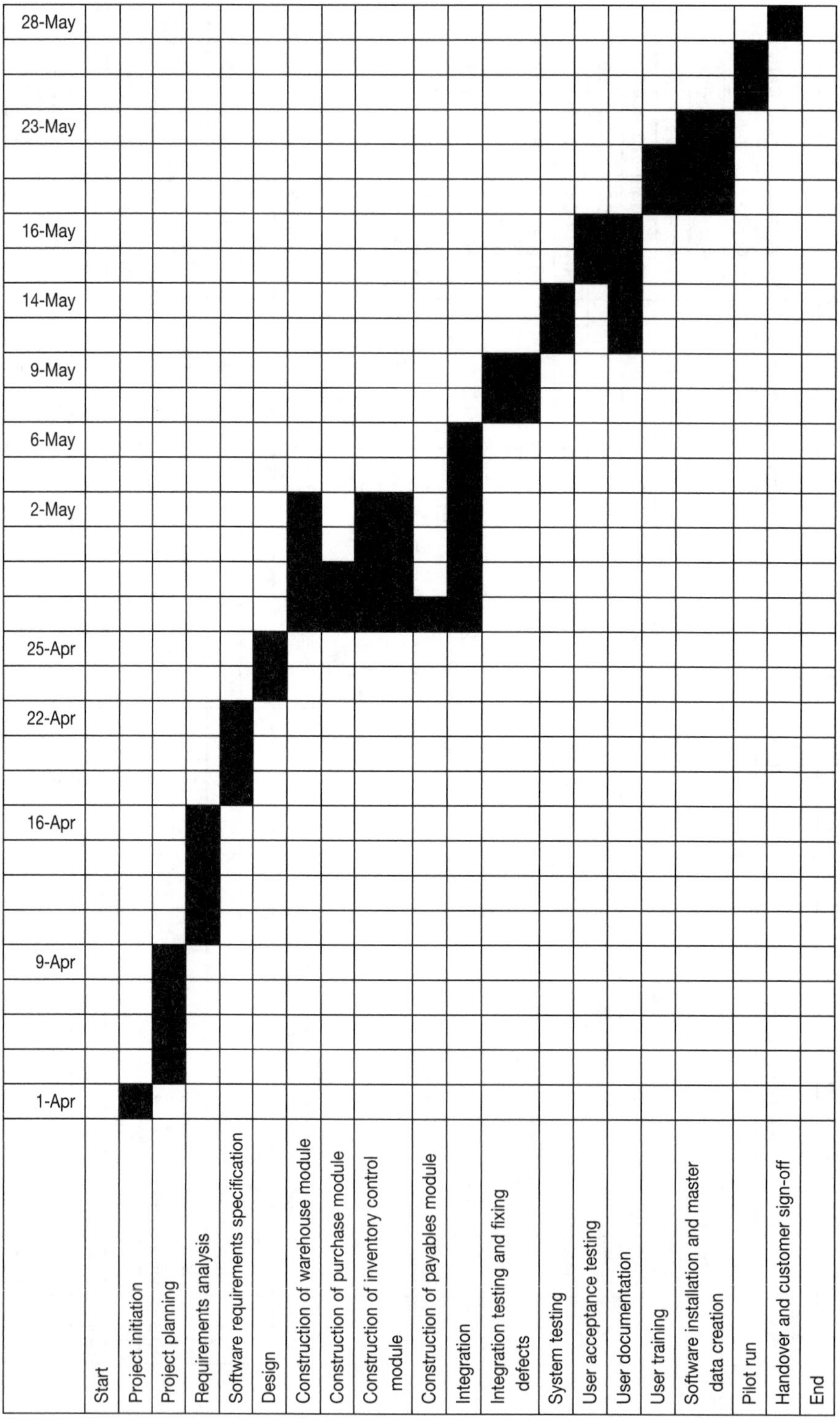

Figure 9.1. Gantt chart.

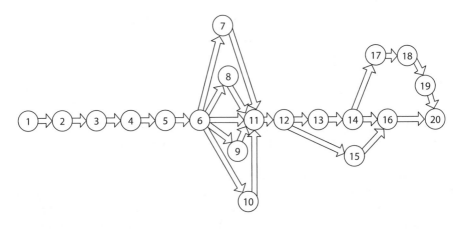

Figure 9.2. Network diagram.

SCHEDULING IN PRACTICE

In actual practice, manual iteration is not required as many times as we have done in our example. Tools such as spreadsheets (e.g., Microsoft Excel) may be used and information can be filled in column by column. Excel's capability for date arithmetic can then be used to our advantage for assigning dates to tasks. Specialized software tools, such as Primavera, Microsoft Project, and PMPal, can also assist in scheduling. These tools take weekends and holidays into account when assigning dates to tasks. Using an automated spreadsheet or specialized scheduling software also makes scheduling easier when a project start date is shifted or if a change in any of the tasks subsequently requires recalculation of the schedule.

GRAPHIC REPRESENTATION OF A SCHEDULE

Graphic representations of schedules are frequently used. Two popular graphic representations are bar charts (also called Gantt charts) and network diagrams:

Bar charts. A Gantt chart is illustrated in Figure 9.1. A Gantt chart is a type of bar chart that illustrates a project schedule. Gantt charts can be produced using Microsoft Excel spreadsheets or scheduling packages such as Primavera and Microsoft Project.

Network diagram. Network diagrams may take various forms. In Figure 9.2, each task is depicted in a circle and is identified by only its task IDs. In more traditional network diagrams, a task is depicted in the arrow of the network and the

Early Start	Duration	Early Finish
	Task Name	
Late Start	Slack	Late Finish

Figure 9.3. Network node diagram.

circle depicts the milestone. In network diagrams currently being used in the software development industry, the arrow represents only a predecessor relationship.

Network node diagram. The most frequently used depiction of an activity, however, is illustrated in Figure 9.3. This graphic representation of a task is in a rectangular shape that is divided into seven sections. Variations of this representation are found in effective scheduling software tool packages, such as Microsoft Project, Primavera, PMPal, EstimatorPal, etc.

10

SOFTWARE PROJECT CLOSURE

INTRODUCTION

Project initiation looks forward to ensure the successful execution of a project. Project closure, however, looks backward: to take stock of what went right and what went wrong and to draw lessons accordingly from these events for use in the future. As a result, project initiation *draws from* the knowledge repository (corporate memory) of the organization and project closure *adds to* the knowledge repository.

When conducted methodically, project closure activities facilitate the reduction of defect injection rates and turnaround time and the improvement of productivity and customer satisfaction in future projects. By contributing to the success of future software projects, project closure activities also contribute to the overall success of an organization. Yet, as important as project closure is to an organization, it is one of the most neglected areas of project management in software development organizations.

Before discussing project closure any further, let's first explore project closure by asking what should be an easy question to answer: "When does a project really close?" Rarely is the answer to this question as simple as one might think. For example, most projects have a warranty phase during which an application will be supported by members of the project team. Usually, the warranty support team is much smaller than the project team. When an application has a warranty phase, the project closes only after completion of the warranty phase. When a project moves to the warranty phase, often the SPM will be retained. In some cases, however, a PL or some other person will be designated by the organization to lead warranty support. (If the SPM is moved out of the project during the warranty phase, all of the project's artifacts are handed over to the person leading the warranty support.) The project will then be closed upon completion of warranty support.

Another possibility is that software maintenance is assigned to the development organization. In this case, sometimes the development project is closed and the software maintenance project is immediately initiated. If the same team continues to support the software during maintenance phase, the project is closed only after the completion of software maintenance. Treating software maintenance as a separate project can have plusses and minuses. For example, software development and software maintenance require people with very different aptitudes. People who efficiently develop software from scratch may not be able to modify code very well. Conversely, people who can efficiently repair code may not be able to develop fresh code well. When this is the case, having different teams for software maintenance and software development makes sense. So, when software maintenance is initiated as a fresh project, the development part of the project is closed as soon as the software is delivered to the client and the project is handed over to the new maintenance team.

In summary, a project may be closed:

- Soon after warranty support is completed, if software maintenance is not assigned to the same organization.
- If software maintenance is assigned to the same organization:
  - The development project may be closed soon after customer acceptance and delivery of the software.
  - The development project may be closed after completion of the warranty period and when software maintenance work is spawned as another project.
  - The project may be closed only after the contract with the customer is terminated, i.e., hybrid development and maintenance may continue as long as the software maintenance work continues.

Several activities are typically performed in project closure:

- Identifying reusable code components and depositing them in the organizational code repository (including allied documentation, such as design and user documents)
- Documenting and depositing the best practices in the organizational knowledge repository
- Documenting and depositing the lessons learned from project execution in the organizational knowledge repository

- Compiling and deriving the final project metrics and depositing them in the organizational knowledge repository
- Conducting a knowledge-sharing meeting with peer SPMs
- Depositing the project records in the PMO
- Depositing the project code artifacts in the code repository
- Conducting a project postmortem
- Releasing the SPM
- Closing the project (and celebrating!)

Let's now discuss each of these activities in more detail.

IDENTIFYING REUSABLE CODE COMPONENTS

Reusable code components are the components that have been developed to meet common technical scenario requirements: dynamic linked libraries (DLLs), stored procedures, or interface routines and any other components that were developed exclusively in the current project in such a way that they are expected to be useful in future projects or for other applications. Factors to be considered when identifying reusable components include:

- Does the organization have intellectual property rights (IP) for the code? (If the IP resides with the client, the organization is not authorized to use any part of the code unless use of the code is specifically negotiated.)
- Are the components generally stand-alone in nature or can they be packaged for a specific purpose?
- Do the components connect to a backend database for achieving database independence?
- Are code components or snippets that are created during the project for current and future use?

Once the components have been identified for inclusion in the organizational code repository, the components are prepared for inclusion by:

1. Removing any hard-coding present in the code (the practice of defining the values for data directly in the code instead of receiving values as input) and replacing it with parameterized code so that the data can be received as input (Removing hard-coding may require adding additional code for reading the data from an external source, e.g., a file, table, or program parameters.)
2. Including in-line documentation to assist future programmers in using a component
3. Removing any trash or dead code present inside the component

4. Preparing design documentation for the component (Preparing the design documentation may involve taking information about the component from the project design document; bringing it up to as-built stage; and adding the additional documentation necessary to include the functionality added to accommodate removing the hard-coding in the component.)

5. Preparing a component usage document that details aspects such as:
   - The functionality of the component
   - Prerequisites necessary for using the component: parameters to be supplied along with the component, details of data files to be created, or database tables necessary for the component
   - Instructions for embedding the component in the code
   - Limitations of the component: size of data and data validations
   - Platform requirements: operating system, programming language, database, and special hardware/software requirements

6. Preparing a note recommending inclusion of the component in the code repository and submitting it to the configuration control board (CCB) of the organizational code repository and following the recommendation through until it is either included or rejected

Typically, the SPM has the responsibility to carry out the activities of identifying all possible reusable components from the project and after obtaining necessary approvals to deposit them in the code repository.

DOCUMENTING THE BEST PRACTICES

Best practices are the processes, practices, or sets of activities that yielded excellent results during execution of a project. Typically, we are interested in capturing the practices that yielded results far above the norm:

- Any software engineering methodology that was used differently or was developed to improve quality and productivity during development of the software
- A new algorithm that solved a tricky issue in a project
- Any project practice, such as work allocation, quality assurance, motivation, configuration management, build preparation, or deployment methods, that reduced the effort necessary and resulted in improved quality
- Use of a new tool or a new way of using an existing tool that assisted the project in any manner to achieve better results

- A new tool that was exclusively developed for the project, but could be used in future projects
- Any new or modified formats and templates that were used in the project that resulted in improved clarity
- Any new checklists prepared for use in the project that were found to be useful in ensuring comprehensiveness in any project activity
- Any new procedure or process developed for the project that yielded positive results outside of the norm

The SPM is responsible for preparing the best practice documents, arranging for their review, and implementing any review feedback. Upon approval, the final step in the process is for the SPM to deposit the new best practices in the knowledge repository.

DOCUMENTING THE LESSONS LEARNED

All projects provide learning opportunities. During execution of a project, the project team and the SPM will at least have learned a few lessons. These lessons are typically a mixture of positives and negatives. (As humans, we tend to extol our successes and play down our failures, but as leaders we must keep an open mind to the possibility of positive and negative impacts on a project.) Only after we have neutralized a problem and recognized the lesson to be learned, do we learn from a negative experience. Once recognized, lessons are only valuable if we then carry out situational analyses using a critical examination technique to draw inferences for the future.

Whenever an unexpected impact is encountered in a project, we need to document the impact and the cause so that we (and others) can learn and benefit from the experience. Only from documentation and learning from others' experiences has so large a body of knowledge been gathered in the scientific world. Software project management is no different. Typically, the areas of project management that are the most conducive for providing lessons include:

- Communications with clients, within the project team, and with other project stakeholders
- Work allocation mechanisms
- Defect resolution mechanisms
- Change request resolution
- Grievance handling
- Software engineering, development platform issues, and solutions

These areas and any other areas that created challenges and opportunities for the project team should be documented. Once documented, they can be submitted for managerial review and then deposited in the organizational knowledge repository.

COLLECTING/DERIVING AND DEPOSITING THE FINAL PROJECT METRICS IN THE ORGANIZATIONAL KNOWLEDGE REPOSITORY

Just as best practices and lessons learned represent holistic views of a project, the activities of collecting, deriving, and depositing the final project metrics provide quantitative information about the project, which involves computing the metrics for the overall project. These metrics typically include:

- Productivity metrics for each of the programming languages used in the project as well as for the other software engineering activities: reviews, testing, requirements analysis, and design
- Quality metrics, including defect injection rates for each of the programming languages and the defect removal efficiency for each of the quality assurance activities implemented in the project
- Schedule variance metrics for the entire project as well as for each of the project execution phases
- Effort variance metrics for the entire project as well as for each of the software engineering activities
- Personnel metrics, including productivity metrics and quality metrics for each of the project team members
- Other relevant metrics: the relative effort spent on various project execution activities (requirements analysis, software design, coding, review, and testing)

These metrics are reviewed against organizational baselines. Variances are then analyzed to determine if they are purely due to chance (random variance) or are due to assignable causes. By leveraging this type of variance analysis, the metrics are reviewed and validated and credible information is extracted and then deposited in the organizational metrics repository for future use.

CONDUCTING KNOWLEDGE-SHARING MEETINGS WITH PEER SOFTWARE PROJECT MANAGERS

A knowledge-sharing meeting is the counterpart of a project kick-off meeting. The audience is the same for both meetings. The kick-off meeting, however, is the first meeting in a project, whereas the knowledge-sharing meeting is the last meeting. One of the goals of a properly conducted knowledge-sharing session is to ensure uniformity of project execution as well as to ensure the success of all projects in the organization.

Once the activities of identifying the reusable components; documenting the best practices and the lessons learned; and deriving the metrics have been completed, the information is shared with peer SPMs. This sharing of knowledge helps to ensure that all SPMs have access to the same depth of rich knowledge so that they can utilize the knowledge gained in their projects. A knowledge-sharing meeting is normally coordinated by the PMO. Representatives of the PMO, the software engineering process group, and the quality assurance department also participate in the meeting so that they also can utilize the information in future projects.

During the meeting, the project's SPM presents all aspects of project execution, including the successes and failures. The SPM also presents the project execution methodology and the results obtained in detail. During the knowledge-sharing session, the SPM also discusses the things that could have been done better as well as the things that were executed better than originally envisaged. All in all, a knowledge-sharing meeting provides a bird's eye view of the project to the participants. To improve their knowledge, meeting participants can elicit additional information from the SPM during the meeting itself or later on.

DEPOSITING PROJECT RECORDS WITH THE PROJECT MANAGEMENT OFFICE

Collating all project records and arranging for the updating of all documents to reflect the "as-built" stage (i.e., so that it reflects the final build of the product) is the responsibility of the SPM. Once the records are collated and updated, the SPM hands over all project records to the PMO for record keeping purposes and for inclusion in the knowledge repository as applicable. Typically, project records include:

- Software estimates
- Project plans
- Work allocation register
- Configuration register
- Defect resolution register
- Change request register
- Issue-resolution register
- Client communications, including commendations and complaints
- Client-supplied documents
- Project-specific guidelines
- Software engineering documents, including requirements specifications and design documents
- Review logs and test logs
- Audit reports and NCRs of the project
- Waivers and special approvals
- Process improvement suggestions

All hard copies, soft copies, and location references are passed on to the PMO by the SPM. Often, most of the documents are in a soft copy form. Therefore, documents are handed over on a backup medium (e.g., a CD/DVD) or are just copied to a PMO-specified location on the organizational server. Some artifacts, such as the configuration, defect, and change request registers, may also be part of a database. In this case, only details of the information are handed over to PMO.

DEPOSITING PROJECT CODE ARTIFACTS IN THE CODE REPOSITORY

The SPM arranges for collation of all code artifacts. Each related set of artifacts is placed in a separate folder with a document describing the folder's contents as well as the nature of the folder's contents. When complete, all of the folders are then copied to a suitable backup media and submitted to the code repository of the organization. Code artifacts of a project typically include:

- The source code of all programs developed in the project, sifted on the basis of the programming language
- Executable code of the software
- Database code, including table scripts, triggers, stored procedures, PL/SQL routines, master data, and parameter files
- Build preparation scripts, including any make files or build routines
- Libraries, including DLLs
- Graphics developed for the project
- Third-party libraries used in the project
- Third-party utilities embedded in the software product
- Macros developed for configuring the intermediate layers of the software
- HTML pages developed for the project.

These artifacts are in addition to the reusable code components discussed in the earlier section.

CONDUCTING THE PROJECT POSTMORTEM

In his novel *Final Diagnosis*, Arthur Hailey spoke of a quote heard in medical circles: "A surgeon knows nothing, but does everything; a psychiatrist knows nothing and does nothing; a pathologist knows everything and does everything, but after the patient has died."[1] A medical postmortem looks at a body dispassionately, with the sole objective of learning the true cause of death. The resulting information is presented at a conference by the pathologist(s) and the lead physician. During the conference, participants discuss the events prior to death, including symptoms, diagnostic investigations, treatment, and cause of death. The intent of the conference is not to assign blame, but to be a platform for collectively learning everything possible from the event. To say that a postmortem is the primary platform for arriving at root causes and developing new treatments to improve survival rates is no exaggeration. Project postmortems are conducted with the same objective: to gain knowledge and to increase the effectiveness of SPMs and the organization as a whole.

The prerequisite for a project postmortem is an investigative audit. An investigative audit reviews variances in the project and the analysis thereof to determine the efficacy of the variance analysis and the inferences drawn from the variances. Once the audit is completed, the auditor who conducted the investigative audit on the project presents the findings to the SPM of the project as well as to all other SPMs in the organization. All findings are dissected so that everyone attending the meeting can learn from the project's issues. The postmortem findings are then included in the project records of the knowledge repository so that they are available to the entire organization.

Note: Some organizations combine the postmortem with the knowledge-sharing meeting. Combining these meetings is not always effective because the knowledge-sharing meeting provides information only from the SPM's experiences, whereas the project postmortem is typically led by an auditor who conducted the investigative audit on the project.

RELEASING THE SOFTWARE PROJECT MANAGER

Before the SPM can be released from a project, all project closure aspects must have been completed. Additionally, performance appraisals of the project team members should have been completed. Typically, the SPM is gradually released from the project because of the overlap of SPM responsibilities with those of the warranty support leader(s). For example, often an SPM is allocated to a different project, but is still required to provide assistance to an earlier project during its warranty phase and sometimes during the software maintenance phase as well (as necessary). As the involvement of the SPM gradually increases in the next project, involvement in the completed project gradually decreases. Only when the new team handling support for either the warranty or the maintenance services is confident that it can handle the project on its own is the SPM completely released from the project.

CLOSING THE PROJECT

When all project closure aspects are completed and the SPM is released, the PMO closes the project. Project closure typically involves the PMO issuing a project closure note to all stakeholders, including senior management; the finance, human resources, systems administration, facilities, and administration departments; and the customer, indicating that the project is closed. Based on the project closure note from the PMO:

1. The finance department allows no further booking of effort or expenditures to the project.
2. The human resources department allocates no further human resources to the project.
3. The facilities department repossesses all seating facilities allotted to the project.
4. The administration department entertains no requests for purchases (or any other requests) for the project.

The project closure note issued by the PMO marks the end of project execution in all respects and is the last document placed in the project's dossier.

THE ROLE OF THE ORGANIZATION IN PROJECT CLOSURE

Just as the organization has a vital role in all aspects of project execution, the organization also has an important role in project closure. But the organization's role is more than just closing a project per se. The organization must also ensure that the knowledge gained from the project is gathered in the organizational knowledge repository, that the reusable components are received in the organizational code repository, and that knowledge is then spread to all concerned members of the organization. The organization exercises this role primarily through three entities: the PMO, the CCB, and the systems administration department.

The Project Management Office

From previous discussions, we know that the PMO is the central project-coordinating agency in an organization. The PMO maintains the organization's knowledge repository, is responsible for updating the knowledge repository with information collated from project closure, and coordinates knowledge-sharing meetings and project postmortems. When initiating a project, the PMO *draws from* the organization's knowledge repository; when closing a project, the PMO *adds to* (or updates) the organization's knowledge repository.

During project closure, the PMO coordinates the project postmortem and ensures that it is conducted objectively and that inferences are drawn professionally.

The PMO also collects all of the information about a project, with the objective of making the project's information available for use in other projects. The PMO takes over the project's records and metrics and the various analyses performed on the project from the SPM. Typically, the PMO scours all of the analyses for assignable causes and includes the validated data for consideration (e.g., to revise the organizational baselines for the next iteration of an activity). While taking over records, metrics, and analyses from the SPM, the PMO ensures that all information has been updated to reflect the latest achievements in the project and that all analyses have been properly carried out. If any shortfalls are uncovered, the PMO obtains the necessary clarifications from the SPM and rectifies the anomalies. After collecting the data, the PMO classifies the information into appropriate categories and stores the information in such a way that it can be located and retrieved easily when required.

The Configuration Control Board

At the organizational level, the CCB takes ownership of maintaining the organizational code repository. The organizational code repository contains all code artifacts developed during the execution of projects. (*Note*: If the contract between the organization and the client stipulates that all the code artifacts must be delivered to the client and that no code artifacts can be retained in the organization, then the code artifacts of such projects are not be maintained in the code repository.)

During project initiation and under the direction of PMO, the code repository is made available to project team members. The repository provides the project team with a "jump start" because it includes all possible tools, reusable components, development tool kits, and third-party code artifacts for efficient and effective project execution. During project closure, the code repository repossesses all of the code artifacts provided during project initiation as well as the reusable components developed during project execution, any client-supplied components, and any third-party code artifacts procured for the project.

Code artifacts repossessed or taken over from projects are the responsibility of the organizational CCB: to ensure that all documentation necessary for future use is prepared and that the documentation is in a usable form. The CCB also conducts sanity testing to ensure that the code artifacts match the respective documentation in terms of functionality and usage. Another important responsibility of the CCB is to ensure that the organization does indeed have the intellectual property rights for the code artifacts being deposited by projects. The code repository typically contains:

- The source code of all projects
- The object code and executable code of all projects
- All project graphics

- All table scripts, triggers, stored procedures, and PL/SQL routines of databases
- All library code (including static libraries, DLLs, and shared libraries)
- All client-supplied code
- All third-party artifacts procured for use in projects
- All development and testing tools used in projects
- All system software (including operating systems, databases, IDEs, debuggers, and all software tools for use in projects)
- Reusable components

All code artifacts in the code repository are properly stored to prevent damage or interference. They are indexed for easy location and retrieval and are periodically checked for integrity.

The Systems Administration Department

The systems administration department takes ownership of the organization's hardware and networking resources. During project initiation and under direction of the PMO, systems administration provides the necessary computer systems, networking, and Internet connectivity to a project team. Systems administration also loads all system software necessary to ensure that the systems provide the intended functionality. Once a project is closed, systems administration repossesses the hardware resources, cleans the computer systems of unnecessary data and software (after ensuring that all backups have been taken and all code artifacts have been deposited in the code repository), and makes these resources ready for allocation to another project.

Some final words about project closure. Project closure is a vitally important activity that needs to be performed diligently. Unfortunately, many organizations do not devote adequate importance to project closure. Often, an SPM dumps the project records on the PMO, the code on the organizational CCB, and the systems on the systems administration department and then moves on to the next project. Project postmortems and knowledge sharing, vitally important activities for garnering organizational experience and enriching an organization's maturity level, are forgotten or forsaken. As they say in HR circles, "Did we execute one project thirty times or did we execute thirty projects?" Project closure is the activity that can make all the difference between executing one project thirty times or executing thirty projects.

REFERENCE

1. Arthur Hailey. *Final Diagnosis* 1959. New York: Doubleday & Company

11

AGILE PROJECT MANAGEMENT

INTRODUCTION

The term *agile* has come to mean many things to many people. The definitions and connotations range from how work is organized within a project to a description of the speed at which work is completed or, alternately, to a radical rethinking of organizational culture. One thing that most practitioners of agile will agree on, however, is that agile is not an abandonment of discipline, but rather a *change* of focus. Regardless of how you define agile, likely everyone will agree that agile methods are now maturing and have become core practices in the software development community. Therefore, all project managers need to have at the least an understanding of agile concepts and the ability to deploy them. We will now approach the subject of agile in three areas: the roles typically held in agile projects, the principles that need to be embraced to effectively use agile methods, and the techniques that are part of agile project management.

PROJECT MANAGEMENT ROLES

When discussing agile project management, our focus will be on three basic roles. Depending on the specific methodology being leveraged, each of these roles tends to be referred to by different names. But regardless of what a role is called, the concepts of the roles are the same:

- Team leader
- Team members
- Customers

The team leader. The team leader facilitates the team's organization and acts as the "grease on the axle," which is the project. This leadership role is often called coach or scrum master. The team leader acts as the interface between the external organization and the team so that the team can focus on the work at hand. The leader handles the overhead common to all organizations that is not directly related to delivering functionality. As a coach, the leader brings forth the best in the team through teaching and support rather than by directing and administrating.

Team members. Team members perform the tasks that are required to execute the project. Depending on the type of project, these tasks can include all of the steps required to deliver functional code, to design a project, and to test the project or a combination of all of the steps needed to deliver a working product. In addition, team members have nontechnical tasks, such as supporting their fellow team members, participating in team activities, and openly communicating status and issues within the team.

Customers. The customer (real or proxy) has a substantial role in an agile project. Customers take the lead in providing information about what a project will deliver, including stories (user requirements) and information about priorities. Prioritization is a process that occurs not once, but on a periodic basis (because customer priorities are expected to change over the life of the project). (*Note*: The reprioritization period depends on the length of the iterations/sprints that a project uses. We suggest using shorter iterations/sprints the more experimental or investigatory a project is.) The customer(s) also provides continual explanations and feedback as the team progresses through a sprint. In a perfect world, the customer would be colocated with the team so that no time would be lost while waiting for the time to have a discussion or to generate answers. Whether due to distance or to the size of the firm, co-location is not always practical. Therefore, proxies or daily planned interaction is sometimes used as a workaround.

AGILE PROJECT MANAGEMENT CHARACTERISTICS

To apply agile project management effectively, we suggest six basic characteristics that your organization needs to embrace to be successful when using agile as a project management framework. All six of these characteristics are important:
- Metaphor

- Teamwork and collaboration
- Guiding principles
- Open information
- Light touch
- Constant monitoring and adjustment

Note: We have seen organizations successfully implement agile as a framework without addressing all six of these characteristics perfectly. But, to a greater or lesser extent, they do address all six of them.

Metaphor

In many agile frameworks, the concept of a central metaphor is used to ensure that the whole team moves in the same direction, even when working on different components. The project leader must therefore help the team develop a vision of what they are trying to achieve. A metaphor is then used to cement that vision. *Metaphor*, in the sense that we are using it in agile project management, is an implicit comparison between two concepts that seem to be unrelated: usually one concept is commonly understood and the other is not. The metaphor is used to provide a path from the understood concept to the concept that is not.

A classic example of a metaphor is from Shakespeare's words from *As You Like It* (1600): "All the world's a stage, and all the men and women merely players." This metaphor equates life to a play. Another example commonly seen in the software process improvement world is a metaphor using a flag stuck in a mountain peak with a specific goal scrawled on it: "CMMI or Bust." This metaphor links the journey to the goal. A metaphor acts as an anchor that a team can reference to ensure that each step moves the team and project in the same direction.

Teamwork and Collaboration

Much of the power of agile methods can be traced to the use of multidisciplinary teams that work and interact well together and are focused on a specific short-term goal. (A short-term goal is used to provide tangible feedback to the team and to the customer.) The term *multidisciplinary* includes mixing customers (or their proxies) with a technical team that may include developers, testers, and designers. An ideal team includes people from all of the various disciplines required to achieve the goal set for the team. *Teamwork* means the team must treat people's ideas and concerns equitably. We use the term *equitably* because for teamwork to be fostered and to grow, ideas must be weighed irrespective of the position or power of each team member. If ideas are not treated equitably, team members will not be motivated to contribute. All ideas, however, are not equal. So, one of the tasks that the leader must accept is that of facilitator. In the role of facilitator, the team leader ensures that opinions, thoughts, and ideas are shared in a positive, nonhostile manner.

Another key characteristic the team leader will help to create is a team that has the ability to make a decision — or the term *collaboration* can be "code" for endless rehashing. The team leader/coach is often the teacher: teams learn how to collaborate and interact together from their leaders.

Guiding Principles

We use the term *guiding principles* rather than *guiding processes* to set metaphoric limits rather than providing a set of perspective rules. Each team therefore has the flexibility to define how they will work together within the limits set by the larger organization. Agile methods do not eschew processes, but rather they *size* the processes needed to the simplest set of processes possible. One exhortation that we do make is that the principles/guidelines must be explicitly stated and understood by the team. We strongly suggest that the principles/guidelines are documented and posted for the team to refer to continually (which also has the side benefit of ensuring that the number of principles is kept to a minimum). In the real world, these principles must fit into the organization's overall management framework, which makes every implementation of agile project management a little different.

Processes, procedures, checklists, and documentation are par for the course in many methodologies (development or management), but in agile they are replaced by guiding principles. In many cases, the level of process definition was originally scaled to the largest, most critical project in the organization rather than to the smallest and then scaled upward to meet the whole spectrum of projects. A project leader needs to focus on having only the principles needed for the work at hand. The project leader must then involve the team in deciding on which principles are needed and how they will be implemented. This process takes time to "gel," which is why highly performing teams should be kept together whenever possible.

Open Information

One of the tenets of classical management theory is that control of information is critical for developing the power required to manage. In agile management, this theory is turned on it head: information is shared so that everyone is free to leverage the power that information provides. Information ranging from requirements (user stories) to project code to status information, to name a few, is considered to be collectively owned by the team.

One means of sharing information is team proximity (co-location). Another technique for creating proximity is to establish team rooms to ensure that team members know what is happening within the project so they can help keep the project on track. Other techniques that are used for sharing what would be typically considered "management status" information include the "big visible chart" (described in extreme programming), burn down charts (defined in scrum; a graphic representation of the work left to do at any specific time and the capacity of the project team), and daily stand-up meetings (also typically attributed to scrum).

Use a Light Touch

Team interaction and self-direction are hallmarks of agile projects. As a standard, each agile project decides on its own guiding principles, allocates work to team members as a team, and deals with team issues inside team boundaries (i.e., all within some set of limits). The role of the leader is to facilitate these processes rather than to direct or make decisions about them. This is perhaps the hardest concept for a typical project manager to adjust to in the agile world. But let's face it, if you have been successful in the past, change is scary. An analogy that we use is that of the sweeper in the sport of curling. The sweeper clears the ice as the rock arcs down the ice without actually touching the rock. Similarly, the team leader acts as a facilitator to help the team reaching its potential. The goal of the project manager is to prepare the way for the team.

Note: Non-agile project managers, when they exist in agile teams, are usually focused on communicating and interacting outward from the team. Non-agile project managers take on the role of resolving issues that are blocking progress and that exist outside the team's boundaries.

Monitoring and Adjustment

The combination of open information, teamwork, and collaboration provides a foundation from which a team and its leader can constantly keep tabs on their progress and at the same time share issues that are blocking progress. Techniques, such as daily stand-up meetings, big visible charts, and other feedback mechanisms, ensure that progress (or lack of progress) toward the goals the team has committed to are examined on at least a daily basis. Daily feedback provides a self-directed team with the information required to adjust tasks and assignments. The team acts as a self-correcting organism based on feedback-consistent mechanisms. Teams without feedback mechanisms are not agile — they are blind. Retrospectives provide feedback at a more macro level that allows the team to alter principles and processes for the next sprint (as needed) so that problematic issues do not recur.

THE NUTS AND BOLTS OF AGILE PROJECT MANAGEMENT

Philosophies are an important and necessary foundation upon which agile management techniques can be implemented. More importantly they are *required* so that agile can work effectively. We think this point is absolutely critical. If an organization cannot embrace agile philosophies, they should not expect perfect results. It is our intent to now review a number of techniques for agile project management in a linear manner. In application, however, these techniques will be applied in an overlapping, iterative manner.

Planning the Work

In non-agile software development models, requirements are typically gathered at the beginning of a project and then "managed" across the life span of the project. In this model, some basic assumptions are made. The first assumption is that users can express what they want in great enough detail that the development organization can quantify and estimate the project. In typical mechanical and civil engineering projects, this is the case. In software projects, however, this statement tends to be less true because software is not physical, but conceptual (at least at this stage).The second assumption is that the business drivers for the work are relatively static in the moderate to long term. The assumption is that the business drivers are relatively static in today's environment. This assumption, however, can be not only wrong, but in some cases be criminally wrong. These are strong statements. They should help shake any complacency you might have. Agile project management leverages several techniques that are designed to address scenarios when assumptions fail.

Agile projects begin by developing a list of requirements. These requirements can be called many things, but one of the most common titles given to these requirements is "user stories." We think the metaphor created by using the term *user stories* is important because it focuses on the list of requirements that satisfy the customer's needs. (The technique for trawling or the eliciting of requirements used by Suzanne Robertson is outside the scope of this book.[1])

The list of user requirements is termed a backlog. The backlog will be revisited and reprioritized periodically during the project. New requirements can be added to the backlog at anytime. Just adding an item to the backlog does not mean that it will be addressed — only that the item will be considered. In an agile project, the project backlog is a starting point, not an ending point.

A tension exists between adherents of using Gantt charts to manage the work and the adherents of backlogs. We recognize that both methods serve the same purpose from a process point of view. Each technique provides a means to judge progress and status. Both are good tools. The difference is wrapped up in the differences in the psychology between agile and non-agile projects.

All projects that have more than one release contemplated have a cadence. The term *cadence* defines the time between releases and/or deliveries. At a more micro level, cadence can also define the time between builds or sprints. Agile projects typically embrace a very quick cadence based on iterations or sprints (the *fast* metaphor slips in) that range from 2 to 4 weeks. (We have seen sprints of 1 week, but do not recommend them except in the most fluid environments.)

Prior to beginning each sprint or iteration, the project team goes through a planning exercise. In its simplest form, the process flow for planning could be summarized as beginning with a review of the progress of the previous sprint, followed by a review and reprioritization of the backlog, and then selection of the user stories for the next sprint. Planning for an agile team includes the customers (or proxies), product personnel, and IT personnel. In the planning process, the customer is the leader. The customer specifies what they want and in what order they want to receive it. (Obviously, product and IT personnel will play an informative role because there are times when you cannot have that bright shiny widget until you build the infrastructure to support it.) We suggest the following planning approach:

1. *Pre-sizing*: Pre-size and evaluate all backlog items. This is a joint activity with overall project leadership. (We recommend Quick and Early Function Points™.)

2. *Product planning*: Periodically prioritize/reprioritize the backlog prior to beginning sprints. This is a customer-lead activity.

3. *Sprint planning*: In sprint planning, the sprint teams evaluate and commit to the user stories prioritized by their customers and based on their capabilities. The sprint teams have a primary role in this activity.

Once a team commits to a set of stories that they will tackle during a sprint, the "die is cast." The team tackles the stories, leveraging feedback and explanations provided by their customer as they move forward, but they do not add to active stories "in flight." Not adding to active stories while in flight is an important concept. The team leader, manager, or scrum master acts as a barrier to keep the outside world from impacting the team. Figure 11.1 provides a graphic interpretation of these concepts when implemented in a scenario in which a project is comprised of multiple teams.

Final planning notes. Change is a given in almost all projects, for reasons ranging from it is hard to know what a customer really wants when you deliver the product to a world that views instant gratification as a right, not a feature. Agile planning recognizes that change will occur and provides a means to embrace change. If you have a known deliverable with a fixed deliverable date, agile techniques are not

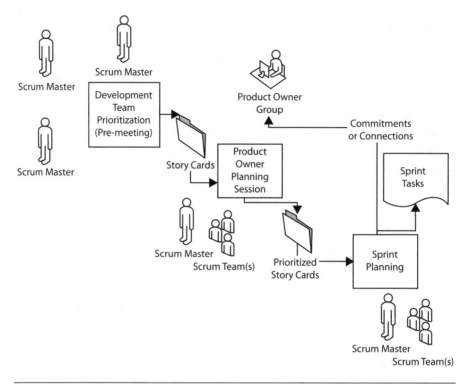

Figure 11.1. A scrum project.

necessary. Agile techniques are effective for most projects, but they are most effective when change will occur.

Remember: Agile project management cannot fix bad project management. Bad project management is bad management, regardless of the technique or method used.

Controlling the Work

Controlling the work covers a significant number of subtopics, ranging from stand-up meetings to configuration management. But before we discuss controlling the work, remember our earlier discussions about guiding principles. Agile project management does not view control through the eyeglass of the old command-and-control model (which we suggest is paternal in nature), but rather through a collaborative filter. A project team guided by agile principles will interpret and react to project data to direct itself rather than to have the project manager tell it what to do. Interestingly, the agile model is the most-used model by modern militaries for training and empowering small teams.

Daily stand-up meetings. A daily stand-up meeting is a common tool used for agile teams to share status information, to seek help to alleviate blocking issues, and to decide on which tasks are going to be done next. The stand-up meeting ensures that each member of the team stays focused on a specific set of tasks and that if there are problems that they will be surfaced. By nature, daily stand-up meetings are short. The team leader facilitates a stand-up meeting and leads the charge to resolve any issues that are blocking progress. The agile leader acts as the voice of the team rather than the voice of management or the voice of the process. The agile leader, also known as a coach, leads the team rather than acting as a director. Each team member typically answers several questions:

- What was accomplished (typically what was completed) yesterday?
- What tasks or activities will be completed today?
- Are any issues blocking progress?

The leader or facilitator must ensure that the questions are addressed and that the discussion does not devolve into explanations or explorations of solutions. Those are conversations that should take place outside the standup meeting. Issues that cannot be resolved within the team should be championed by the project leader.

Displaying measurement data. Measurements and free access to information provide primary control techniques within any agile project. Numerous techniques capture and display measurement data at the sprint or iteration level. Critical measurement components include:

- Accepted stories and broken tasks required to accomplish a story
- Team capacity
- Work accomplished and work remaining on stories or on the tasks currently being addressed

Using these pieces of data, an agile team can create a burn down chart to graphically represent the work left to do at any specific time and the capacity of the project team. The pending work (or backlog) is often shown on the vertical axis with the time shown on the horizontal axis. The capacity of the team is generally represented as the straight line going from the initial amount of work to be done to the end of the sprint.

Using a big visible chart (defined in extreme programming) puts a critical set of metrics in front of the project team on a daily basis. (A "high touch" approach is updating the chart daily by hand.) Metrics that are important to the team can change over time, e.g., the team's velocity (the ratio of estimated development time and calendar time), the number of tasks still outstanding, the number of test issues, etc. We suggest letting the team have input in (or *crowdsource*) the metrics that will be tracked. When a measure attains a consistent 100% level, it is no longer worth measuring. We suggest replacing a metric that has consistently attained a 100% level with the next most important metric.

So, how do team members know when there is no more work to be done to complete a story or a sprint? Each agile project creates a definition of the word *done* that supports delivering functional software. Definitions vary and depend on how organizations organize work, but typically *done* means:

1. Code is complete.
2. Code is commented and checked in (including tested if this is part of the environment),
3. Functionality is peer reviewed (unless built using pair programming).
4. The code builds without errors.
5. Unit tests have been written and executed (and passed).
6. Relevant documentation has been produced and checked in.

The list could go on, but as you can see, the concept of *done* represents a disciplined process that generates *functional* code. Functional means that the code *works* without defects and that the *relevant* documentation is produced (relevant being the critical term). If a particular type of documentation is not needed to support functional code, an agile team would be hard pressed to describe it as relevant.

Configuration management. Another core practice within agile projects is configuration management. The practices and processes used for configuration management supplement the basic concept of project management. In discussing configuration management, we will touch on code and relevant documentation. Code should be checked in when complete and the overall set of project code is built (and tested) on a daily basis. Problems with the build should be tackled and resolved as they occur. Because developers are committing to activities and tasks on a daily basis, they should be able to check-out the required code and **know** that it is functional. (Remember that testing is listed in the definition of *done*.) The use of automatic testing suites has made the concept of the daily build combined with unit and smoke testing a very powerful tool for making configuration management valuable at the coder level (notice the *smoke* metaphor).

Information requirements. Agile projects operate within organizations that have needs and requirements for specific information. Specific information might be driven by software projects for other organizations that might have contracts with defined service level agreements. Another set of specific information needs might occur when coding and design standards are set at the organization level. Sometimes financial records are required for tax purposes (or others) in many projects. To satisfy these information needs, specific deliverables may be required. So, each project should begin by reviewing (and in some cases negotiating) the types of non-code deliverables that are required. Upon agreement, these deliverables should be maintained as if they were code (check-in, check-out, testing, and approval).

Testing. We have been asked to describe the role of a testing group in an agile project many times. In its simplest form, the answer is that the role of an independent testing group does not have to change. Although the role does not change, the *approach* may change. Some types of testing (such as functional testing) can be incorporated directly into the development teams. We consider embedding testing personnel into the development testing teams (to keep the matrix reporting intact) a best practice. Embedding testers helps facilitate transferring knowledge training to the project team and can ensure that the issue of testability (and simplicity) stays at the forefront of the team. As features and functions are combined into their final forms, many organizations begin testing sprints. In these testing sprints (iterations), the teams apply the same processes and rules as in development sprints. When testers are embedded in a development team, the testers typically are drawn back into the testing group to provide deeper subject matter expertise of the functionality and functional code.

Sprint review meeting. The final control step in an agile project, iteration or sprint, is the sprint review meeting. As noted earlier, a sprint begins with planning meeting in which the teams commit to what they will do. A sprint review meeting "plays back" what was actually completed (i.e., met the definition of *done*) for all of the stakeholders. The power of peer and organizational pressure is applied in the processes of public commitment and public demonstration, providing a level of control that a project manager cannot. The commitment and review processes are bookends and to some extent can be viewed as management by peer pressure. If a deliverable does not work, and therefore does not meet the definition of *done*, the team cannot hide from their failure. "Spin" has no place in a sprint review.

PROCESS IMPROVEMENT

Retrospectives provide opportunities to generate team memory. They provide an agile team with a platform to figure out what worked, what did not, and what needs to be changed. The bottom-line goal of most retrospectives is for a project team to change how it is doing work (rather than to create lessons learned deliverables for outsiders to consume; that is not to say, however, that if action items are created that they should not be captured and pursued). In projects with multiple iterations, all teams should take time for a retrospective after the first sprint and then periodically afterward, with one of the retrospectives occurring at the end of the project. (Because they have learned to share and communicate, teams that have operated together for long periods of time generally do not have as great a need for a retrospective after each iteration or sprint.) When global issues are identified, the team leader/coach should take the lead in making sure these issues are brought forward.

Some final words about agile project management. Agile is about focusing on the tasks and activities that add value to functional code. In this sense, agile is very similar to the concept of lean manufacturing. Agile projects define what the term *done* means before they begin. So, although the bottom line of a software project is *working* software, *working* typically means more than just being functional — *working* includes being tested **and** the inclusion of relevant documentation.

REFERENCE

1.   Suzanne Robertson and Robertson, James C. *Mastering the Requirements Process, Second Edition* 2006. Reading, MA: Addison-Wesley.

12

PITFALLS AND BEST PRACTICES IN SOFTWARE PROJECT MANAGEMENT

INTRODUCTION

Because there are numerous viewpoints on the subject, discussing the pitfalls and best practices in software project management is a bit difficult. All practices are contextual to an organization, and based on an organization's culture, management is also unique. Often people in an organization think that the way they manage is the "best in the world" because they are producing results. Producing results is certainly a very important aspect of management. More important, however, is that the results are achieved in an effective manner, with optimal costs, productivity, quality, and morale. The achievement of results also ought to be sustainable — so that the organization is maintained in an ever-expanding upward-moving results' spiral. Best practices ensure several objectives: optimal costs, productivity, quality, and morale. Best practices also ensure that an organization's performance improves with every completed project and that the organization continues to move in an ever-improving direction.

Pitfalls can bring an organization down: from excellence to mediocrity or worse. To avoid pitfalls and to grow and prosper, adopting best practices is therefore necessary. We will now examine some common pitfalls in software project management and the best practices for approaching them to achieve successful software project management and organizational excellence. Because effective software project management requires organization-level support in addition to diligent efforts by software project managers, we will discuss pitfalls and best practices at each of these levels. We will also discuss some overall best practices.

ORGANIZATIONAL-LEVEL PITFALLS AND BEST PRACTICES

Organizational-level processes and practices establish the platform on which an SPM will perform software project management. Organizational-level practices also "set the tone" for an SPM to orchestrate and produce results.

Process-Driven Project Management

A process-driven approach to work facilitates the predictability of results. A person-driven method, however, is dependent on the personal capabilities of the individual doing the work. Many organizations use person-dependent processes in their organizations, and these processes certainly do not preclude them from being successful, but as an organization grows and concurrently executes larger numbers of projects, person-driven processes can lead to unpredictable or inconsistent results. Leveraging process-driven approaches such as the ISO- and SEI-defined certification models will generally achieve consistent success. (The process-driven approach to software project management is covered in Chapter 2.) Many organizations that have adopted the process-driven approach have even obtained appraisals and certifications. Unfortunately, however, some organizations chase obtaining an appraisal or certification without actually embracing the continued adaptation and implementation of the process-driven approach.

Best practice: We strongly recommend the process-driven approach to project management as a best practice — with the proviso that you define the process that is "right" for your organization based on the size and number of concurrently handled projects. Once the process is determined, another best practice is to continuously monitor the results being delivered by the process and improve the process as necessary in a regular manner. (The alternative is a common pitfall.)

An Ineffective Project Management Office or No Project Management Office

A significant pitfall is failing to see the importance of having an efficient and effective PMO. Some organizations perceive that the role of the PMO is to just create the project initiation note (PIN) document and nothing more! Sometimes the PMO is attached to the software delivery manager. A secretary then becomes responsible for generating the PIN and maintaining the project documents in a file. At other times, a "refugee" from one of the technical teams is assigned to the PMO and given the role of initiating projects and being the custodian of project records. This type of PMO is generally ineffective. It cannot provide aid to SPMs when needed because of its administrative slant. Additionally, the necessary references cannot be provided to an SPM during project initiation. So, every project is started in just the same way as a new organization initiates its first project — without references to knowledge that has been captured earlier. The SPM is therefore left to his own resources when planning and executing the project. This situation is akin to "reinventing the wheel" — and in all likelihood, the same issues will confront the SPMs and the same mistakes will recur in almost all projects because the experience gained from the execution of projects is not made available to the SPMs when necessary.

A well-organized PMO with a competent staff goes a long way in an organization to ensure the success of projects. An effective PMO is actively involved in providing support to projects. At times, getting the best resources for a project is not always possible. In such cases, the PMO can play an important role by providing mentoring and expert assistance. The PMO is also involved during project execution by giving exception reports to senior management and providing support to the SPM. One aspect of this involvement includes measuring the project's "health" with metrics, such as earned value, quality, and productivity, and assisting the SPM in any course corrections that are required.

We suggest having a robust PMO because the benefits generally outweigh the costs. An effective PMO performs several functions:

- Acts as the central agency for all matters relating to project execution in the organization (The PMO should continuously capture organizational experience from project management: collating all the best practices, bad practices, and lessons learned; subjecting them to analysis; and maintaining them in the organizational knowledge repository.)
- Takes ownership of the organizational repository of project management knowledge (Ownership includes gathering relevant knowledge from internal and external sources; organizing the data in a meaningful manner so that it can be retrieved quickly and easily; and ensuring that the data is made available to all SPMs when they need it.)
- Initiates software projects in such a manner that the SPMs can leverage the organization's experience from similar past projects
- Takes ownership of organizational metrics related to software project management, including deriving the organizational performance and productivity baselines; collating metrics on a regular basis and analyzing them; and continuously updating the organizational metrics repository with credible metrics data

- Takes ownership of the project closure process, including the project postmortem; knowledge sharing; variance analysis of actual versus estimated/planned values; and taking possession of project records
- Scans the technological horizon continuously for developments and improvements in project management and ensures that the organization's SPMs have access to such developments and improvements
- Mentors SPMs in the organization, including providing necessary training to perform project management effectively
- Participates in project progress monitoring meetings and provides information and assistance to SPMs to help correct the course of a project when necessary

The PMO should be headed by a competent professional who has the necessary support personnel. This person should be a senior SPM who has executed software projects. The PMO assumes a senior staff role by providing specialist assistance in project management to SPMs. Some organizations rotate their SPMs in the lead role in the PMO so that they better understand the concerns of other SPMs as well as those of the organization. Although some organizations see the role of PMO lead as being suitable for an entry-level SPM, our opinion is that only senior personnel are able to do justice to the role.

Best practice: Have a robust PMO and, based on the size of the organization and the number of projects being executed in the organization, add supporting staff as needed for effective execution within the PMO.

Poor Project Initiation

Project initiation is a very important step in ensuring the successful execution of a project. Poor project initiation can significantly impact the possibility of a project succeeding, effectively or not. Yet, in some organizations, project initiation has become the mere formality of handing the project dossier over to the SPM. So, these organizations experience the pitfall of poor project initiation: preparing only the PIN document, filing the purchase/work order, and including the technical specifications in the project dossier and then handing it over to the SPM. (Project initiation is discussed in Chapter 4.)

Best practice: Treat project initiation as an essential step in ensuring the success of a project.

Poor Software Estimation

Robust software estimation helps to identify the "right" resources and the "right" amount of these resources needed for efficient execution of a project. Many organizations, however, do not treat software estimation as an important activity. They do not collect metrics on effort actually spent and contrast them with estimated effort or use normalized baselines for planning. Many organizations also do not even leverage a standard software size measure for their organization, resorting to the view that the software they produce is unique and therefore cannot be measured. In these organizations, a ballpark estimation is the most-often used software estimation technique. But overestimating and underestimating result in an imbalanced application of project resources. Significant estimation errors do not augur well for project health during execution.

When software estimation is not diligently performed, a project's schedule will also not be practical. At best, the team will only have a "best guess" schedule. When a schedule is not practical, it likely will slip: either the project's completion is delayed or the resources take on a lot of extra stress to complete the project on time. In the ensuing haste for completion, quality will also take a beating. In short, the project will not be completed satisfactorily. To say that poor software estimation is a major cause of project failure may not be an exaggeration.

Best practice: Treat software estimation as an important activity. Provide training on software estimation and on the use of metrics to aid in accurate estimation. Define an excellent software estimation process for the organization and carry out software estimation using that process. Then develop and implement organizational estimation standards. Monitor the performance of these processes and standards regularly and improve them by using actual values that are collected and analyzed to correct organizational baselines. Maintain all estimates prepared in the organization in the organizational knowledge repository and make them available to SPMs.

Poor Project Planning

Remember the quote attributed to Abraham Lincoln in Chapter 5? It says, "If I were given six hours to fell a tree, I would use the first four hours sharpening the axe." This quote is the best advice that we can offer to describe the importance of planning because several pitfalls are associated with planning.

SPMs who do not understand the value of planning often take project plans from an earlier project. They then do a "Save As" to arrive at project plans for a new project.

Best practice: Make new plans. But completely doing away with the practice of "Save As" is unnecessary. Instead use parts of previous plans in a "Cut/Paste" mode when appropriate to allow fresh thinking based on the requirements of the new project.

Some SPMs equate project planning solely with generating a project schedule (e.g., using a Microsoft Project schedule as a plan). Software project planning goes far beyond just generating a schedule.

Best practice: Ensure that plans have adequate detail to make implementation easier during project execution.

A common complaint heard in some organizations is that planning requires too many documents. Sometimes the planning process does go overboard and bureaucracy replaces efficiency, particularly in organizations that treat project planning as an exercise in creating documents just for the sake of meeting process requirements. Such organizations create plan documents and then put them aside and execute the project on an ad hoc basis. Yet, planning is not an exercise to create documents. Planning is a time when an SPM focuses on what is to be achieved and how it is to be achieved. Planning is looking ahead and making provisions for the required resources so that a project will be executed smoothly and without any surprises.

Best practice: Ensure that all processes are lean (just enough to meet the needs of the organization) and scalable (smaller projects need less rigor than larger projects). *Scalability* suggests that for small and short-duration projects, creating a single overall plan (with all other plans embedded in it) will be adequate; for large projects that are especially prone to failure, create separate plans in greater detail. Treat project planning as an important and critical activity rather than as an exercise in creating a set of documents that is required for a quality audit or an appraisal.

The Wrong Service Level Agreements

Another frequent pitfall we have seen is providing the "wrong" service level agreements (SLAs) for a project. Having poor SLAs between a project and the service departments will lead to project failures, delays in delivery, or poor-quality deliverables.

Software development activities typically need the support of other departments in the organization, such as the quality department, systems administration, the PMO, and the HR department. One way of achieving support is to negotiate the needed support on a case-by-case basis. The service department, for example, would then indicate the turnaround time whenever the project team approaches the department for support. Another approach is to define an SLA for each department and then conform to it. A third way is to define the SLAs on a project-by-project basis. The issue or balancing act is whether to optimize the capacity utilization of the support department or to provide full support to project teams. Cost control or delivery is another way to state this question. The aim of case-by-case SLAs and department-level SLAs is to control costs, but perhaps at the expense of project delivery. The aim of project level-SLAs is to strengthen delivery, but perhaps at the risk of increasing support costs. Software development organizations have to balance these two objectives.

Any project needs timely responses to its needs, especially when provisioning resources, troubleshooting when an issue arises, and obtaining expert assistance when projects are stuck with an issue, just to name a few. If the SLAs provided for these types of support are not in tune with project requirements, the consequences will be undesirable, regardless of why. Providing the SLAs necessary for a project rather than asking the project to live with generic SLAs proffered by the support groups is therefore necessary. If support groups have resources or tools limitations, the PMO should interact with senior management to facilitate removal of the hurdles that the support departments have in providing the required SLAs. We have often seen situations in which a project is asked to adjust to substandard SLAs rather than asking the support groups to provide the SLAs that meet the project's needs.

Best practice: The organization has a leading role in providing appropriate SLAs to projects. Usually, the PMO champions the provisioning of SLAs between the service departments and SPMs. One best practice is to have each service department define a set of SLAs which is then published. SPMs plan project execution in keeping with the service departments' SLAs, but if an SPM needs any above-normal SLAs, the SPM leverages the PMO to broker a resolution. Another best practice is for the PMO to receive the SLAs needed from an SPM(s) and then obtain commitments from the service departments for these project requirements. If a disagreement is encountered, the PMO will negotiate with the service department and the SPM to achieve a mutually acceptable SLA.

Poor Standards and Guidelines for Software Development

Standards and guidelines are established to assist a development team in achieving predictable quality for an end product. A high-quality set of standards and guidelines will go a long way in executing projects in an efficient and effective manner. Yet, some organizations pay lip service to the concept of having high-quality standards and guidelines or, if they have them at all, they implement the standards/guidelines poorly. A badly defined set of coding standards will cause quality issues and rework. So, organizations that totally neglect defining standards and guidelines, define sketchy standards and guidelines, have ad hoc standards, or pay lip service to following them, do so at the risk of poor quality.

Organizations that neglect the development and implementation of standards and guidelines argue that standards and guidelines stifle creativity and innovation and thereby promote mediocrity. This statement is untrue. What standards and guidelines stifle is unbridled experimentation in the name of innovation (which is more akin to random movement than true experimentation), not true creativity and innovation. No organization wants experimentation on a live project. In any process-driven organization, facilities to improve processes, including standards and guidelines, are always available. SPMs may freely offer improvement suggestions for all aspects of the process. Furthermore, SPMs may volunteer to develop new standards or modify the existing ones and then pilot the standards on a project they are managing. We acknowledge that emergencies do arise (although not very many). When faced with an emergency, the urgency of the project should allow the leverage of a process waiver request.

Best practice: Define excellent standards and guidelines for development. Have coding guidelines for all programming/scripting languages used in a project. Coding guidelines are critical for ensuring the quality of a project's deliverables. A well-defined set of coding standards facilitates achieving excellent quality levels and reduces project rework. Also facilitate improvement of organizational standards and guidelines in prescribed manner.

Poor Project Oversight

Inadequate project oversight is a common pitfall for senior management. Oversight can be inadequate if it is infrequent or overdone, i.e., "breathing down the neck" of an SPM. So, what is the right approach? The answer is that no universally accepted "right" interval exists for reviewing a project's progress by senior management. Oversight should therefore be at some regular interval — short enough to facilitate timely intervention, but long enough to allow some space (breathing room) for the SPM. Set oversight intervals based on the planned duration of a project. For shorter-duration projects, weekly monitoring may be adequate, whereas monthly monitoring may be adequate for longer-duration projects.

Best practice: Determine oversight intervals on a project-by-project basis. Then record the decision in the project's software project management plan and conform to it.

Inadequate Project Management Training

Project management training is conducted to ensure that an organization's philosophy, processes, standards, and guidelines are imparted to trainees. The training is based on the software project management body of knowledge that exists within the organization. Training results in homogeneity among all SPMs in the organization and promotes predictability in project management. The course content is subject to regular improvement (as are the organizational processes, standards, and guidelines). If the training stifles creativity or innovation, the training program needs to have closer examination and be improved. In some organizations, however, project management training is frequently neglected.

Most SPMs have a background in a technical specialty, such as being a programmer. Using the example of a programmer, a common progression is for a programmer to rise from being a coder to a module leader (or team leader) to a project leader and then to an SPM. During this transition, the programmer has generally learned the basics of software project management from on-the-job observation of superiors. Unless the former programmer works under the supervision of a number of SPMs, and on all types of projects, the knowledge gained is likely to be limited by the practices of the SPMs that the programmer has observed.

So, in the absence of a formal well-designed training program, most newly promoted SPMs will imitate the SPMs that they have worked under. This problematic situation tends to be accentuated when SPMs are recruited from outside an organization. These SPMS arrive with their own project management philosophies, which may not be (and in most cases are not) in sync with the project management philosophy of the organization. When SPMs in an organization have different philosophies of project management, discord is likely.

Organizations that neglect project management training frequently argue that their senior project managers will use mentoring to smooth out any "rough edges" on new SPMS. Another argument sometimes made (albeit rarely) is that training has the potential to stifle innovation in SPMs. In essence, this argument says that if given a free hand, new SPMs will develop innovative and new methods and that the resulting discord and conflict are just a normal part of any organization and can be managed. (Very convincing, aren't they?)

Best practice: Conduct software project management training (either full syllabus training or refresher training) for all SPMs before allocating them to manage projects. Subject the training curriculum to regular enhancement in line with the organizational process for improvement.

SOFTWARE PROJECT MANAGER-LEVEL PITFALLS AND BEST PRACTICES

Although organizational-level processes and practices establish the platform on which an SPM performs project management, even so, the SPM has a critical role in ensuring the success of a project. We will next address some pitfalls and best practices from the SPM-level point of view.

Fair Treatment of Project Human Resources

Project management includes achieving work through the actions of subordinates. A well-motivated project team can reach unimaginable heights of performance. An SPM can add to (or detract from) the prevailing morale of a project team. If a project team perceives that the SPM is not treating team members fairly, morale will deteriorate. Some SPMs fall into the pitfall of showing favoritism to their cronies, something that will be noticed in no time at all.

Best practice: Treat team members fairly and equally to ensure that high levels of motivation are maintained in the project team. Refrain from giving special treatment to any team member. Remember that it is not enough to be fair — but to be seen as being fair.

A Balanced Workload

Each member of a team wants to perform his or her share of the work and to achieve the best possible results. And no team members want to see another team member laze around when they are working hard. SPMs may not perceive that team members are keeping tabs on them, but team members absolutely do. So, any imbalance in loading work to team members is noticed immediately. So, balancing the workload equitably is essential.

Best practices: Best practices in work allocation include:
- Maintain a formal work register for all work allocations. The register helps to quantitatively assess the workload of each of the team members when allocating work or when reviewing individual contributions of team members. A formal work register also allows team members to see their individual contributions as contrasted with others. A formal level is needed in large projects. Using informal methods makes ensuring workload balance very difficult. The absence of a formal work register also makes answering any accusations of overloading by a team member very difficult.
- Make the formal work register available to all team members so that they can assess for themselves how equitably the workload has been allocated.
- Measure actual achievements, productivity, and quality for each team member and make these measurements part of the work register.
- Acknowledge achievements when a team member is allocated with more work and attains that level of contribution.

Equitable Rewards

Dispensing rewards is another area in which an SPM can be perceived as being unfair. Sometimes only positive results are rewarded. To be equitable, however, positive performance should receive a positive reward and a negative performance should receive a negative reward. To refrain from acknowledging either scenario or failing to deliver the appropriate reward will certainly cause less motivation among team members. Douglas McGregor (1906–1964; MIT Sloan School of Management) recommends that discipline ought to be like a hot stove. A hot stove burns anyone who touches it. The burn is immediate. The amount of the burn is directly proportional to the amount of touch. The stove is impartial (it burns everyone irrespective of rank or importance). (*Note*: Numerous websites may be consulted for additional information about the theories of Douglas McGregor.)

Best practice: Reward positive and negative performance equally. Remember the adage, "Justice delayed is justice denied." When applied to rewards, this adage says that rewards must be in close proximity to the occurrence of the performance that deserves the reward.

Poor Software Estimation

Software estimation must be pursued with diligence at the organizational level. The SPM for a project is responsible for ensuring that software estimation is carried out as diligently and as accurately as possible. If software estimation goes haywire, project planning and execution have little chance of being successful.

Best practice: Focus attention on estimation and then perform the estimation activity with all diligence.

Poor Project Planning

In the sections discussing organizational-level pitfalls, common pitfalls included treating project planning as a document creation activity and using plans from a completed project for a new project. SPMs can also indulge in the pitfall of treating project planning as a document creation activity. Taking documents from an earlier project, to have "Save Them As" plans for a current project, makes sense only if the older documents are used as a vehicle for thinking through the project and making provisions for every foreseeable contingency in the project plan.

Best practice: Use the project planning exercise to think through a project and to carry out the planning activity with total diligence.

Informal Issue Resolution

Issues crop up in most projects. As noted previously, we recommend using a formal mechanism to record every issue and to track the issue through to resolution. Also report the status of every issue in the weekly status report. A common pitfall is to not record every issue, but to try to resolve it informally ("off the record"). In particular, project stakeholders should be kept informed of every significant issue that arises in a project and should know about these issues early enough to avoid unpleasant surprises.

Best practice: Use a formal mechanism for issue resolution. Record every issue and report every issue in the weekly status report. Keep all project stakeholders informed about the status of issue resolution.

Poor Change Management

Failing to handle change management with a well-planned strategy is one of the most common pitfalls encountered in project management. Often a project begins with a sense of overconfidence that the customer will not ask for changes or, if the customer does make change requests, that the team will have the ability to take care of them informally, without impacting the budget, quality levels, or the delivery date. This kind of informal handling of change requests can evolve into project failure and even litigation (we have seen it happen).

Best practice: Follow a formal strategy for handling change requests. Include change management in the project plans. Regularly report the status of change requests to all project stakeholders.

Poor Record Keeping

Execution of a software project generates a host of information. When properly analyzed and included in the organizational knowledge repository, this information can facilitate manyfold improvement in an organization's efficiency. Improved efficiency can generate a significant amount of savings in monetary terms — savings that can end up directly on the organization's bottom line. An SPM is responsible to ensure that all information is properly recorded so that it can be processed and analyzed. If an SPM does not keep diligent records, all further analysis will yield incorrect results. Any modifications of organizational processes or baselines that are based on these wrong indicators will be disastrous for the organization. (Remember the adage, "Garbage in, garbage out?")

Poor record keeping is an easy pitfall to fall into for a project manager. But why does this happen? Typically, SPMs do not set out to gather bad data. Instead they view record keeping as an overhead activity that is not directly linked to delivering software (something that is easy to do) and often neglect it. Typically, poor or inadequate record keeping is not caught until an investigative audit is done as part of a project's postmortem.

Best practice: Diligently maintain project records so the records provide useful, worthwhile information about project planning and execution

ADDITIONAL BEST PRACTICES FOR SOFTWARE PROJECT MANAGEMENT

We will now address some additional best practices for software project management. These are in addition to the pitfalls and best practices discussed at the SPM- and organizational-levels.

A Knowledge Repository

A well-organized knowledge repository (not just a dumping ground for records of completed projects) will greatly enhance the chances for success in project initiation and execution. A well-stocked repository can significantly simplify an SPM's work and be of great assistance: to get records for relevant projects at the time of project initiation and then again if needed by the project team.

Continuous Process Improvement

Continuous process improvement ensures that the best practices are incorporated into organizational processes and that the bad practices are eliminated. Continuous process improvement activities help to enable SPMs to be successful in project execution. Having a well-structured software engineering process group (SEPG) with a competent support staff to support serious process definition and improvement activities within an organization is a best practice. (*Note*: An SEPG is now known as an engineering process group or EPG by the Software Engineering Institute.)

Project Postmortems

If a patient dies in a hospital, a mandatory medical postmortem is conducted to determine the real cause of death. A medical postmortem helps physicians to assess if the patient's diagnosis and treatment were correct and allows them to learn lessons for the future diagnosis and treatment of patients. We recommend conducting a project postmortem for all software projects, regardless of whether they succeed or fail. We find, however, that the project postmortem (regardless of what it is called) is often skipped, with the argument that a postmortem takes a significant amount of time that could be otherwise spent on revenue-earning activities. Sometimes we hear an explanation about a customer satisfaction survey being quite enough to assess a project's performance. We find these arguments to be shortsighted.

At other times, we see a project closure meeting being treated as the project postmortem. A project closure meeting and a project postmortem, however, serve very different purposes (see Chapter 10 for a more in-depth discussion of project closure and postmortems). The goal of a project postmortem is to identify all of the pitfalls that were faced by the project and all of the best practices that were discovered. Analyzing and critically examining the causes for these pitfalls and best practices will facilitate process improvement. The best practice is to conduct a postmortem for every completed project.

Training in the Soft Skills

Training for SPMs should cover more than the software project management training described in a previous section. The SPM and the project team should be trained in the soft skills that are required for the team to be effective. Soft skills training should include topics such as problem solving, communication, interpersonal relationships, conflict management, motivation, and morale. These soft skills will help the SPM and the project team to maintain a harmonious atmosphere during execution of the project. Role-based training is also sometimes neglected in an organization. So, in the absence of formal training, resources tend to imitate a boss or the most charismatic person in the organization, which may not be in the best interests of the organization. A best practice is to conduct formal training for all resources involved in project execution.

Information Sharing

Formal and informal sharing of information should be encouraged among SPMs. Within an organization, information sharing can be achieved through holding meetings designed for information sharing between SPMs, by attending seminars (internal and external), and by providing a bulletin/discussion board. Any of these activities can be implemented in an organization without incurring significant cost.

Management Support

Presented last, but in no means being the least in importance, management support and funding are vital for any success to be achieved in an organization. Management must recognize that software project management is just as essential to the success of a project as programming. All of the best practices cited above can be implemented only if management sponsors them.

We know of a chairman of a mid-sized software development company (300 programmers) who has stated, "I do not want to have managers in my organization. I want only programmers." We also know that this organization's success rate is not very high for large projects and that the organization survives only because of small projects. Now we ask you: "Can that organization get out of the rut of doing small projects and ever achieve the capability of handling large complex projects without a change in management attitude?"

SOME CLOSING WORDS

Software development has grown into a complex activity. The size of software products has steadily increased. The facts that MS-DOS used to come on a 360-KB floppy disk in the 1980s and now Windows comes on a DVD should bear witness to this phenomenon of the ever-increasing size of software products! "Back in the day," computers were "programmed," now we are "developing software." Large teams of software engineers work on software development and the work is now treated as a "project." Software engineers develop the software; SPMs ensure that they do so efficiently, effectively, and with the best possible quality. Software development therefore should be managed so that the project not only delivers the software, but also delivers functional, defect-free software at the greatest speed and at the lowest cost and with the highest quality.

In this book, we have endeavored to present you with the art and the science of project management as applicable to the software development domain, drawing from our own experiences as well as those from the available literature and from our learnings from experienced SPMs. Our hope is that you will derive benefit from this work of ours. We welcome your feedback. Please feel free to email murali@chemuturi.com.We promise to respond to every email.

APPENDIX A

MANAGEMENT OF SOFTWARE DEVELOPMENT PROJECTS

BACKGROUND

Numerous articles, books, and other types of literature are available on the topic of management. Many management models, tools, and theories are also available. These models, tools, theories, and literature are all largely derived from and focused on manufacturing organizations, with modifications to some extent based on the services industry (e.g., retailing, banking, and insurance). Most manufacturing organizations started out being "person-dependent," but over time they grew to be "technology-dependent," with a goal of leveraging their processes to reduce dependency on the *inscrutable* resource — human beings. The software development industry, however, the industry which has helped other sectors to reduce person-dependency, is still woefully person-dependent.

Several aspects of the software development industry and the manufacturing industry are contrasted in Table A.1. In a nutshell, manufacturing industries need blue-collar workers and the software industry predominantly needs professionals or white-collar workers. Management of these types of workers requires vastly different strategies and tactics. Appendix A looks at management from the standpoint of a manager, in particular a software project manager. We will provide as much information as possible on the subject of management in this limited space, describing a number of topics briefly:

- Project planning
- Project execution and control
- Motivation and morale
- Interpersonnel relationship management
- Communication

Table A.1. Comparison of the Software Development Industry with Other Industries

Predominant Aspect	Software Development Industry	Manufacturing Sectors
Type of workers	White collar (professional workers)	Blue collar
Education	College	Some school
Number of college-educated persons	Mostly	Few
Knowledge-gap between the managing and the managed	Very little	Vast
Type of work	Mostly new, with some amount of routine	Mostly routine
Pay/salary	High	Low
Environmental change	Frequent	Infrequent

WHAT IS MANAGEMENT?

Management may be viewed from three angles:

- As the group who is responsible for running the affairs of an organization: here the word *management* connotes a group of individuals. An example illustrates this usage: "*Management* decided to reduce working hours from 48 to 40 hours per week, which will take effect beginning the first of next month."
- As an art (and a social science) that is practiced to get things done through other individuals in an environment in which authority is not absolute and the procedures/processes are somewhat vague (e.g., matrix management): here the word *management* connotes a process. An example illustrates this usage: "The *management* of professional workers is entirely different from the management of blue-collar workers."
- As a body of knowledge on the subject of management: here the word *management* connotes a social science. An example illustrates this usage: "Besides the responsibility for results, *management* science specifies that delegation and motivation are essential responsibilities of a manager."

Appendix A looks at the term *management* from the second viewpoint: as a process and the art of getting work done through other individuals.

But why do we use the word *art* when describing the word *management*? The answer is because the topic of management consists of a large body of knowledge. This body of knowledge has been collected empirically by practitioners themselves or from studying other practitioners. Adopting this body of knowledge generally produces predictable results. Additionally, many mathematical models, such as linear programming, the transportation problem technique, and management games, as well as other topics have been developed to assist managers in making objective decisions and obtaining predictable results. Although many aspects of management are scientific, many of these aspects are still not measurable. So, no formulas can objectively predict consequences precisely. Regardless of the slow and steady progress that is evolving management into a science, it is, as yet, at least partially an art.

EVOLUTION OF THE MANAGEMENT DISCIPLINE

The word *management* itself signifies that something is *not* under control! Consider this adage: "If we can, we control it. If we cannot, we manage it." This adage brings to mind a second adage: "If you cannot surmount it, then circumvent it." So, management can have a number of varied objectives:

- To achieve what you originally set out to do
- To attain your goal; to reach your target
- To not win the race, but to stay in it and complete the course (to finish it)
- To keep all concerned parties from becoming unhappy/dissatisfied

Perhaps, we should also have said that the word *management* signifies that if something is not desirable to be controlled (or is not controllable), then it is better for it to be managed. But *control* can sometimes beget a penalty-avoidance type of performance. At times therefore using control is not always desirable —letting things happen and then managing (maneuvering) to get innovation and thus better-than-average performance is better: "If we can, we administer. If we cannot, we manage!"

Management has evolved from a base process of oversight and ensuring that everyone worked to their full capacity. From this base process, Frederick Winslow Taylor (1856–1915) proved that full capacity is not really the same as maximum output. Taylor used physical experiments and coined the term *scientific management*. He advocated studying the work being carried out and then using that study to design the proper methods for carrying out the work. Taylor also advocated that providing rest breaks increased output. Taylor's work has lead to new fields of "work study" (method study and work measurement), industrial engineering, ergonomics, "a fair day's work for a fair day's pay," productivity, and quality assurance. Taylor's work caused significant evolution in work design and workstation design. (Several websites can be consulted to obtain additional information about Taylor's work.)

The evolution of management continued with Henri Fayol (1841–1925). Fayol's work vastly influenced the process of management and was the forerunner of present-day management thought.[1] Fayol began as an apprentice engineer and went on to become the managing director of a mining company in France. His management background is reflected in his later theories. (Fayol wrote a book entitled *Administration Industrielle et Générale* in 1916. This book was translated and published in English as *General and Industrial Management*.) Fayol classified management functions into five categories:

- Planning
- Organizing
- Commanding
- Coordinating
- Controlling

These categories have subsequently been modified to:

- Planning
- Organizing
- Staffing
- Directing (leading)/coordinating
- Controlling

and then further refined to:

1. Planning
2. Organizing
3. Leading
4. Controlling

Henri Fayol also offered fourteen management principles:

- *Division of work* (specialization): Work should be divided into packages that foster specialization among the workers. (This division of work principle is said to be the harbinger of assembly lines in manufacturing, which led to a reduced cost of goods.)
- *Authority*: Those who have the responsibility for results should have the authority to issue commands and exact obedience.
- *Discipline*: Personnel should be disciplined and perform their functions diligently.
- *Unity of command*: Each employee should have only one boss. An employee should not receive commands from multiple individuals. (In organizations using matrix management, especially software development organizations, practice of this principle seems to have dropped significantly.)
- *Unity of direction*: Each position should have a single objective. (In today's business environment almost every executive position has multiple objectives.)

- *Subordination of personal interest* (to the organization's best interest): Pursue organizational goals when at work and do not look for personal aggrandizement. (This principle seems to be directed more at management personnel, but the principle applies to everyone.)
- *Remuneration*: Pay workers a fair wage for their services. (This principle may be the harbinger for the "need-based minimum wage" concept.)
- *Centralization*: Make decisions at the top of the hierarchy and everyone else will follow orders.
- *Line of authority*: Hierarchy is defined as a pyramidal structure for the organization.
- *Order*: There is a place for everything and everyone and everything and everyone should be in its place. (This concept of segregation of work and strict order is still followed by the armed forces.)
- *Equity*: All personnel should be treated in a fair and just manner. (Henri Fayol advocated kindness in the treatment of employees.)
- *Tenure for personnel*: Ensure that employees work longer for the organization. (The basis for this principle is the recognition that the loss of a trained employee has substantial impact on an organization. Job insecurity is not good for any organization. Fayol recommended putting steps in place to lessen the chances of a good employee leaving the organization.)
- *Initiative*: All employees should demonstrate initiative.
- *Esprit de corps*: Promote team spirit in which a team pulls together to achieve a goal.

MANAGEMENT IN A PRESENT-DAY CONTEXT

As discussed previously, Fayol's initial five categories of management function were eventually refined to four categories. Present-day management is now understood to be:

- Planning
- Organizing
- Leading
- Controlling

Present-day managers are expected to perform these four tasks as primary responsibilities. The scale, however, differs for each type of manager: a project manager performs these tasks at a project level and a senior manager performs them at a group or organizational level. We will now briefly discuss the four tasks.

Planning

Planning is defined as "the intelligent anticipation of resources required to perform a predefined endeavor successfully at a future date in a defined environment." The key terms contribute the following meanings:

- *Anticipation* indicates that planning precedes performance and that it is a best guess (no matter how diligently the guess was derived).
- *Resources* refer to the four M's (4 M's) of men (individuals, male and female), materials, methods (includes information), and machines (equipment) plus time (duration).
- *At a future date* indicates that the work has not already been performed and that it is consistent with the anticipation of resources.
- *In a defined environment* indicates that the location of the work (where it will be carried out) is known and defined. (Any variation in the environment will have an effect on the plan. The environment also refers to the working conditions, including work and workstation design, methods of management, prevailing morale at the workplace, etc.)
- *Predefined endeavor* indicates that the scope of the work is known.

To accomplish planning, several activities need to be performed:

1. Size and effort estimations for the human resources required
2. Scheduling to estimate the calendar time resource within the constraints of the existing facilities and the availability of other resources
3. Cost estimation to define the monetary resources needed (also called budgeting)
4. Definition of the environment to determine the requirements and to allocate the physical resources
5. Documentation of all estimates and plans

Organizing

Organizing refers to creating the work environment. Organizing includes several tasks:

1. Breaking down activities of the organization into departments/sections/teams so that work can be performed efficiently and effectively
2. Designing and arranging the workstations that will be used to accomplish the work (A workstation is a combination of the machine and human resources that are required to accomplish the work assigned.)
3. Breaking the work down into its constituent components so that that they may be allocated and executed at a workstation

4. Defining and developing methods, standards, and processes for all types of work, including quality assurance, to be carried out in the organizations

Leading

Leading is concerned with guiding the team that works for a manager/leader toward achieving the objectives. More specifically the tasks include:

- Providing direction
- Providing guidance
- Providing assistance/removing obstacles to performance
- Providing motivation and ensuring team morale
- Setting targets:
  - Productivity
  - Quality
  - Schedule
  - Technical goals
- Conducting performance evaluations
- Pursuing team goals and tracking them until they are accomplished successfully
- Coaching and mentoring team members

Controlling

Controlling involves ensuring that the execution of a project adheres to the plan. Tasks in controlling include:

1. Continuously measuring progress
2. Comparing actual performance against the planned performance and identifying gaps in achievements (if any)
3. Taking corrective action to align actual performance with planned performance:
   - Adding resources
   - Providing expert assistance
   - Providing better tools/methods
   - Changing the plan when required
4. Taking preventive action so that future occurrences of slippage are prevented and the time lost is made up so that final deliveries are not affected adversely

THE PRIMARY RESPONSIBILITIES OF MANAGERS

The primary responsibilities of managers fall into four categories:

- Work management
  - *Division of work*: Break down the product to be developed into work packages that may be allocated to individuals for execution. Breakdown of the product should ensure that the output of the work packages can later be assembled/integrated into the specified final product in an efficient manner. The division should also facilitate inspection/testing of the packages to ensure that quality is built into the product. The work packages must also facilitate measurement of productivity. When breaking the work down, a manager should ensure that the packaging does not necessitate frequent work allocations (there is no minimum duration, however, having allocated work take at least 1 day is better).
  - *Allocation of work for execution*: Allocate work in such a way that the individual receiving the assignment has the ability to execute it. The allocation of work should be done in such a manner that the targets for schedule, productivity, and quality are achievable. The targets must also be commensurate with the skill level of the individual given the work. Whenever possible, ensure that all individuals have a similar workload: the fair allocation to all of available individuals should be perceived as being fair.
  - *Integration of the product*: Arrange work so that assembly, testing, and delivery of all components as designed are accomplished and made ready for delivery to the client.
  - *Ensure quality*: Implement all planned quality control activities to ensure that work is executed in conformance to organizational standards and quality norms.
  - *Ensure productivity*: Implement all measures necessary so that the work carried out meets or exceeds organizational productivity levels.
  - *Deliver, install, commission, train, and hand over*: Deliver the product to the customer while also meeting schedule and quality specifications. Delivery typically includes assisting in the implementation and rollout of the product and lastly obtaining acceptance from the client.
  - *Get paid*: Arrange for billing and collection for services rendered, which may include any follow-up with the client.

- Expectations management
  - *Senior management*: Senior management expects that the project will be executed with minimal necessity for their intervention and with maximum client satisfaction; while also meeting or exceeding organizational norms for schedule, quality, and productivity; that they have access to correct project information when needed; that managers will maintain team morale; and finally that the project will earn revenue.
  - *Clients*: Clients expect to have access to progress information; that the team will adhere to agreed-upon schedules and quality norms; that there will be cooperation in the resolution of issues and change requests; and finally that the team will pay attention and provide quick turnaround of their communication.
  - *Peers*: Peers expect sharing of knowledge and experience; assistance in reviews; assistance when interviewing recruits; and assistance in process improvement initiatives.
  - *Teams*: A team expects fair work allocations; assistance in trouble-shooting issues; fair performance appraisals; transparent and fair performance targets; fair recognition, including rewards and punishments; and grievances to be redressed.
- Morale management
  - *Self*: A central component of personal morale is self-confidence. Self-confidence is a personal belief in your ability to deliver the expected results and that management will support your actions.
  - *Team*: Central to team morale is being confidant that other team members can achieve their objectives and strongly believing that their manager (you) will support the team.
  - *Organization*: Just as people do, organizations have a culture and morale. An organization's morale should invigorate managers and their teams and provide a sense of confidence that the organization has the ability to support the teams.
- Resource management
  - *Humans*: The goal of human resources management is to use team members effectively, efficiently, and wisely.
  - *Time*: Management of time resources boils down to one critical resource: the calendar time (unless you have access to a time machine!). Calendar time is a consumable resource. If used poorly, calendar time can rarely be recovered. Optimize the utilization of time so that targets and schedules are met.

- *Equipment*: Computers, system software, and development tools should be used efficiently. Maintain them at peak capacity to support the management of human and time resources.
- *Monetary*: Monetary resources include expenses and revenues. Both must be managed well and accounted for completely. Your goal is to use expenses and revenues optimally.

Keep these primary responsibilities in mind while performing software project management. Translating these responsibilities into action requires specific tactics, which we will now discuss.

Delegating

The job of a manager is to get things done. This means that unless you manage a one-person project, you, as a manager, will need to work with and through other individuals. You will therefore need to delegate work to subordinates. An important aspect to keep in mind is that although you can delegate authority, you *cannot* delegate responsibility! As a manager, the responsibility for results always remains with you. In other words, you may delegate something to a subordinate to do, but if this subordinate goofs up, you are still responsible for getting the delegated task done. As a manager, however, when you delegate authority to your subordinates, you also extract accountability from them.

Consider this exaggerated example: a cashier in a bank steals some money. Who is responsible for answering to the customers and depositors? Will the depositors only shrug their shoulders and say, "That poor bank manager — what can he do if a cashier just runs away? It's just our bad luck. Let's not blame the manager." No way would that ever be the case! Bottom line: the bank manager is responsible for his subordinate's actions. But will the subordinate get off scot-free? No. The cashier will be accountable for his or her actions. The bank manager will file a report with police to track down, arrest and jail, and recover the stolen money from the cashier.

Managing People

People management is vast topic, which is beyond the scope of this appendix. We will therefore devote a separate appendix to people management (Appendix C). A few points related to people management, however, are pertinent for inclusion in this appendix: interacting with subordinates, peers, and superiors.

Interacting with Subordinates

At times, you will need to deal with subordinates in ways that are similar to how a concerned and disciplined father treats and disciplines his teenaged children. We use teenaged children as an example because a teenager:

- Is not yet fully "grown-up"
- Is sharp and smart, but immature
- Is capable, but likely to be somewhat irresponsible
- Requires proper handling (firmness coupled with love)

Proper handling of these characteristics can produce astounding results. Treat subordinates with firmness that is coupled with compassion — you will see them respond to (not react to) you.

Interacting with Peers

Treat peers as a true friend treats his friends. We use the word *friend* because a true friend:

- Is still a friend even when you are in need (Likewise, when a peer has a need, you step in to help — no invitation is needed.)
- Listens patiently and gives complete attention to a friend's ideas and views
- Bridges gaps in a friend's performance
- Is willing to teach a new skill to a friend
- Does not expect anything in return from a friend

Friendly interaction with peers, however, does not include gossiping and sharing personal information. Life (as well as the workplace) is full of competitors. Be careful what you share. (Refrain from gossiping and inappropriate sharing of information. Your career might end with a note on Facebook!)

Interacting with Superiors

Treat superiors like a responsible son or daughter treats their father. We use the comparison of a father and a child because generally a child:

- Has no suspicions about his father's intentions — he believes his father
- Wants to take care of her father
- Takes reprimands better from her father (her ego and self-confidence are not affected as much)
- Wants to do better than his father
- Wants to please her father and to get words of praise from him

By exhibiting these characteristics, your superiors will slowly but surely begin to exhibit fatherly behavior with you.

But are these recommendations sure to get results — always? Difficult people are everywhere. So, you may not always get the results promised from following our recommendations. (This topic is discussed in more detail in Appendix C.)

WORK MANAGEMENT

As a manager, you have the responsibility for conducting certain activities that are necessary to ensure that work is carried out by your subordinates. Activities performed for getting the work done and for making delivery to clients include:

1. Work allocation
2. Assisting and facilitating the subordinates who are carrying out the work
3. Arranging quality control activities, such as inspection, walk-through, review, and testing, to ensure that the executed work and deliverables conform to the organizational standards and design
4. Arranging for integrating disparate components into a single entity: product or deliverable
5. Arranging for acceptance testing by the client
6. Delivery

Management Levels

First level. The first level of management if often called *technical management* or *line management*. Technical management is the conduit between the individuals who do the work and the individuals who manage the work. Technical managers are therefore very close to where the work is being carried out. The day-to-day job of a technical manager is primarily concerned with providing leadership for the technical aspects of the work (the "how" of getting things done). The control aspect of technical management therefore focuses on guiding the work and the people. Often the planning role for technical management is primarily work allocation.

Second level. Second-level management is typically called *middle management* (for devotees of Dilbert, picture the pointy-haired boss). Second-level management supervises first-level managers and interacts with other management layers. Often second-level management has multiple levels and names, including manager, senior manager, deputy general manager, general manager, etc. The list could go on and on. The primary concern of this layer of management is to ensure integration, cohesion, results delivery, and fire fighting and to be the bridge between senior management and first-level management.

Senior level. Senior management is concerned with the profitability of their unit. Senior management takes full ownership of a unit or a division or a group or a company. The key measure of success for senior-level management is *results* — the results that are expected by top management.

Top level. Top-level management sets and manages strategy and sets the ultimate goals of the organization. Top management is concerned with the direction, survival, and growth of the organization.

In large organizations and in large projects, a software project manager is in the middle-management level. In smaller organizations or smaller projects, an SPM is in the first level — technical or line management.

SO, WHAT DOES A SOFTWARE PROJECT MANAGER DO?

We gave thought to this question and we came up with an answer . . . *plenty*. So, we made a list:

1. Delivery functions
   - Manage work
     - Plan
     - Organize
     - Allocate
     - Progress chasing
     - Completion of individual assignments
     - Integrate
     - Deliver as specified
   - Manage quality
     - Plan
     - Implement verification and validation
     - Allocate verification and validation activities
     - Progress chasing
     - Completion of quality assignments
     - Monitor and measure quality continuously
     - Improve quality continuously
   - Manage productivity
     - Plan
     - Monitor and measure productivity
     - Improve productivity

- Manage team morale
  - Plan
  - Monitor morale
  - Motivate the team continuously
- Manage the schedule
  - Plan
  - Monitor work progress vis-à-vis schedule
  - Implement preventive and corrective actions as required
  - Deliver on schedule
2. Reporting functions
   - Report to management
   - Report to the client
   - Report to the quality department (or SEPG)
   - Participate in meetings
3. Organizational assistance functions
   - Participate in strategic initiatives
   - Participate in quality initiatives/certification
     - Process improvement activities
     - Participate in audits
     - Conduct audits
     - Verification and validation assistance to peers
   - Assist in recruitment/interviews
   - Assist in human resource development (training, recruitment)
   - Assist in project acquisition
4. Miscellaneous functions as required (i.e., do what it takes to deliver value)

Performing the delivery and reporting functions well is critical to the success of an SPM.

Some final words about management and SPMs. In Appendix A, we have tried to present the art and science of management in a nutshell as we think is relevant to SPMs. Many books address this subject. To learn more about the art and science of management, we strongly recommend that you read the good ones.

REFERENCE

1. Henri Fayol and Gray, Irwin. *General and Industrial Management* 1984. New York: Institute of Electrical and Electronics Engineers.

APPENDIX B

DECISION-MAKING FOR SOFTWARE PROJECT MANAGERS

INTRODUCTION

Decisions, decisions, decisions … sometimes we make decisions, postpone making decisions, jump to making a decision, sit on decisions, and face tough decisions and sometimes we delegate making decisions. Decisions are part of everyday life — and even more so for a manager. Your job description as an SPM likely includes "the ability to make quality decisions" as one of the key result areas. Appendix B presents some of the aspects of decision-making. In some instances, the material presented is quite brief (which might induce you to study the subject further and master it).

But first, let's attempt to define decision-making. Decision-making is "choosing between alternatives in a *volatile* environment, while having *incomplete/ unreliable* information about the scenario at hand and with *uncertain* and *unpredictable* outcomes for the available alternatives. Speed is needed, mainly for the sake of *expediency*." Now, let's look at the key words in this definition.

Volatile. In the software project environment, the environment is described as being *volatile* because software project execution is never stable (e.g., the human resources are inherently nonlinear systems and therefore chaotic). By definition, a project is also not a continuous endeavor: it is temporary, with a defined beginning and ending. Additionally, a specific project is executed only once and for the first time, people are temporarily assigned to the project; as well, the client is new and changes in requirements are certain. So, how could we define this situation as being anything but a volatile environment?

Incomplete and unreliable information. The terms *incomplete* and *unreliable information* are included in the definition of decision-making because in the project environment, we do not have time to wait for *perfect information* to be received. Deadlines always loom large on the horizon. So we also cannot wait to ensure that the information is *complete*. The information at hand therefore will always be incomplete and unreliable (even though the degree of unreliability and incompleteness will certainly vary). We cannot expect to have better than a 90% level of completeness and reliability of information. (If you have complete and reliable information, then you can make authoritative judgment calls instead of decisions.)

Uncertain and unpredictable outcomes. Similarly, the terms *uncertain* and *unpredictable outcomes* are used because a volatile environment is not conducive to having *predictability* of outcomes. (Again, if you know the outcome and its certainty, the decisions would be called judgments.)

Expediency. We also use the term *expediency*, a term which is not synonymous with "aiming to do justice." Decisions are often made in organizations to "tide them over" in a current situation/difficulty, to solve an immediate problem/issue, or to simply get things moving. Decisions therefore render injustice at times. We do not condone being unjust in the name of expediency; we are merely confirming the facts of life in decision-making.

A prevalent misunderstanding is that decisions are judgments, which is far from being universally true. True, judgment is used to make a decision, but rarely are the terms synonymous. Now that we have a definition, let's move forward with our discussion of decision-making.

CLASSIFICATION OF DECISIONS

Decisions may be classified for better understanding. Our taxonomy includes:
- Strategic and periodic decisions
  - Selection decisions
    - Products/services
    - Process
    - Location
    - Layout
    - Equipment
    - Workforce

- Design decisions
  - Product design
  - Service design
  - Job design
  - Process design
  - Control system design
  - Capacity design
- Recurring decisions
  - Target setting
  - Scheduling
  - Sequencing
  - Inventory control
  - Cost control
  - Maintenance
- Planning decisions
  - The system
  - Usage of the system
- Organizing decisions
  - Organizational structure
  - Jobs
  - Staffing
  - Work and workstation design
  - Standards of performance
  - Compensation systems
- Controlling decisions
  - Quality
  - Quantity
  - Schedule
  - Inventories
  - Costs
  - Maintenance

Although all of us make some of these decisions, very rarely does any given decision-maker make all of the decisions in the list — except, perhaps, entrepreneurs.

Decision-Making Styles

Decision-making styles differ from person to person. And obviously the same style of decision-making is not appropriate for every scenario. Even though individuals have their own particular style of decision-making, having knowledge of the various decision-making styles allows us to have flexibility in adopting the appropriate style to fit the scenario at hand. Let's look at some decision-making styles.

Judgment-/hunch-based. The judgment-/hunch-based style of decision-making is used by people who have a vast amount of experience. Experience builds knowledge about the possible consequences that can result from a decision. Experience therefore hones hunches to a fine edge. Some people are inherently "convergent thinkers," meaning that they look for one single best solution for a situation. Convergent thinkers tend to use the judgment-/hunch-based style of decision-making. This style is also best suited for situations in which the experience/knowledge gap is wide between the decision-maker and the decision-implementers. Some scenarios include:

- Trainee/novice decision-implementers and a more experienced or knowledgeable decision-maker
- Emergency situations (such as a battlefield-like or fire-fighting scenario)
- Breakdown maintenance

Analytical. Analytical decision-making implies that a thorough analysis has been carried out in which all possible alternatives as well as their costs and the possible outcomes have been considered. After all of the possible paths are analyzed, the optimal alternative is selected. Analytical decision-making is used by knowledgeable individuals who are somewhat less experienced in their particular field. The scenarios in which analytical decision-making is appropriate include:

- Strategic decisions that have a long-term impact, especially selection and design decisions
- When time is available for developing all of the alternatives and making the decision

Precedence-based. A precedence-based decision-making process uses established practices and policies to make decisions. (A precedence that has been well repeated is also known as *organizational policy.*) The precedence-based decision-making style is used to ensure uniformity between different decision-makers, perhaps at different locations. Scenarios for precedence-based decision-making include:

- Senior management who sets the policy and middle managers who make the decisions
- Headquarters that sets the policy and branches that make the decisions

Participative. Participative decision-making is sometimes called *consultative* decision-making. In the participative decision-making style, the decision-maker consults stakeholders to get their perspectives on the scenario at hand to ensure that all concerns are taken into consideration, and that those concerns can be addressed, before making the decision. Possible scenarios for participative decision-making include:

- Target setting
- Sequencing
- Scheduling
- Inventory control
- Preventive maintenance

Democratic. In the democratic style of decision-making, the decision-maker simply lets the decision-implementers make the decision. Democratic decision-making is especially useful in public-interfacing scenarios. The decision-maker formulates guidelines (or sets boundaries) and then allows the decision-implementer to make the decision. The democratic style of decision-making is prevalent in knowledge realms, such as research and development organizations, educational institutions, high-tech fields, and aid distribution work.

Consensus building. In consensus building, a decision-maker generates acceptance for a decision from individuals who have different, and sometimes conflicting, interests in the matter at hand. The decision-maker consults all of the involved parties and finds out about their concerns and their levels of acceptance for a proposed decision. The decision-maker then negotiates with the involved parties to arrive at a consensus. The decision-maker then rolls out the decision. The consensus-building process is normally followed by committees in which peers come together to discuss and finalize a decision that concerns all parties. The trick is to arrive at a win-win situation for everyone. Usually, everyone has to give up something to get something. The consensus-building process needs a decision-maker who is mutually acceptable to all parties and who is thoroughly knowledgeable in the field and in the decision scenario.

Dominant Factor in Decision Scenario

At times, a dominant factor influences decision-making. For example, a mining company may have no alternative but to open a plant that is near a mine, or a maritime shipping company's liners may need to be docked at a seacoast. The location of a company's market is another dominant factor. Although locating a company away from its market is possible, typically being close to customers is more efficient. Other dominant factors in decision-making include emotional factors that influence an entrepreneur, such as using a native location when opening a company, and the expertise of an entrepreneur, such as selection of the product, etc. In day-to-day affairs, however, a customer's preference usually becomes the dominant factor. A statutory obligation can also be the dominant factor. In some cases (e.g., Y2K), even the calendar is the dominant factor. When a dominant factor is present in a decision-making scenario, the decision will be affected by the dominant factor and our understanding of the factor. We therefore have to manage around dominant factors (they guide and direct).

When a dominant factor is absent, or using a dominant factor is not preferable, tools and techniques may be used. Some of these tools/techniques are described in the next section.

TOOLS AND TECHNIQUES FOR DECISION-MAKING

Over time, tools and techniques have been developed to improve the quality of decision-making and to reduce dependency on a given manager's capacity to arrive at a good hunch-based decision.

Critical Examination

Critical examination is an excellent technique for bringing more clarity to a scenario and to evaluate the available alternatives. Critical examination is based on two types of questions:

- *Primary*: "What" and "why" questions are used to clarify a scenario.
- *Secondary*: "What else" and "what should" questions are used to discover alternatives and to focus on a selection.

Using questions can illuminate the five aspects of any scenario:

- Purpose (why)
- Means (how)
- Place (where)
- Sequence (when)
- Person (who)

Use of these questions is shown in Table B.1. Answers to the questions in the *What Should* column provide the decision.

Critical examination can be used "all by itself" or in combination with other tools in any decision-making scenario. For example, answers to the questions in the *What Else* column can be obtained from another tool and yet another tool can be used for evaluating the alternatives and to arrive at the best possible decision.

Queuing Theory

Queuing theory facilitates analysis of the workload at a single workstation so that the number of workstations needed to optimize capacity utilization and service

Table B.1. Critical Examination Questions

Question	What	Why	What Else	What Should
Purpose	What is done? Is it necessary?	Why is it done?	What else could be done?	What should be done?
Means	How is it done?	Why is it done this way?	How else could it be done?	How should it be done?
Place	Where is it done?	Why is it done there?	Where else could it be done?	Where should it be done?
Sequence	When is it done?	Why is it done then?	When else could it be done?	When should it be done?
Person	Who does it?	Why is it done by them?	Who else could do it?	Who should do it?

levels can be planned. Queuing theory allows us to visualize the work arrival and execution rates at a given workstation and provides us with a set of equations for making decisions, especially in regard to the building capacity that is adequate to execute the tasks at hand effectively and economically. Some examples of places where the application of queuing theory can be seen and used for decision-making include service departments in software development organizations, retail checkout counters and counters where tickets are issued, and in automobile service departments (e.g., by mechanics).

Linear Programming

Linear programming (LP) is a mathematical optimization technique that allows us to define objectives and constraints. LP provides a procedure for optimizing a process to meet an objective. Optimization includes either maximization (such as revenue or profit) or minimization (such as cost or tardiness). The solution is derived by a procedure called *simplex programming*. Using manual means for simplex programming is impractical. Computer assistance is more or less essential for the use of this technique.

The Transportation Problem Technique

The *transportation problem* technique deals with reaching a number of places (m), originating from a number of places (n), while optimizing travel, usually by reducing distance or time. Originally this type of decision-making was typically applied to determining how to distribute items from a number of warehouses that were located across a country (or for that matter, now the world) to a number of sales points that were also located across the country (or the world). By using the transportation problem technique, this distribution problem can be optimized by using a number of iterations. Each of the iterations involves making an assignment of originations and destinations and then computing the costs between these points. The assignment of originations/destinations is iterated until a satisfactory solution is found. For real-life problems, computer assistance is essential when using the transportation problem technique.

PERT/CPM

PERT (the Program Evaluation and Review Technique) originated in the research and development (R&D) field as a tool for visualizing the activities to be performed for completing a program. The PERT process also supports handling the uncertainty involved in the R&D domain with the aid of probability theory. CPM (the Critical Path Method) originated in the construction industry as a tool for determining the completion time for projects and for identifying critical activities (the activities which should not be delayed if the project is to be completed on schedule). Both techniques are based on building and utilizing a network diagram. Over time, these techniques have come to be used and referred to together. PERT/CPM techniques help us visualize the activities and their sequence of performance to complete a project; to deal with uncertainties; and to identify the critical activities in the project. PERT/CPM is performed best by using computer assistance. (PERT/CPM is discussed in greater detail in Appendix H.)

Management Games

Management games (or game theory) are a tool that helps to analyze the competition's strategy. Game theory helps us to know the outcome of strategies between two or more parties. The basic form of the game theory decision-making tool is expressed in the popular example of the prisoner's dilemma. In the prisoner's dilemma, two men are caught at the scene of a theft. They are taken to a police station and interrogated in two separate rooms. Now, if neither confesses, they might go scot-free or be given only the minimum sentence. But if either one (or both) confesses and implicates the other, one of these men will certainly receive the maximum sentence. The dilemma is that neither prisoner knows the strategy of the other.

More often than not, a manager finds himself (or herself) in a similar situation. But instead of a jail sentence, the dilemma concerns the consequences of profit/loss or gaining/losing a deal. Game theory helps us to work out the possible outcomes for a number of strategies/counterstrategies and then to select the optimal strategy.

Delphi Method

The Delphi method consists of consulting knowledgeable persons in an anonymous manner and soliciting a response or a decision from each; comparing the answers and sharing the rationale for all or at least the outliers; and then iterating until a consensus has been reached on the decision at hand. Crowdsourcing is a variant of the Delphi method.

Decision Trees

Decision trees allow us to graphically explore the possibilities for the consequences of our actions. The following diagram is an example of a decision tree:

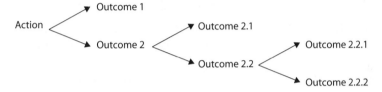

The branches of a decision tree can contain any number actions and outcomes. A side benefit of the graphical nature of a decision tree is that it helps organize seemingly disparate thoughts that can "grow" in any direction.

Interpolation and Extrapolation

Historical data provide a source of substantial information. Interpolation and extrapolation are statistical techniques for forecasting future trends using historical data. *Interpolation* is for forecasting an intermediate value; *extrapolation* is for forecasting a future value. These techniques are also referred to as time series analysis.

Sampling

Sampling is a technique used for the gathering information. In data gathering, the sampling technique is used to test assumptions, theories, proposed decisions, and quality control. The basis for using sampling plans is the underlying assumption that a randomly drawn sample truly represents a homogenous population. Key terms used in the context of sampling include:

- *Universe or population*: includes the whole gamut of data of all relevant candidates that can be included (A population is generally very large, so large that it is impractical to cover every member of the population.)

- *Sample*: a small section of the population or universe, drawn at random
- *Candidate*: represents each data item in the population or universe that will be considered for inclusion in the sample

For sampling to be successful, the key aspects are (1) the population or universe is homogenous and (2) the sample is randomly drawn. On many occasions, however, we find that the population is not homogenous and that the sample is not truly random. Therefore, we use several techniques and strategies to ensure that sampling produces better results.

Techniques for drawing samples. Some commonly used techniques for drawing samples include:

- *Random sampling*: used in a homogenous population in which sample candidates are drawn based on a lottery or by using random numbers
- *Judgment sampling*: a selection process based on our judgment about a candidate's ability to truly represent the population
- *Convenient sampling*: a technique in which we select candidates who are readily available to us (exertion of effort is hardly required)
- *Stratified sampling*: a more powerful manner of sampling used in populations that are not truly or fully homogenous; a technique in which the population is divided into various strata and a random sample is drawn from each stratum
- *Cluster sampling*: a technique similar to stratified sampling in which the population is divided into representative clusters and then sample candidates are drawn from each of the clusters using a random sampling technique

Strategies for sampling. Strategies, such as the single sampling plan or the double sampling plan, are also used in the context of sampling:

- *Single sampling*: A single sample is drawn from the population and used for drawing conclusions about the population.
- *Double sampling*: Double sampling plans use two typical methods: drawing samples sequentially or concurrently.

Sequential sampling. In the sequential sampling method, one sample is drawn and tested. Then, if the results of this first sample are found to be unsatisfactory for some reason, another sample is drawn from the same population and this sample is tested. A decision(s) is then made based on the outcome of testing the two samples. The one-sample method is popular in lot testing. Lot testing is done when large numbers of products are to be tested. A sample is drawn and tested. If the first sample fails the criteria for lot acceptance, a second sample is drawn. If the second sample confirms the findings of the first sample, the lot will be rejected. But if the first sample fails the criteria for lot acceptance and the second sample passes the criteria, the organization's process is followed. This process could be to accept the lot or to carry out 100% testing or to take another sample and then use the majority outcome.

Concurrent sampling. In the concurrent sampling method, two samples are concurrently drawn from the same population and tested concurrently by two independent agencies. The results are then compared. A familiar example that comes to mind is from the medical community: laboratory testing for cancer via a biopsy. In this example, two tissue samples are sent to two different laboratories and the findings are compared.

Statistical Analysis

Statistical analysis is a set of methods (tools) that allows managers to extract information (and perhaps knowledge) from data. (We will even go so far as to say that every manager uses statistics — in that managers use averages and trends.) Because descriptions in this section are not comprehensive, our recommendation is that you educate yourself about these techniques by studying more elaborate material about them. In fact, our recommendation is that every manager who is interested in making good decisions should take a basic course in statistics. We will now describe a few statistical techniques that we think are the most valuable for decision-makers:

- *Central tendency, dispersion, and skewness*: The measures of central tendency, dispersion, and skewness help us to draw inferences about a population. The three measures of *central tendency* for data are mean, mode, and median:
  - The *arithmetic mean* (usually called the average value) is used to summarize data. We use such terms as mean time between failures, average defect density, and average duration of a project (just to name a few of the common metrics). The arithmetic mean is a good measure to use when we have a large number of observations. Use of the mean, however, may not be appropriate for a small number of observations.
  - The *statistical mode* (modal value or the most frequently occurring value) is typically more suitable for small samples of data.
  - The *median* (or the middle value) is another measure of central tendency.

The measures of *dispersion* describe the variability of data. Commonly used measures of dispersion are standard deviation (represented by Greek letter sigma, σ) and variance. Other measures of dispersion are quartile deviation, percentile deviation, etc. *Skewness* is a measure that indicates if the data is uniformly distributed or is skewed in some way. We must check for skewness because normal decisions cannot be made from data that is skewed in one way or another.

- *Correlation*: Correlation (or covariance) is a method to determine if one set of outcomes is related to another set of inputs. A common question can be examined/confirmed by this measure: "Would increased inspection ensure higher quality? We compute the coefficient of covariation and, based this computation, draw an inference about whether one is dependent on the other or not. But remember one important thing about correlation: correlation and causality can be two very different things!
- *Probability distributions*: Three popular probability distributions are normal, binomial, and Poisson:
  - *Normal* probability distribution assists us in making inferences about normally occurring values. In many populations, for example, there is one central tendency with an equal number of observations occurring on either side of this central tendency, but with fewer observations occurring the further away they are from the central point.
  - *Binomial* probability distribution assists us in making inferences about values that are binary in nature, such as in tossing a coin: in a coin toss, only two possible values (outcomes) are possible (we will ignore the possibility of the coin standing edgewise!).
  - *Poisson* probability distribution assists us in making inferences about rare events, such as fires, floods, and earthquakes.

Other probability distributions, such as beta distribution, gamma distribution, and T distribution are used for specific purposes. Statistics handbooks may be consulted for in-depth information.

- *Tests of goodness of fit*: *Goodness of fit* is a set of techniques that is used to validate the results obtained from statistical testing. We compute the measure of goodness of fit from the interaction of expected values and the actual values (χ^2, chi-square; pronounced with "ch" as in "kay").
- *Hypothesis testing*: Hypothesis testing is a set of techniques that assists us in designing tests (or experiments) and using sampling of data to determine if a hypothesis is valid or not.

Consultants

More often than not, a manager will need to manage a particular knowledge area, but the manager has less knowledge than he or she would prefer to have. Another possibility is that the manager has no experience in the particular decision scenario, i.e., he or she is has no experience in defining and assessing the alternatives, in assessing the possible outcomes, or even in properly defining the problem in the first place. In scenarios such as these, using a consultant can come in handy. A properly chosen consultant brings his or her knowledge and training to the decision-making process to assist in all areas: from problem definition to development of the decision scenario, to enumerating the alternatives, and to generating the possible outcomes, which enables the selection of the optimal decision.

THE DECISION POSTMORTEM

We should learn from the outcomes of all of the decisions that we make. Possible decision outcomes include:

- *As expected*: In this outcome, we need to examine if we made a really good decision or if control of the decision's implementation ensured the expected result.
- *Better than expected*: In this outcome, we need to analyze what caused the improved outcome so that we can use that aspect in making all future decisions (assuming the outcome was more than just a random variation).
- *Worse than expected*: In this outcome, we need to analyze what caused the failure. Why did the decision we made result in failure and how could that failure have been prevented so this pitfall can be avoided in the future?

So, should we conduct a formal postmortem for the decision outcome with all concerned and then document it? Our recommendation: If a decision is important enough to be approached formally, then the answer is "yes." In general, documenting the results of a decision is always a good idea because the information will be available for future reference, even if only for us. If a decision involves others, documentation is optional. Having the documentation, however, will allow us to have flexibility in the future because we may or may not involve others. Get the facts/data, analyze the decision, and then decide what to do in the future.

Some closing words. Everyone makes decisions. We therefore need to be aware of decision-making theory, techniques, and tools. Mastering as many tools and techniques as possible enriches a software project manager.

APPENDIX C

PEOPLE MANAGEMENT

INTRODUCTION

Our opinion is that people management is the oldest form of management. The word *management* itself contains the word *man*, which represents human beings as being at the beginning of the word. Ever since humans have organized themselves to accomplish a task, they have required some form of management (some would say manipulation) to achieve a desired result. The endeavors of management can vary from waging wars to building edifices or growing food. Any endeavor requires that some form of organization be performed (even if it is done inefficiently). To accomplish any task with more than just a few people also requires some combination of exhorting (motivating), judging/measuring performance, rewarding, promoting, punishing, and possibly even demoting individuals or groups.

In software project management, as in all other endeavors, people are managed to achieve the objective of delivering a software product, while meeting the goals of being on time and being within the allocated budget, and at the same time maintaining and improving the morale of the team members. In software project management, people management includes carrying out several activities:

- Estimating the human resources requirement
- Acquiring the required human resources for project execution
- Allocating work to team members so that project execution is efficient and effective
- Motivating team members to higher levels of achievement
- Maintaining team morale at desirable organizational levels
- Disciplining team members as necessary
- Developing and mentoring people who are suitable for higher responsibilities
- Releasing human resources when the project is completed

Let's look at each of these activities in greater detail.

ESTIMATING THE REQUIRED HUMAN RESOURCES

Arriving at a project's human resources requirements is achieved from the effort estimate that has been made for the project in conjunction with the project's technical specifications. A software project needs human resources who have various skill sets. Some of the usual skill sets include:

- Systems analysts/business analysts who collect user requirements, either directly from the end users or from documentation or from reverse engineering an existing product, and then document them in such a way that software designers can carry out the software design activity
- Software architects/designers who develop the designs for a software product, including the software architecture, navigation, inputs, outputs, and processing, and document the software design in such a way that programmers can develop the software
- Programmers who develop the required code based on the design documents (A project may use multiple programming languages. If so, each programming language will need programmers with different skills.)
- Database specialists who are experts in the data handling aspects of the software project (Database specialists design the database and develop stored procedures/triggers that assist the programs in handling data efficiently. Database specialists also guide the programmers in developing efficient data handling routines.)
- User interface designers who develop the user interface screens in a manner that is aesthetically pleasant for end users and also develop the necessary graphics, icons, and buttons that are required for the screens
- Testers who carry out software testing for all of the components as well as the testing to ensure that the end product of the software project conforms to the project's testing plans

To determine the human resources requirements, we apportion the effort estimated for the project among the skill categories (and possibly others) and then round the estimates off to the nearest day. (Allocating a person for part of a day may be ideal; however, allocating a person for less than a full day is often impractical.) Based on the effort required for each of these categories, we determine the persons who are required full time and those who can be allocated part time. Full-time people are for the activities that require significant duration continuously. Part-time people are best applied to those tasks that are required for only a short period of time or for those tasks that are needed intermittently over a long period of time, but in which each requirement is of a short duration. The SPM will also need to develop the schedule for project execution so that the period during which each of the skill sets will be required is understood and can be easily communicated.

Based on the needed skill sets and the schedule, we can request human resources from the organizational entity vested with the responsibility of allocating human resources to projects. In this request, we detail the number of people needed, the dates on which they are required, and the skill sets needed by them. (A sample resource request form is presented in Chapter 4.)

ACQUIRING THE REQUIRED HUMAN RESOURCES

To execute a project, people (as necessary) have to be acquired either from within the organization or from external sources. Sources *internal* to the organization include:

- People "on the bench" who are not currently allocated to any project (People on the bench could just have been de-allocated from a completed project and be awaiting allocation to another project or they could be new recruits who are waiting for allocation to their first project.)
- People working on other projects who are likely to be released by the required date(s)
- People in the recruitment pipeline who are likely to join the organization and who therefore will be available by the required date(s)

Sources *external* to the organization could include:

- Consultants from consultancy organizations who are taken on as temporary hires
- Freelance consultants who are taken on as temporary hires
- New recruitments for the regular rolls of the company

The project management office is responsible for acquiring the required number of people with the desired skill sets for the project and for arranging for their allocation. Based on the resource request, the PMO (or the entity that is vested with the responsibility of making people available to projects) allocates the people.

A situation that plagues many SPMs is the differences in the skill levels of the people in the organization: in any organization, the skill levels of the people will vary from poor to super, with fair, good, and very good skill levels in between.

When estimating effort, however, we assume an *average* level of skills (i.e., good skills). Ideally, the total number of allocated persons will equal the number of requested people when the skill levels are factored into the equation. Yet, when actual allocation takes place, the SPM could get a mix of skill levels that range from poor to super skills. For example, suppose an SPM requests five persons who have average skills. But when the actual allocation is made, the SPM receives one person with very good skills, two persons with good skills, and four persons with poor skills — for a total of seven persons. When we normalize the allocated number based on the individual skill levels allocated, the total number of people allocated is five. The allocation is therefore as the SPM has requested. The PMO needs to ensure that the allocation matches the normalized request for personnel from the SPM and then, if necessary, to convince the SPM that a fair allocation of people has been made to the project. (Appendix D, *Productivity for Software Project Managers*, deals with this concept and the aspects of productivity in greater detail.)

ALLOCATING WORK TO TEAM MEMBERS

Once human resources are acquired and allocated to the project, they should be allocated work in such a manner that project execution can begin and run efficiently and effectively. The following activities are part of work allocation:

1. Organize work into work packages that can be executed by one person or by a small team of two to three persons working together. Include the work's scope and instructions (documented) for carrying out the work in each work package. Work packages typically include developmental as well as quality assurance work (as appropriate).
2. Estimate the effort required to complete the work based on the skill of a person putting in an average (good) level of skill.
3. Allocate work to the persons who are responsible for its completion by:
    *   Entering the work allocation in a work register
    *   Providing the scope of the work and instructions for carrying out the work
    *   Providing schedule, effort, and quality targets
    *   Negotiating and then finalizing the targets with the assignees
4. Monitor progress and ensure completion.

The subject of motivating people to put forth super effort and to achieve higher levels has received significant attention. In fact, motivating teams and maintaining their morale are such large topics that they are subjects unto themselves. Full coverage of them is therefore beyond the scope of this appendix. Numerous works are available that discuss the motivation of people in great detail. Online material is available as well. We recommend that SPMs educate themselves on these topics so that they can perform the vital function of motivation effectively.

MOTIVATING TEAM MEMBERS

Concerning their occupational work, people typically have two primary objectives: to earn a livelihood and to perform the work that has been assigned to them. These primary objectives are followed by a host of secondary objectives: the possibility of advancement, earning more money, achieving satisfaction from doing work, and receiving respect from society and from others. Regardless of the secondary objectives, the first objective is to earn a livelihood! (Remember Maslow's hierarchy of five basic needs?[1])

Of course, the people who still come to work even though their livelihoods have already been taken care of by their ancestors (or spouses, good fortune, etc.) are an exception. For these people, their primary objectives might include:

- Gaining the respect of others and the self-satisfaction that comes from working (i.e., for the purpose of enhancing their personal sense of self-respect)
- Acquiring knowledge (e.g., to learn about a business so that they will be able to start a similar one)
- Having social interaction and using time productively

Thus, the work is generally a means to an end rather than a goal unto itself.

In addition to the objectives for working, people can be classified in several simple ways:

- By their *purpose*
  - Straightforward (open)
  - Scheming (closed)
  - Normally straightforward (unless in a situation that affects them personally)
- By *pleasantness*
  - Pleasant
  - Disagreeable
  - Neutral (no pronounced inclination to either characteristic)
- By their *expectations*
  - Easy to please
  - Difficult to please
  - Usually easy to please, but can be difficult

- By their level of *desire*
  - Ambitious
  - No ambition
  - Somewhat ambitious
- By their level of *acceptance* (of you)
  - Willing
  - Reluctant
  - Usually willing (except when you have bad news)
- By their level of *responsibility*
  - Responsible by nature
  - Irresponsible by nature
  - Mostly responsible
- By *age*
  - In the prime of life
  - Well past the prime of life
  - Slightly past the prime of life

Classifying people by age, the last category, is illegal, especially for recruitment or advancement, in North America and in Europe at a minimum. Nevertheless, individuals in any organization naturally fall into certain age categories. In all of these classification schemes, however, notice that types one and two are the extremes. Type three is typically found in most organizations, but an individual can be any combination of these classifications:

- Straightforward, pleasant, easy to please, ambitious, willing, responsible, rich, and in the prime of age (obviously a best-case scenario!)
- Scheming, unpleasant, difficult to please, no ambition, reluctant, irresponsible, poor, and well past prime

The list can (and does) go on with a multitude of combinations and permutations. Given this level of complexity, how do we motivate people to perform their tasks to the best of their ability?

History is replete with examples of ordinary people performing extraordinary feats when motivated by necessity, fear, or some reward. Motivation schemes include:

Carrot and stick. One of the most common and effective techniques is *the carrot and the stick.* (Why? It works with many types of people!) The carrot and stick technique rewards excellent performance and punishes poor performance. This reward/punishment process can go a long way in maintaining performance in ordinary situations. A cardinal rule for this technique, however, is that the technique must be exercised fairly, without fear, and without favoritism. Any perception of bias or hesitation when exercising this technique renders it ineffective (including taking umbrage during extraordinary situations and avoiding application of policy). (*Note*: A limitation to the carrot and stick technique is that SPMs are rarely in a position to reward or punish on their own or with the desired immediacy, which might mean using this technique in modern, progressive organizations is not all that feasible.)

Stimulus-response. The second most effective technique is the *stimulus-response theory*. This technique is based on the assumption that people will respond visibly and positively to a positive stimulus. The alternative is also true: people respond negatively to a negative stimulus — albeit not always in an explicit manner (which can be misleading). In most cases, for example, a negative response comes sooner rather than later, but maybe not when we are ready for it or at a time that we would prefer. So, take care to ensure that a negative stimulus, when given, is administered in such a way that a positive response is generated — doing so is very important. (Remember the words of Mario Puzo in his novel *The Godfather*: "It is not easy to say 'no' and one needs training in administering negative stimuli."[2])

Expectancy. Another theory we need to learn about is the motivational theory proposed by Victor Vroom (Yale School of Management) in 1964.[3] According to Vroom's *Expectancy Theory*, people have expectations when they come to an organization and put in the effort required to complete their assignments. In addition to earning a salary, these expectations can include fair treatment, career advancement, recognition, rewards, and punishment (e.g., for lack of performance, violations, errors, etc.). In Vroom's Expectancy Theory, when positive performance results in a realization of positive expectations and negative performance results in a realization of negative expectations, an individual will be motivated to better performance. (*Note*: A point of interest is that most individuals watch how the expectations of others are being met. If they perceive that certain individuals are getting more positive or fewer negative rewards, they are likely to become de-motivated. Numerous books and online articles that discuss Vroom's Expectancy Theory in great detail are available.)

Laissez-faire. Remember from our discussion of the *laissez-faire* leadership style that it is a "hands-off" style in which a manager provides little direction concerning the assignment and completion of tasks and gives team members as much freedom as possible. The team members have the power to make decisions and solve problems on their own. Having this added responsibility can be a source of motivation to the team. The manager does not, however, ignore the team. The manager is available to answer questions and provide/

supply information as required. But even in laissez-faire management, a manager must still be fair, and also be perceived as being fair, in all of his/her actions by all concerned parties. (If a manager is unfair, yet seen as being fair, or vice versa, any motivational actions taken tend to result in failure.) The laissez-faire philosophy is sine qua non (absolutely indispensable) in people management and motivation situations.

Behavioral correction. An important aspect of motivation is delivering *behavioral correction* to people who are not performing in a way that is commensurate with the exigencies of the work, the abilities of the person, and the compensation being given to the person. Behavioral correction is best achieved through coaching and counseling. Coaching provides expert guidance to a person on how to achieve better performance. The "how to" is provided by training (either classroom or on-the-job) and expert assistance by a senior person that is followed by periodic progress assessments. Counseling is resorted to when the skills are present, but an "attitude correction" is necessary. The first form of counseling is typically friendly — counseling in which the correction needed is pointed out in nonconfrontational manner. Nonconfrontational counseling may be used when an individual is unintentionally exhibiting an undesirable behavior — the individual does not realize the consequences of his/her behavior and is therefore receptive to counseling. Even after friendly counseling, sometimes an individual's undesirable behavior continues. When an individual knows that he/she is exhibiting an undesirable behavior, confrontational counseling is used. Confrontational counseling involves presenting the individual with the expected behavioral correction as well as irrefutable evidence of the undesirable behavior and the consequential damages. Confrontational counseling also includes outlining the consequences to the person if the required behavioral correction does not materialize. (Outlining the consequences of not making the desired behavioral correction requires management's approval.) We recommend training in the art of confrontational counseling for all SPMs so that they will be equipped with the skills necessary to better deal with difficult situations. Training can be through formal training or by self-study.

MAINTAINING TEAM MORALE

Think about the classic movie entitled *Charge of the Light Brigade*, a film that is based on the poem *The Charge of the Light Brigade* (by Alfred Lord Tennyson) and history of the Crimean War (1853–1856).[4] As in this film, even underdogs can be exhorted to incredible actions if their morale is extremely high. In sports, we often see that a team with higher morale wins over a team with lower morale, even if the two teams have similar skills. Keeping team morale at the levels desired by an organization is also extremely important for successful project execution. Yet, even if every team member is positive, the team's morale can still be low. Some reasons for low team morale include:

- A perception that the project is not important to higher management or that it is not important within the organization
- A perception that the technology used in the project is obsolete
- A perception that the human resources are being treated unfairly by the project's management
- A perception that team meetings and reviews do not receive adequate importance
- A view that the targets are either too lax or too tight
- The presence of rumor mongers and gossips on the team

Many other reasons lead to lower morale. But what is important is that an SPM should continuously monitor team morale and strive to maintain it at a desirable level.

DISCIPLINING WHEN NECESSARY

Although all precautions and actions are taken to motivate team members and to maintain team morale at higher levels, sometimes disciplining an errant subordinate becomes necessary. Disciplining a team member is usually necessary, however, only if the team member is found to be willfully indulging in some act(s) that is detrimental to the health of the project and to the morale of the project team. For example, an unintentional delay in an assigned task or a task taking more effort than has been estimated might necessitate counseling and coaching, but not disciplining. A subordinate might also act out as a result of some unresolved grievance. So, before subjecting a subordinate to disciplinary action, ensure that:

- All grievances have been resolved.
- Some reasonable expectations of the individual have not been met by the organization.
- The infraction is not the result of an innocent action(s).
- The offending act is indeed willful.
- Other persons are not engaged in a conspiracy against the employee.

When these criteria have been addressed, disciplinary action(s) can be taken with the assurance that a mistake is not being made. Remember a cardinal rule: the punishment should be commensurate with the infraction. Terminating the services of an individual is akin to capital punishment. Additionally, recruiting a new employee and training this person costs much more than correcting and retaining an existing employee. The result of a disciplinary action therefore should be targeted at correcting the behavior (if possible) rather than being punitive. If discipline is inevitable, we recommend that a manager should carry out the disciplinary procedure/policy of the organization, diligently giving the errant individual every opportunity to redeem himself/herself.

We should also note that infractions typically do not just "crop up overnight." Most behavioral issues tend to be the culmination of a number of incidents that have occurred over a period of time. We typically find that the need to discipline is a failure of management: it could have been prevented through the proper use of motivation and behavioral correction. (Consult textbooks and other types of books on industrial relations for more information on disciplinary procedures.)

DEVELOPING AND MENTORING SUITABLE PEOPLE FOR GREATER RESPONSIBILITIES

SPMs are uniquely positioned to spot potential leadership talent in software engineers in an organization. Once leadership potential is discovered, an SPM is usually the first person in the organization who can develop this potential into a reality. How? The SPM puts the latent talent to practical use. By allowing an individual with potential to exercise his/her latent leadership talent, the SPM creates a development opportunity for the individual. Continued mentoring by the SPM involves the individual in decision-making and provides leadership opportunities, beginning in a small team environment, with continuous coaching of the individual, and then gradually increasing his/her independence from supervision over time. We recommend exposing latent leadership talent to senior levels of management so that he/she can be evaluated by senior management and so that the individual's development will continue from the enhanced opportunities provided from being allocated to other projects. By being allocated to other projects, the developing leader will also have opportunities to work with other SPMs within the organization.

RELEASING HUMAN RESOURCES UPON COMPLETION OF THE PROJECT

Remember from previous discussions that a project typically follows a general cycle:

1. They start with a minimum set of people to carry out the project initiation activities.
2. More people are then added to carry out the business/systems analysis and to carry out the software design.

3. Even more people are added to develop the source code and to build the software product.

4. When software design is complete, some of the people who carried out the business/systems analysis and software design may need to be released because they will be required in smaller numbers during software construction.

5. As development progresses, software testers may need to be ramped up to test the developed software.

6. As software construction nears an end, generally programmers need to be released because they will be needed in smaller numbers.

7. When testing is completed, fewer testers are needed.

8. After delivery of the software, most of the project team may need to be released (except those assigned to software maintenance activities).

9. At the close of the project, typically everyone is released.

Also remember that software projects are not static. So, to be effective and efficient, projects generally require that human resources be continuously ramped up and down. *Ramping up* involves conducting induction training for new team members. *Ramping down* involves conducting performance appraisals for the team members so they can understand how they performed on the project.

Releasing human resources from a project involves following a set of activities for each individual:

1. Carry out a performance appraisal. After agreement from the individual has been obtained, give the performance appraisal to the HR department.

2. Update the skills database of the organization with the new skills that have been acquired by the individual during project execution.

3. Take over all project-related artifacts, including source code, code libraries, and the development kit.

4. Archive project-related communication that may need to be preserved as part of project records for future reference and possible use (a legal requirement in some countries).

5. Recover hardware resources from the individual.

6. Prepare the project release communication (a formal letter or an email) and hand the individual over to the PMO (or the agency in charge of reallocating employees to another project).

7. Document the best practices, worst practices, or any other events that deserve special mention. Forward the documentation to concerned management personnel.

8. Take software artifacts, communications, and hardware resources from the individual to concerned agencies in the organization for further maintenance and reallocation.

9. Update the project information to reflect the release of the individual.

Release of contractors would entail similar activities.

BEST PRACTICES IN PEOPLE MANAGEMENT

We have several recommendations to help you manage the human resources of a project well:

- Communicate continuously and coherently with all team members. In the absence of official communication, team members will listen to the organization's grapevine, which can distort facts so that they become detrimental to the project's (and organization's) well being.
- Monitor morale continuously. Strive to keep morale at a sensibly high level. *Remember*: A team with high morale can scale unimaginable heights.
- Motivate continuously. Learn about the team members and try your best to motivate them. To some extent, motivation is unique to an individual. It pays to show team members individual attention.
- Discipline only when you are absolutely sure you are taking the correct action. Make every effort to not only be fair, but to also appear to be fair to the entire team. *Remember*: Unless you administer discipline very skillfully, your actions can end up de-motivating the entire team.

MANAGING DIFFICULT PEOPLE

As a software project manager, you will need to deal with various individuals, ranging from your own team members to peers, superiors, and customers. Typically, all of these individuals are well educated and highly intelligent. Most of them are good individuals and will perform well what is expected of them, but a few will be "difficult." Will these few difficult individuals really matter? Consider what George Bernard Shaw once said, "The reasonable man adapts himself to the world; the unreasonable one persists in trying to adapt the world to himself. Therefore, all progress depends on the unreasonable man."[5] Also noteworthy to consider is the effect of the "insignificant majority and significant minority." Identifying the significant minority and insignificant majority is commonly used in ABC analysis (Always Better Control), VED analysis (Vital, Essential and

Desirable), etc. (Although ABC analysis and VED analysis are beyond the scope of this section, we refer to them to forewarn you of the significant minority so that you can more effectively manage people.)

Our discussion of difficult people reminds us an amusing anecdote: a psychiatry professor was giving a lecture to her students about the behavior of the abnormal man. This was the fifth time in a row. When the professor began a continuation of the lecture the sixth time, a student raised his hand and asked her: "Professor, when are you going to start telling us about the behavior of the normal man?" She replied, "When we find him, we cure him."

So, are any people easy to handle? The answer: "Yes, but often only for a period of time." People who are easily managed for a short time include:

- *Trainees*: until their training has been completed and they are on the permanent rolls of the company
- *New employees*: until they have successfully completed their probation period
- *Employees*: until they have received an expected promotion (and still wish to receive it)
- *Employees*: who are low on performance, but high on pleasing the boss (and thus survive)
- *Eager beavers*: who always want to please their bosses (just for the sake of pleasing)

Wise individuals, however, understand their role as well as yours as a manager and perform their duties diligently, irrespective of your provocation (e.g., at times when the message from upper management is not good or the tasks are challenging, etc.), and are always easy to handle. The percentage of these people in an organization is usually miniscule. The remaining percentage is to some degree difficult to handle.

What Are Some Types of Difficult People?

We will now profile the difficult people and give you some tips for handling them. Is your first thought, "But why should I even try to deal with difficult people? Our answer: "Because you cannot avoid dealing with them." Difficult people are part of every organization (and who knows, maybe you are difficult to handle for some people).

We classify difficult people into twelve types:

- The two-timer
- The backstabber
- The first chapter expert
- The martyr

- The prima donna
- The manipulator
- The gossip
- The breather-down-the neck
- The buck-stopper
- The "no" man
- Mr. Justice
- The carrier pigeon

So, where do you find these people? You find them everywhere. They are among your subordinates, your peers, and your superiors.

The two-timer. The two-timer is a person whose stand depends on the situation and the people involved. He puts on a "public smile," but a "private snarl." What he says in public is different from what he says in private. He is completely undependable. We easily spot him the first time he two-times us. But do not treat the first occurrence as a mere coincidence. No person two-times unintentionally. Two-timers can be subordinates and peers as well as superiors. How do we handle a two-timer? If he makes a private commitment to you, do not depend on it unless you get the commitment in written form: an email or a chat in a messenger forum. Save the email or messenger conversation. When you deal with him, always try to have a witness. When you have a meeting with him, record minutes of the meeting.

Backstabber. Backstabbers betray your confidence, particularly if doing so will get them positive "points" with upper echelon managers. Backstabbers are often not your enemies, but your friends. Spotting backstabbers or proving that they backstabbed you is very difficult. Backstabbers are only identified through using secondary sources. For example, if a boss-type person exhibits animosity toward you for no apparent reason, someone has likely backstabbed you. And that someone has likely suddenly become quite "friendly" with the boss-type person. Backstabbing people are among your peers and subordinates. Rarely is backstabbing behavior found in superiors. A backstabber obtains the information that assists him in backstabbing you — from you! He uses charm, encouragement, and sympathy to egg you on, particularly to criticize senior persons. Remember the advice from World War II: "Loose lips sink ships." Never criticize a senior person in the workplace in the presence of others, especially someone who is powerful. Remember that a backstabber can hurt you only when you turn your back on them. So never show your back to anyone, including your most charming friend.

The first chapter expert. The first chapter expert knows something about every scenario, technology, and person in the organization. She never allows anyone to go into detail about something because her knowledge is limited. Her knowledge is limited to the introductory chapter of some book on the subject at hand. So she ends up using her limited knowledge to shoot down any positive proposal by "picking holes" in it — holes which are plugged in subsequent chapters in the book. Arguing with a person with half-baked knowledge on a subject is extremely difficult. First chapter experts are also easy to spot. You see her discussing new topics everywhere, but she disappears as soon as someone else goes into detail about the topic. First chapter experts are mostly found among your peers. You can deal with a first chapter expert by giving the details first and then by giving her some credit, saying something like: "As Jane can probably explain to you because she knows ...." This usually shuts her up.

The martyr. People who are overlooked for promotions often become martyrs, particularly the people who have a long tenure in the organization, who lack the academic credentials to allow them to reach the top echelons, or who are not on the career progression fast track. These people often exhibit the attributes of a martyr. Martyrs have a negative spin on everything, especially in private. They usually do not express a negative spin in public for fear that they will be fired from the organization. Martyrs are easy to spot. When something goes wrong, a martyr comes to you and says, "I told you (thought) so." If there is a new initiative, he will tell you privately that it is going to fail. Although a martyr is harmless, he can discourage you from coming up with new initiatives or taking up a challenging opportunity. Martyrs are found among your peers and superiors. You handle a martyr by indulging him, but never taking his discouraging words seriously. He is actually a great source for pointing out the other side of your proposals. So use him as your personal quality assurance person for proposals and initiatives.

The prima donna. A prima donna is a stickler for the rules, regulations, conventions, practices, etc. Often a prima donna is a petty-minded person. Prima donnas are found in the security department, as secretaries to bosses, as auditors, as parking lot attendants, etc. For example, have you ever had an experience with a parking attendant who waits until you have parked your vehicle, locked it, and are ready to go before he slowly ambles over to tell you that you have parked wrongly or are in the wrong place and that you have to park where he says. You think (and maybe say): "Why didn't you just tell me before I parked"? This parking lot attendant is a prima donna. Perhaps you are visiting a client and his secretary tells you to wait. But you soon see that she is polishing her nails and not making any attempt to communicate your arrival to her boss. You then remind her gently, only to be reprimanded. She is a prima donna. These people have limited power, and just to annoy you, they use it to its full extent. So how is a prima donna handled? Give the parking lot attendant a friendly greeting when you enter the parking lot. Put on your charm and best manners with the secretary. The trick is to give them the impression that you respect their position and power; then you can get along well with them.

The manipulator. Manipulators act as if they are very busy either to avoid work or to pass it on to you. Manipulators always look haggard and as if they are under pressure. Often they are slow workers or do something else during working hours. A manipulator eventually comes to a peer saying something similar to: "I'm really busy right now. Can you help me by doing this?" Sometimes a manipulator goes so far as to tell her boss: "Even though it's my job, Mark is best person because of his experience and special skills (real or imagined) and he seems to be free of any work right now." Manipulators are mostly found among your peers. To handle a manipulator, put on that same haggard look yourself when you notice the "always busy-as-a-bee" person and approach her to see if she is free to help you out. But wait — are we telling you to become a manipulator yourself? You bet we are! No medicine is better suited for a manipulator than to give her a dose of her own medicine.

The gossip. The problem with gossips is that they hear the words of someone thinking out loud or they hear part of a conversation and then put two and two together to make eight and pass the result off as fact. If they cannot find anything worth circulating, they often invent some piece of juicy information. The impact of a gossip is best illustrated by a quote attributed to Mark Twain: "A lie travels half-way around the world before truth gets its boots on."[6] Gossips sow distrust, prejudice, and suspicion among other people. They also waste a lot of time — yours, theirs, and everyone else. For some reason, a gossip seems to have a lot of spare time. He is also a very good conversationalist and can narrate with great skill to hold your interest — so well that listening to him can even become somewhat addictive and make you want to ask for more information. Gossips are found among your subordinates and peers. The best way to handle a gossip is to avoid him or avoid being drawn into a gossip session with anyone. Remember that if a gossip is giving false information to you about someone else, then he surely will do the same about you with others when you are not present.

The breather-down-the-neck. A breather-down-the-neck is an uneasy delegator. She is usually in a supervisory position (a boss). Perhaps due to some past bad experience with her subordinates, she is not comfortable delegating work. She is also insecure about her position. When a person who normally works alone is promoted to the position of a boss, that person also often becomes a breather-down-the-neck until he/she attains maturity. Even a boss with a few subordinates will resort to breathing down the necks of their subordinates because they have little else to do (or nothing else better to do). If a boss is a breather-down-the-neck, understand that she may just be maturing into the skills needed to be a boss and give her some space. Something that gets a breather-down-the-neck off your back is to meet a deadline the first time and a few more times so that she becomes more confident with your commitments. Then she will not be so overbearing. The trick is to give her a sense of confidence about your commitments.

The buck-stopper. Anything that goes to a buck-stopper stays there. It never comes out. If you want the buck to be moved, you have to chase down the buck-stopper. A buck-stopper never says "no," but neither does he give a commitment or an actual response. His desk is a bottomless pit. You can put something on it, but getting it back will be very difficult. A buck-stopper generally dodges all of your queries about the status of a task or for a commitment to a date for completion of any action expected from her. You find buck-stoppers among your peers and handling grievances or complaints in service departments. A buck-stopper's thinking is that "if it's really urgent, someone will come and ask about it in person." To get something done by a buck-stopper, you need to push him. Pay a visit to him to get what you need.

The "no" man. A "no" man is able to say "no" to everything you say. A no man uses excellent logic to deny your proposal or a request. Even if you were to say, "The sun rises in the east," a no man would say, "No — the sun does not rise in the east." If you press on with an argument, he will say that the east itself is ill-defined, that the physical north pole and the magnetic north pole are not the same, that the Earth itself is slanted, etc. A no man is easy to spot. The most frequent word spoken by him is either "no" or "not." No men are found among your peers, particularly in service departments. Although negative, no men are eager to make proposals. So, to get a no man to say "yes" (or something similar), ask him to make proposals on your behalf. Instead of telling him what needs to be done, consult him and make suggestions, but let him think that your proposal is in fact his proposal.

Mr. Justice. Mr. Justice has grown up hearing the stories of class struggle. Mr. Justice therefore divides the world (and the organization) into the "haves" (those who have power or the management) and the "have not's" (staff, workers, professional workers, etc.). Mr. Justice sees injustice in every action taken by management. He denigrates the benefits, but always accentuates the side effects. More often than not, Mr. Justice (or Ms.) is active, directly or indirectly, in a trade union and some other similar type of association. Mr. Justice also opposes the recognition of meritorious persons. He instead advocates seniority for receiving awards and rewards. Consequently, Mr. Justice types are low performers. They hover around the penalty-avoidance level of performance. Mr. Justice is mostly found among your subordinates. Rarely is he found in your peers. Confrontational counseling, using quantitative data, is the best way to bring Mr. Justice in line — and it will be a continuous and periodic chore. If you miss a single confrontational counseling session, Mr. Justice will revert to using trade union jargon.

The carrier pigeon. The bearer of good news is always well received and rewarded. You have seen this scenario in movies when the heroin hugs or kisses the postman who brings a letter from her distant lover or from someone informing her of good news. Some people in an organization take on this role of the postman. When some achievement is made or something great is done, the carrier pigeon immediately visits the boss to inform him — before the person actually making the achievement has a chance to talk to the boss. A carrier pigeon always keep her antennae up, scanning the horizon for newsworthy items to report to the boss. This behavior is harmless, but the excitement for you, the achiever, is gone — you have been beaten to the punch! Your success is already "old hat" to the boss. Carrier pigeons are easily spotted by observation. They constantly poke their noses into other people's affairs. If something important is going on in the organization, a carrier pigeon always manages to be in close quarters irrespective of whether she is involved. She is usually at places where she is not needed. Carrier pigeons are mostly found among your peers. Obviously, carrier pigeons have the ear of the boss. So, be careful about what you say to a carrier pigeon. She not only carries good news, but she also carries tales. If you criticize the boss in a carrier pigeon's presence, know for certain that your message will be carried. Discretion is therefore your best safeguard. If you are on the verge of some success, keep it to yourself. Remain calm and wait to show your excitement in the presence of your boss.

Some final words about handling difficult people. Humans are basically difficult to handle because humans are unpredictable. Most of the time, another person's response is not commensurate with your stimulus. A person's personality attributes can also change over time. So not necessarily is "once a thief always a thief" always correct, but "forewarned is forearmed" is certainly better than being ignorant. As an SPM, you need to know how to motivate people toward success and you need to practice motivating them diligently, but being prepared to handle difficult people is also necessary. The purpose of Appendix C is to "forewarn and forearm" you.

REFERENCES

1. http://en.wikipedia.org/wiki/Maslow's_hierarchy_of_needs.

2. http://en.wikipedia.org/wiki/The_Godfather_(novel).

3. http://en.wikipedia.org/wiki/Victor_Vroom.

4. http://en.wikipedia.org/wiki/The_Charge_of_the_Light_Brigade_(1936_film).

5. www.quotationspage.com/quotes/George_Bernard_Shaw.

6. http://www.twainquotes.com/Lies.html (Although often attributed to Mark Twain, this quote has not been verified as actually originating with him. The quote may have originated with Charles H. Spurgeon, a fundamentalist Baptist preacher, in a sermon in 1855.)

APPENDIX D

PRODUCTIVITY CONCEPTS FOR SOFTWARE PROJECT MANAGERS

In general, *productivity* is a term that is used in the context of human beings. There are various ways to define productivity. One definition is "the rate of output per unit input" (sometimes called industrial productivity because of the initial definition of productivity that stems from the practice of industrial engineering). Another definition can be expressed as a certain number of units of output per person-day or a certain number of units of output per person-hour. Another definition can be expressed as a ratio of output to input. Still others invert this equation and call it *productivity*, albeit the actual term for that metric is *delivery*. Perhaps the simplest conceptual definition of productivity is "the rate of achieving or accomplishing something in a human endeavor." In this appendix, productivity is defined as "the rate of producing some output, using a set of inputs, during a defined period of time, leveraging a defined work environment by a qualified person who is acclimatized to the working environment and who is using a defined set of methods at a pace that can be maintained day after day without any harmful physical effects."

CONCERNS WITH PRODUCTIVITY

Our observation is that the software development industry confuses the terms productivity, capacity, and efficiency, substituting the word *productivity*. So, at the outset, let's distinguish our understanding of the terms *productivity*, *efficiency*, and *capacity*. These terms have similar meanings, but markedly different distinctions:

Productivity. In addition to the previous definitions, productivity can also be defined and expressed as the amount of output per unit input. The term *productivity* is normally used in the context of human beings who are performing work. Productivity is also used in reference to one type of homogeneous activity. A person's productivity depends on the activity and the working conditions. Productivity lends itself to improvement by using better methods, tools, and techniques, but without the addition of more workstations.

Efficiency. Efficiency is output divided by input and is expressed as a percentage. The term *efficiency* is normally used in the context of a process or machinery. For example, the efficiency of fuel in generating heat, the efficiency of a machine, or the efficiency of peer review processes.

Capacity. Capacity is the throughput of a system. For example, a car factory produces 5000 cars per day. The term *capacity* assumes that several disparate activities with varying rates of achievement are being performed within the system. Capacity therefore accounts for the final output of multiple heterogeneous activities. Capacity is also used in reference to an entity, such as an automobile manufacturing plant or a software project team. The capacity of a facility or plant is designed before the facility or plant is actually set up. Once a specific capacity has been designed and built, increasing the capacity is not possible without adding new workstations, changing the efficiency of the machines or processes, or increasing productivity.

The software development industry is obsessed with giving a single, empirical, all-activities-encompassing figure for productivity. Attempts are made to express productivity numerically, e.g., 10 person-hours per function point, with a rider that this number (figure) could vary from 2 to 135 person-hours, depending on the product's size and other factors. Sometimes ranges are given, such as 15 to 30 hours per use case point. At other times, empirical formulas are used that depend on a set of factors such as those used in the COCOMO (constructive cost model) method of software estimation. These productivity figures lump all software development activities (i.e., requirements analysis, design, coding, review, testing, etc.) into a single measure. But in reality, the skill requirements for each of these activities are different, the tools used are different, the inputs are different, and the outputs are different. Therefore, combining all of them under a single head of "software development" and giving a single figure of productivity can at best offer only a rough estimate — never an accurate one.

Currently focus in the software industry is on *macro* productivity (which is really capacity), using a single figure to represent the productivity of all of the activities of software development. This approach needs to change. Focus needs to shift from macro to *micro* productivity, using a figure for each specific activity involved in developing software. To achieve this, we either modify our timesheets (if we use empirical methods to determine productivity) or we have industrial engineers arrive at the productivity for each activity of the tasks that lend themselves to this level of measurement. The benefits of productivity at a micro level include:

- Better predictability of software development (because the effort for each specialized activity is separately estimated)
- More accurate estimates for pricing assistance during project acquisition and sanction stages
- More precise target-setting when assigning work
- More accurate cost estimation
- Better prediction of skill and resource requirements
- More precise variance analysis (which can lead to process improvement and establishment of productivity norms)

STANDARD TIME AND PRODUCTIVITY

The American Institute of Industrial Engineering (AIIE) defines standard time as *the amount of time taken to accomplish a unit of work performed using a given method under defined working conditions by a qualified worker after adjustment at a pace that can be maintained day after day without any harmful physical effects.* Needless to say, standard time is the unit of measure for productivity. The key terms and phrases in the AIIE definition include:

- *Unit of work*: The amount of work is in its smallest possible size (which implies that there must be an accepted unit of measure for the work for which productivity is being defined).
- *Given method*: The method of performing the work must be defined and the person performing the work must adhere to that definition in letter and in spirit.
- *Qualified worker*: The person performing the work has the knowledge and skills to carry out the work (either by certification or by training).
- *After adjustment*: The qualified worker is not performing the work for the first time (i.e., he/she has put in some amount of time in the organization and has adjusted to the work environment and the methods of working).
- *At a pace that can be maintained day after day*: The pace must be such that it can be achieved every day and will not affect the person's health in any manner (physical or psychological).

An analogy for pace. Consider this illustrative analogy. The Olympic record for the 100-meter dash is between 9 and 10 seconds. But the Olympic record for the marathon, 26 miles or 42 kilometers, is disproportionately longer than what would be obtained mathematically by using the Olympic record for the 100-meter dash in calculations. But an average person is not an Olympian, so in this context, the pace of working is the pace of a normal person (an average person) who is running a marathon race, not that of an Olympic champion running a 100-meter dash.

We have now defined productivity (using standard time), but we still need to consider the aspect of an organization having personnel with a mix of skill levels. *Maynard's Industrial Engineering Handbook* defines five skill levels:[1]

- *Super skill*: a person who has extensive experience and who knows all there is to know about the work, including all the best practices and all the shortcuts (This person is an authority who can guide others on the subject.)
- *Very good skill*: a person who has a lot of experience and who has learned all there is to learn about the work, but who perhaps has not personally applied all of this knowledge (This person knows all the best practices and most of the shortcuts and can guide others on the subject.)
- *Good skill*: a person who has adequate experience and is capable of delivering results, but who perhaps needs to refer to documents or seek guidance from senior colleagues in advanced aspects of the work (This person does the work, but may not be able to guide others.)
- *Fair skill*: a person who is not a trainee and who has some experience, but who needs reference documents or assistance from senior colleagues to complete the work (This person needs occasional guidance.)
- *Poor skill*: a person who is a new entrant and who has not completed a formal training period in the organization (This person needs continuous guidance from senior colleagues.)

Another aspect we need to consider is the level of effort put into performing the task:[1]

- *Super effort*: no trial and error, not a second lost, all available time used, allowed breaks not taken, all effort focused on the task
- *Very good effort*: no trial and error, very effective use of time, all allowed breaks not taken, all effort focused on the task
- *Good effort*: very little trial and error, uses time fully, takes only allowed breaks, all effort focused on the task
- *Fair effort*: some trial and error, uses most of the available time, takes all allowed breaks, most effort focused on the task

- *Poor effort*: keen to experiment, uses as much of the available time as possible, takes all allowed breaks and more, all effort not focused on the task

As you have no doubt deciphered, the output of a person with super skill, but who is putting in poor effort, may be equal to that of a person who has poor skill, but is putting in super effort.

Remembering our Olympian analogy, *productivity* is defined based on a person of good skill level who is putting in good effort — an average person. Organizations have a mix of workers with different skill levels, however, which raises three questions:

- *As advocated, if productivity is defined based on an average person, how do we reconcile the output of a super-skilled person and a poor-skilled person?* Obviously the productivity of a super-skilled person is much higher, but at a higher cost than that of poor-skilled person. So, our expectation is that the costs will be different for people of different skills. We use an "average person" as the basis for estimating, but during execution, target setting will be commensurate with the skill levels of the persons to whom the tasks are entrusted.

- *A mix of skill levels results in the actual time varying from the estimated time, right?* Absolutely! But in large projects, the combination of mixed skill levels and mixed effort levels tends to average out. So, the overall actual time to complete the tasks required for the project should come very close to the estimated time. (And, of course, the skill level is only one source of variance between the estimated values and actual values.)

- *So, how does resource allocation occur if resource estimation is performed using the parameters of average skill and average effort, knowing that the organization has a mix of resources?* Resource allocation is not just making the requested number of resources available. For example, when an SPM makes a request for ten software engineers, the request typically means ten resources of average skill. But if we allocate super-skilled resources, we will not need to allocate ten of them (unless ten super-skilled resources have been specifically requested). Similarly, if we allocate all poor-skilled resources, we will need to allocate more than ten. When resources possess different skill levels, the person in charge of allocating resources to projects needs to ensure that a project has an *equivalent* of the requested number of average skilled persons. To accomplish equivalent allocation effectively, an organization should maintain conversion rates for converting one level of skill to another level (e.g., one super-skilled person is equal to three poor-skilled persons).

Table D.1. Conversion Rates for Skill Levels

Skill Level	Conversion Rate
Super	2
Very good	1.5
Good	1
Fair	0.60
Poor	0.50

Table D.2. Example of Resource Allocation Using Conversion Rates

Skill Level	Number of Resources Actually Allocated	Equivalent Number of Average-Skilled Resources
Super	2	4
Very good	2	3
Good	1	1
Poor	4	2
Total allocated	7	10

An example. Suppose an SPM has requested ten resources from the development pool. The person allocating the resources would use conversion rates (as shown in Table D.1) to ensure that an equivalent of ten average (good) skilled resources is allocated to the project). An allocation can be any combination of skill levels (as shown in Table D.2). (Note that sometimes an allocation plan will require an absolute number of physical resources due to the multithreading of the work. This requirement must be communicated to the appropriate person if the SPM is not allocating resources himself/herself.) As can be seen in Table D.2, even though the actual number of resources allocated is seven, the allocation meets the *equivalent* requirement of the SPM.

Concerning the effort per day or per period expended, all resources are expected to put in average level of effort. Therefore the onus of the SPM is to ensure that all resources expend the level of effort required of them. If the SPM can find ways to motivate the team to expend more than an average level of effort, the project will be completed before its scheduled date. Conversely, if the SPM fails to ensure that everyone on the team expends an average level of effort, the project will be completed later than its scheduled date.

THE PRODUCTIVITY PATH

Remember from our earlier discussions that software development involves (but is not limited to) the following activities:

- Preproject activities
  - Feasibility study (proposal in the case of external projects)
  - Financial budgeting and approvals for the project (negotiations in the case of external projects)
  - Approvals, both financial and technical (receipt of purchase order in the case of external projects)
  - Project go-ahead decision (project initiation in the case of external projects)
- Project start-up activities
  - Identification of the project manager
  - Allocation of the project team
  - Setting up of the development environment
  - Project planning
  - Setting up of various protocols
  - Service level agreements and progress reporting formalities
  - Project-related training
- Software engineering activities
  - User requirements analysis
  - Software requirements analysis
  - Software design
  - Coding and unit testing
  - Testing (integration, functional, negative, system, and acceptance)
  - Preparation of the build and documentation
- Rollout activities
  - Installation of the hardware and system software
  - Setting up of the database
  - Installation of the application software
  - Pilot runs
  - User training
  - Parallel runs
  - Rollover
- Project cleanup activities
  - Documentation of good and bad practices
  - Project postmortem
  - Archiving of records

- Releasing of resources
- Releasing of the SPM to enable him/her to take up another project
- Initiation of software maintenance

Industry "rules of thumb" for productivity are not clear as to how many of these software development activities are included in the productivity figure. Rules of thumb are good to help confirm assumptions and paradigms, but they are not exact tools. So, do not stake your career on a productivity figure that is an industry rule of thumb!

Let's draw a parallel between software development activities and the manufacturing industry. The following activities (tasks) are involved (in order) in the activity of punching a hole in a steel sheet:

1. Set up machine
2. Set up tool
3. Load job
4. Punch hole
5. Deburr hole
6. Clean up
7. Deliver work piece to next operation

If multiple holes are punched, the time to complete Activity 4 will be a multiple of the number of holes to be punched: the number of holes punched is multiplied by the time per hole. The times for the other activities remains unaltered because these activities are one-time activities.

If we take the task of coding a unit (under "software engineering activities" in our list of software development activities), micro activities could involve:

1. Receiving instructions
2. Studying the design document
3. Coding the unit
4. Testing and debugging the unit for functionality
5. Testing and debugging the unit for unintended usage
6. Deleting trash code from the unit
7. Regression testing the unit
8. Releasing the unit for the next step

Similarly, we can have micro activities for each software development phase.

CLASSIFICATION OF SOFTWARE DEVELOPMENT ACTIVITIES

The major classes of software development work include:

- *Requirements analysis*: involves understanding what the user needs, wants, and expects and then documenting this information so that the software designers can understand and design a system in strict conformance with them (Requirements analysis depends greatly on external factors.)
- *Software design*: involves considering the alternatives available for hardware, system software, and development platforms; arriving at the optimal configuration; designing an architecture that will meet the stated requirements and fulfill expectations, yet be feasible with the current technologies; and documenting the design in such a way that the programmers understand and can deliver a product that conforms to the original user specifications (Because several alternatives are possible, software design is a strategic activity. Errors made during software design have strategic consequences.)
- *Construction*: involves developing software code that conforms to the design and is as defect-free as possible
- *Reviews of requirements, design, and code*: involves walking through the requirements, design, and code developed by another person; deciphering the functionality; and unearthing any possible defects
- *Testing*: involves trying to unearth all defects remaining in the software (An accepted fact is that 100% testing, or testing for every eventuality, is just not practical.)
- *Build preparation*: involves linking all of the components into one software product and preparing the product for rollout (Depending on specific project, multitiered software and architectures can cause this stage to become a major specialist activity in itself.)
- *Documentation*: includes user guides, operation manuals, user training materials, and troubleshooting manuals (Developing this level of documentation for a new application can be a major activity in large projects. Many organizations employ specialist technical writers for this task.)

When considering the variety in the nature of these activities, it soon becomes obvious that the productivity of the activities cannot be uniform: the pace of work is different for each of these activities and the activities depend on the amount of software code produced as well as on other factors such as:

- Requirements analysis depends on the efficiency and clarity of the source of requirements, such as users or documentation.

- Software design depends on the complexity of processing, alternatives available, and constraints within which the functionality is to be realized.
- Code review depends on the style of coding.
- Testing depends on the density of residual defects: the more defects found, the more time required to test and retest.
- Coding depends on the quality of the software design.
- Build preparation depends on the number of tiers and components in the software architecture.
- Documentation depends on the size of functionality achieved by the software product.

Having separate productivity figures for each of these activities is therefore only logical.

SO, HOW DO WE ARRIVE AT PRODUCTIVITY?

Productivity (standard time) can be determined in two distinct ways: empirical methods and work measurement.

Empirical Methods

Empirical methods involve collecting actual data from a large number of projects and then computing an average productivity (statistical mean, mode, or median) and a standard deviation. The software industry, to a large extent, follows the empirical methods technique.

A reliable and easily obtained source of credible data is the historical data from timesheets, provided timesheets have been filled out accurately and diligently. Most timesheet software used in the industry is oriented toward payroll and billing, however, rather than toward capturing data at the micro level so that it can be used to arrive at productivity figures. In addition to date and time, most timesheets only capture data at two or three levels: the project level is always the first level; the second and third levels are either at the module and component levels, the component and activity levels, or some other similar combination. But to derive reliable productivity figures, timesheets need to capture data from five levels: project, module, component, development phase, and task accomplished. These levels are in addition to the date and time for each employee. If timesheets supply such information, the "right" data will be available for establishing productivity data empirically and in a realistic manner.

A word of caution. Our observation is that some individuals in the software development industry perceive the term *average* to mean *arithmetic mean*. The drawback with the arithmetic mean is that it is influenced by extreme values (values which result from extreme circumstances). Using the arithmetic mean produces skewed results. The *statistical mode* is a better measure to use to arrive at average productivity because the statistical mode is the most frequently occurring value in a population and therefore is not influenced by extreme values. A matter of concern is that after nearly three decades of intense software development activity, no universally accepted norms have been established for arriving at productivity in the software development field. The result is that software development is poorly managed and costs more for the end-users.

A recommendation. If empirical methods are selected to arrive at productivity, use the statistical mode, not the arithmetic mean, to arrive at an average. The nature of the statistical mode, i.e., of not being influenced by extreme values, allows for better accuracy within the software development environment.

Work Measurement

In the early 1980s, the International Labour Organization (Geneva) released the *Compendium for Professional Workers*, adding a third category to the organizational workforce: the professional worker (the original two categories being workers and management).[2] This compendium treated software developers as professional workers. Although the ILO compendium separated programmers from management, providing them with certain benefits and facilities enjoyed by other workers, it did not suggest methods for measuring their work as it did for other workers. The premise was that programmers' work is creative and therefore cannot be measured. (*Note*: This premise is true when the programming work performed by a programmer is not mechanistic and the programmer does not work with the assistance of a design document. It is not true, however, when software developers are working in a contract development scenario. These developers work with defined user requirements and a design document. In this case the work is mechanistic and cannot be described as creative by any stretch of the imagination.)

Work measurement involves defining the unit of measure for the work and setting the standard time required to perform it. The ILO has approved a few methods for this activity, including:

- Time study
- Motion study
- Therbligs
- Synthesis
- Analytical estimation
- Work sampling

The method most often associated with work measurement is the *time and motion study*. Although time and motion study techniques are commonly used in the manufacturing industry, using them in the software industry is not feasible. Factory workers do not sit in cubicle. Supervisors in factories can scan each workstation from his or her location to ensure that work is being carried out. In the software industry, this type of supervision is impossible. In many cases, all a supervisor can see is that the programmers are in their cubicles staring intently at their screens with brief periods when their fingers fly across the keyboards. Most programmers do work productively, but sometimes a programmer:

- Sends personal emails
- Surfs the Internet
- Chats with an online friend
- Prepares his/her résumé for submission to a recruiter
- Does some similar type of non-work-related activity

Not all of these activities are necessarily bad. Substantial literature suggests that some level of personal or non-work-related activity actually increases productivity and creativity.

In the past, white-collar productivity was thought to be unmeasurable, but it is now, and norms for office-type work have been established. Using work measurement techniques is now possible in the software industry. So, should productivity norms be set for every programming language used in the software development industry?

In the software industry, common understanding is that programming languages differ vastly from one another. The productivity of programming in different languages is also thought to vary vastly. This thinking, however, is a myth. Let's look at some facts:

- All programming languages have facilities for input, output, and data manipulation functions as well as other miscellaneous functions. Although the syntax and semantics vary, the philosophy remains the same: to achieve the given functionality with a defined quality in the minimum amount of time. (Before you protest, one of the authors has programmed in many languages and makes this statement from personal experience.)
- Software is written by programmers who are proficient in the language being used and with the help of a design document.
- Although the work is not purely mechanical and repetitive, because programmers write programs with the help of a design document (just as factory workers use a drawing to perform their work), very little creativity is involved (similar to the scenario in job-order manufacturing, such as ship building, air craft manufacturing, construction, etc.).

Another myth is that some programming languages are more complex than others. For example, COBOL language has been called "top of the line" in the past (we've actually heard that), but now, after the turn of the century, this same COBOL language is considered to be "bottom of the line." Pascal, C, dBase III Plus, Oracle, and VB have gone through a similar journey. Programming language is always complex when it is new. Few teachers are available for a new programming language. Programmers therefore have to educate themselves so they can master and write code in the new language — a tedious task. But as time elapses, the new language becomes manageable and actually easy to master. As more teachers and experts become available, programmers are able to more easily learn the language, get help when they are stuck, and master the language.

For Java programmers, Dot Net is complex (and vice versa!), but by its general nature, no programming language is any more or less complex than another. So, where does the myth that some languages are more difficult than others spring from? (Perhaps it is from the programmers who have spent a considerable amount of time learning a new language on their own and therefore believe that they deserve a premium!) The difficulty associated with a programming language is more about learning and mastering the language, than using it. Another difficulty is that many organizations have a shortage of programmers who are skilled in a particular new language (or programmers are unavailable).

A programmer might also say that more time is required to produce 100 LOC (lines of code) in Java than in Dot Net, but why? Because Java requires more characters per line to achieve a given functionality than Dot Net does? Or because the programmer is not as well versed in Java as he is in Dot Net? If a programmer says that Dot Net takes more lines to achieve a given functionality than Java, this statement might be accurate (and suitable for testing), but more than likely the same amount of time will be taken to produce the same number of LOCs, irrespective of the programming language. We base this statement based on the following assumptions:

- Dot Net and Java programmers have similar skills (proficiency) in their respective languages.
- Dot Net and Java programmers are assisted by similar design documents.
- Dot Net and Java programmers type characters at a similar speed.

So, what might the limiting factor be? Could it be typing speed? A speed of 10,000 keystrokes per hour is the accepted norm for data entry operators, which is comparable to a typing speed of approximately 35 words per minute (with each word assumed to have five characters on average). In typewriting and stenography circles, however, 35 words a minute is considered "lower." (Stenography circles classify typewriting speeds as either lower, i.e., 35 words per minute, or higher, i.e., 45 words per minute. Typewriting and shorthand "species," of course, are more or less extinct today after being very common just 25 years ago!) So, perhaps the problem is that not very many programmers practice typewriting. (Typewriting courses are not part of a software engineering curriculum, although in our opinion they should be because software engineers spend their most of their lives punching keys and their speed is approximately 15 words per minute!)

Using the work measurement technique for factory workers, we prefix and suffix two activities to the actual work when measuring work:

- Setup time (pre-work) or the time taken for receiving instructions, collecting information, and studying the information to understand it
- Cleanup time (post-work) or the time taken for delivering the output, clarifying any issues, and handing over the artifacts

Carrying out time studies to set standard time (productivity) for a good number of software development activities is both feasible and possible.

How to Conduct a Time Study in a Software Development Organization

The technique of work sampling can be used to conduct productivity studies in a software development organization. Work sampling involves observing employees at work without causing any interference and recording how much time they spend on various activities — productive and nonproductive activities. Nonproductive activities (e.g., personal matters, meetings, etc.) are usually classified into various categories for analysis purposes. Then productive time is separated from the time spent on nonproductive activities and set as the *basic time*. Basic time is then corrected using the "rate (pace) of working," which is a percentage of "normal working" (an average level of effort by a person of an average level of skill). Consider two examples of established benchmarks in which the rate of working is considered to be 100% if:

- Hand movements compare well with the motions of dealing cards when 52 cards are dealt in a minute in a game of bridge.
- When walking, the walking rate is 3 miles per hour

From these examples, we can easily see that having a rate of working that is more than 100% is possible for some people.

Basic time, after correction using the rate of working, is called the *normal time*. We add a relaxation allowance based on factors defined by the ILO to obtain the *standard time*.

Stopwatches are used for time studies in factories (because the operations often take only minutes). Ordinary watches, however, are adequate for carrying out work sampling for software development activities. Work measurement can be carried out and productivity norms set for all of the seven types of software development activities that have been described earlier in this chapter.

CAPACITY VIS-À-VIS PRODUCTIVITY

As stated at the beginning of this appendix, our opinion is that some in the software development industry confuse the terms *capacity* and *productivity*. When dealing with the *overall throughput* for a facility, we use the term *capacity*, e.g., we say that an automotive plant has a capacity of 5000 cars per day or that a shipyard has a capacity of 10 ships per year. *Capacity* implies that various activities are performed at different workstations, that each activity may need different skill sets from the staff, and that each worker might have a different productivity (or rate of achievement). *Capacity* can also refer to the overall output from a facility. In other words, capacity can be a certain number of units per a defined time period. For example, in an automotive plant or a shipyard, the workflow is routed through different workstations. Some workers at their workstations take more time to complete their assigned operations than workers at other workstations do. In this situation, the workstations taking more time are considered fully utilized and the remaining workstations are considered to be underutilized and to have spare capacity. The capacity of a plant is therefore limited by the fully utilized workstations. Thus, to increase capacity (to produce more automobiles), the plant needs to add only those workstations that are fully utilized.

So, if an automotive plant has 500 persons working (or 500 person-days of effort) to produce 5,000 cars per day, and production needs to be increased to 10,000 cars per day, the required manpower and workstations would *not* double. Why? Because, some spare capacity already exists in the plant. We just need to add machines and persons as required after considering each workstation and the number of units that it can produce. This process of increasing the capacity to produce more units is an exercise called "line balancing" and "capacity planning." Therefore, less than 1,000 person-days of effort are required to produce 10,000 cars. We also cannot say that because 500 person-days are spent to produce 5000 cars per day that 1 person-day produces 10 cars. Why? The production depends not just on the person, but also on the machinery and the tools used.

Capacity is finite at each workstation irrespective of utilization. Think of a car with five seats. The car always has five seats: if only one seat is occupied by the driver or if all five seats are occupied. Similarly, a plant is designed for a certain capacity. But producing less than the designed capacity increases cost per unit. Well understood and accepted is that some amount of "waste" is built into the production system. (Capacity planning is an altogether different subject that is beyond the scope of this book.) So, in software development, we need to design a facility for a specified capacity and then populate it with personnel to fill the required roles (e.g., with architects, designers, business analysts, programmers, testers, etc.) to achieve the capacity goals of the organization.

To develop (produce) software, the skill sets previously mentioned in this appendix are needed. In practice, we can allocate a person for a minimum period, but we cannot allocate a person, say a designer, for eight different activities in a day without impacting his effectiveness and efficiency as well as his motivation.

DETERMINING PRODUCTIVITY

Our recommendation is to set up productivity norms using work sampling techniques, a method that produces a fair result, a result that is arrived at through scientific study by unbiased, independent experts. Setting norms from past project records requires accepting data without knowing the causes for the pace of working (be it slow, average, or fast), which could result in having skewed norms. Using skewed norms is not fair to programmers or to the organization. Conducting time studies to set standard time is also fair to staff and to the organization because time studies set the "right" expectations and predictability for human endeavors and work results.

REFERENCES

1. Kjell Zandin, Editor-in-Chief. *Maynard's Industrial Engineering Handbook, Fifth Edition* 2001. New York: McGraw-Hill Professional.

2. http://www.ilo.org/public/english/bureau/dgo/.

APPENDIX E

ISSUE RESOLUTION IN SOFTWARE PROJECT MANAGEMENT

WHAT IS AN ISSUE?

The word *issue* has multiple meanings in a dictionary, ranging from a *topic* to a *subject*, a *problem*, or a *concern* as well as several others. For this appendix, the word *issue* indicates a *concern* or a *problem*. So, why is the word *issue* used? Why not just use the word *problem* or *concern*? The answer is because during software project execution, we sometimes encounter a situation that might not be a problem or a concern. Instead, the situation requires focus and resolution from various agencies other than the project management team. Consider these scenarios:

- During requirements specification, the end user (or the customer) held one or more requirements as a TBD (to be decided later).
- During the course of project execution, the project team found that one requirement (or more) was unclear, ambiguous, or open to multiple interpretations. To obtain the correct interpretation, all unclear requirements need clarification.
- During the course of project execution, the project team found that it may be unable to implement one requirement (or more) fully (or perhaps even partially). A concession is therefore needed from the end user or customer concerning alternatives for implementing the requirement(s) in question.
- Some approvals or reviews needed from the end user/customer did not take place or the results of discussions have not been received by the project team.

Situations such as these are not problems (yet), but they need resolution before they do become problems. These scenarios are known as *issues* in software project management parlance.

THE ISSUE-RESOLUTION PROCESS

Often heard are simplistic statements such as: "If you have an issue, pick up the telephone and make a call. Don't make it so bureaucratic." If a single telephone call can solve all of the issues, excellent. In small projects, or even when the number of issues is limited, those approaches are indeed adequate. (In the agile approach, co-location of a customer allows more opportunities for interaction using simple person-to-person approaches that are adequate for issue resolution.) But when a situation becomes even somewhat complicated, "things can fall apart."

Many attributes can complicate a project's environment: the project is large, the duration of execution is relatively long, too many TBDs, etc. Complications associated with attributes such as these tend to require a more formal approach for adequately tracking all of the issues to resolution. Our opinion is that generally a process-oriented approach is necessary for effective issue resolution. Consider this scenario: a customer/end user needs to consult their project team because the true decision-makers are waiting for another vendor to come up with the specifications for a particular component. In this case, the issue has to be kept pending because its resolution is awaiting action from the other vender. If not recorded, the issue could be forgotten until it becomes a more significant problem. This scenario provides just one of the reasons why a procedure or a process is needed for issue and resolution tracking. Issue resolution has three components:

- *An issue register*: a place where all issues can be recorded and exchanged between the project team and the end user/customer
- *A communication vehicle*: to be used to assist resolving issues (in addition to an issue register, emails, teleconferences, video conferences, and face-to-face meetings)
- *An escalation mechanism*: to be used to provide an escalation mechanism to raise the level of visibility of an issue when a resolution is either not forthcoming or if the resolution offered is not practical or satisfactory

Let's now discuss these components.

An Issue Register

Often an issue register is maintained using a spreadsheet (e.g., such as can be generated in Excel or by some other software tool). This register contains numerous

Table E.1. Sample Issue Register Format

Issue ID	Issue Category	Reported by (Name)	Priority	Description of Issue	Date Originally Reported	Closing Date (Project Team)	Assigned to (Project Team)

Solution by (Name)	Client Comments/ Reply	Project Team Comments/ Reply	Final Status Closed/ Open (Client)	Date Closed (Client)	Status (Project Team)	Remarks/ Attachments

types of information: the issue ID number, an issue description, the date that the issue was raised, the name of the person raising the issue, the category defined for the issue, a description of the resolution date on which the resolution was provided, the status of the issue (open or closed), the date on which the issue is closed, and any other information that a particular organization may need to manage issues.

When an issue is discovered by the project team, the issue should be recorded in the issue register. The register is sent to the customer as a communication vehicle for issue resolution whenever a new issue arises (or periodically if real-time communication is not possible). The customer then records a resolution to the issue raised and sends the register back to the project team, usually within one business day (particularly for issues developed by the project team). If the end-user or customer has any issues from their side, these issues may also be recorded in the register. The project team will then record resolutions against the issues raised by the customer. Only one copy (in addition to backups) of the register is maintained. At any given time, control of the register is either with the project team or the end user/customer. As execution progresses, issues in the register will move to "closed" status. A recommended format for an issue register is illustrated in Table E.1.

Communication for Resolving Issues

Sometimes, the description of a resolution issue is large enough to warrant a separate document. If so, a reference to the document is recorded in the issue register.

The document itself is archived by the project team. If feasible, the document should be embedded in the register itself. Sometimes a discussion is needed:

- To explain the resolution in greater detail
- To elicit details about an ambiguous definition of the issue
- For "thinking out loud" between both parties about the possible alternatives/approaches to resolve the issue

If discussion is needed, holding a teleconference or a videoconference may be very useful. Many tools (e.g., Skype, Dimdim, Webex, Centra, etc.) are available for conducting conferences in a very cost-effective manner. We strongly recommend capturing meeting minutes and either archiving them or embedding them in the register.

If a discussion is needed, the person who raised the issue begins the process by explaining the issue and its impact on the project. If a straightforward resolution is possible, the resolution is explained and discussed among the concerned parties. If alternative solutions are possible, each solution is discussed and the optimum solution is selected. If a resolution is not possible during the meeting, the estimated resolution date for the issue is recorded along with the name of the person who is responsible for resolving the issue. Several aspects should be described when documenting a resolution:

- An explanation (with elaboration) of the issue resolution provided earlier in the register if requested by the originator of the issue
- Additional explanation (with elaboration) of the issue if requested by the person resolving the issue
- Any issues encountered in implementing the resolution as originally described
- A discussion of the various alternative solutions that are available for the issue
- Status of the resolution

Record all discussions in the meeting minutes (MM; also MOM, minutes of the meeting). The MM must also contain the person responsible for the issue resolution as well as the target date for the resolution and any other information discussed. Update all resolutions arrived at during the discussion in the issue register.

The Escalation Mechanism

Sometimes a project team or a customer needs to escalate an issue(s). Scenarios that could necessitate an escalation of issues include:

- A customer or end user thinks that the project is tardy and that their entreaties are falling on deaf ears.

- A customer or end user thinks that a crucial requirement is not being implemented by the project team due to some technical reason.
- Project team members think that approvals are not being given in a timely manner and therefore are hampering progress.
- Project team members think that a customer or end user is insisting on an immediate implementation of the requirements that could hamper the project's progress (this situation would not be possible in an agile project).

An escalation mechanism defines:

1. Name of the person (with contact details) for the first level of escalation (The first level of escalation is typically to a person concerned with the project who is one level above the concerned parties.)
2. Name of the person or persons (with contact details) for further levels of escalation if needed (Further levels of escalation are normally to a senior level of management that is concerned with the project.)
3. A final decision-maker if a conflict occurs that needs to be recorded
4. A description of the circumstances under which escalation can be invoked (These circumstances can be triggered if one of the parties is causing unreasonable delays or unreasonably holding to a stated position without giving consideration to the other party's limitations.)
5. The communication process for escalation, including the means of communication (e.g., a telephone call, email, a template or format, etc.)
6. Approvals required for escalation (if necessary)

The software project management plan (SPMP) contains a section on escalation mechanisms. All escalations have the potential to damage relations between the project team and the customer. Escalation therefore must not be undertaken (or resorted to) frivolously. No escalation should be made until very careful consideration has been given to the situation. Concurrence from senior management must also be obtained. Escalations by the project team are frowned upon. Escalations by a customer, however, are likely to occur more frequently, something that can perhaps be avoided through tactics such as co-location.

A project's SPM should continuously monitor customer satisfaction with all pending issues and take any actions necessary to prevent a customer from becoming dissatisfied. When a customer does escalate an issue, action must be taken. (Remember that an issue can be escalated not only to the persons mentioned in the SPMP, but also to marketing, the person who is handling the CRM functions in the organization, senior management, and even top management.) Escalations cause disturbances in an organization and raise doubts about an SPM's ability to ensure customer satisfaction. Remember the adage about prevention: "an ounce of prevention is worth a pound of cure."

Should an escalation take place, an SPM needs to be prepared to satisfactorily resolve the issue: first internally and then with the customer. When an escalation from a customer occurs, senior management typically asks for an explanation. (*Note*: If you suspect that escalation of an issue is imminent, obtaining buy-in from senior management will be helpful. So, whenever an issue cannot be resolved to the satisfaction of the customer, promptly escalate the issue internally to senior management. Senior management will then be prepared to make a proper response if the customer ultimately escalates the issue to a higher level.) We recommend providing the following information to senior management:

- Reasons for the issue
- Efforts taken to resolve the issue
- Present status of the issue-resolution process
- Barriers to meeting the customer's expectations for resolving the issue
- Possible alternative solutions for resolving the issue as well as the concomitant merits and demerits
- The optimum solution in the SPM's opinion

When supplying information to senior management, focus on the issue. Avoid bringing personalities into any discussion. The goal is to provide senior management with information that will facilitate gaining an understanding of the issue from an accurate perspective. Having knowledge helps senior management to deal with an escalation in a way that arrives at an amicable resolution of the issue for all.

Issue escalation occurs during project execution even when all reasonable efforts have been made to maintain friendly relations with a customer. Recognizing that escalations do take place and having mechanisms in place to handle them successfully helps ensure that escalation issues will have better resolutions rather than damaging customer relationships.

Status Reporting for Issue Resolution

A summary of the status of issues is usually a part of a project progress report (weekly or monthly). The total number of issues raised, the number of issues resolved, and the total number of open issues should be reported in the project progress report. Issue status should also be reviewed and monitored along with other aspects of the project during project progress-monitoring sessions.

Some final words about issue resolution. Issues are part and parcel of software project execution. Under even the best of circumstances, issues will occur during project execution, and some of them will be escalated to senior management. Organizations and project teams must therefore plan for issue resolution by including the proper methodology for resolution in the SPMP. Having a defined process for issue resolution is essential. A defined process ensures that there is uniformity in handling issues across the organization. A defined process also ensures that as issues are raised, they will be recorded and tracked to closure. As much as possible, however, foresee the potential for an issue to occur and take steps to prevent escalation of the issue by a customer (or vice versa). When escalation does take place, handle it promptly and carefully with the objective of arriving at an amicable resolution.

APPENDIX F

MEASUREMENT AND METRICS IN SOFTWARE DEVELOPMENT ORGANIZATIONS

INTRODUCTION

A diligent measurement process and metrics program goes a long way in understanding an organization's health and in determining whether the organization's management of software development is effective or not. The ISO 9000 Series of Standards and CMMI (Capabilities Maturity Model Integration of the Software Engineering Institute of Carnegie Melon Institute, U.S.) emphasize measurement and make measurement mandatory for achieving certification of (or achievement of) a higher level of maturity. This appendix will shed some light on the metrics used in the software development industry, with specific focus on software project management.

Change in the information technology arena is happening at phenomenal speed. By the time a baseline is established, a newer technology is established. So, the available baselines become indicators of past achievements, but they are not useful for predicting future performance.

The software development world does not have a standards organization, which is unfortunate because other industry segments have organized to form industry associations to generate standards and then to generally encourage compliance with those standards. Our opinion is that not coming together and failing to standardize are unique to the software development industry. Part of the issue may be that intellectual property rights legislation and legal actions are more prolific (and more serious) in the software industry than in any other. Have you ever heard of a copyright suit because a new car looks like an existing car? Yet, in the software industry, examples of litigation equivalent to that include dBase going to court against FoxBase alleging copyright violation and Lotus 123 going court against VP Planner for the same reason. The lack of a single industry standard makes measuring the efficacy of software development essential within each organization. (There is hope that organizations such as SPIN, the Software Process Improvement Network, and SPMN, the Software Project Managers Network, will help support standardization and encourage the use of standards.)

MEASUREMENT AND METRICS: THE PRESENT SCENARIO

The ISO 9000 Series of Standards stipulates measurement and metrics as being mandatory. The SEI stipulates that measurement and metrics are part of their CMM (Capability Maturity Model) and their CMMI (CMM Integration) that came later. Unless measurement and metrics are ingrained into the organization, Level 4 of CMM could not be achieved. IEEE Standards 982.1, 982.2, 1045, and 1061 and SEI's handbook[1] set the guidelines for measurement in software development organizations.

Most organizations, however, do have a department dedicated to collating and analyzing metrics. Some organizations delegate this responsibility to their quality department; others vest it in their PMOs. These departments collate metrics from the reports of the SPMs, maintain them in a repository, and analyze and present them to their respective managements as well as to external assessment/certifying/auditing agencies.

Every organization has its own "cadence" for discussing metrics. In many organizations, quarterly metrics reviews are held; in other organizations, reviews are bimonthly. The reviews are typically part of a management review meeting (also known by many other names). During the meeting, the department in charge of maintaining the metrics repository presents the metrics. The metrics analysis is then discussed and decisions are made so that preventive action can be taken.

Project-level metrics. Project-specific metrics are reported by SPMs (manually or in an automated manner), using reporting vehicles such as weekly or monthly status reports. In some organizations, only a monthly metrics report is collected from SPMs. SPMs compute productivity metrics, taking effort and size data from their work allocation and management systems. Quality defects are computed utilizing data from peer reviews, testing, and defect reports from clients. (Many organizations have defect reporting and management systems in place that are used to automatically generate defect/quality metrics reporting.)

Schedule metrics are computed using data from project schedules (planned and actual).

Organizational-level metrics. At the organizational level, computing a single metric for productivity is elusive because of the wide mix of platforms used to meet the needs of clients that is coupled with a fast-changing technological environment. And generally, organizations do not specialize in only one technology.

In most organizations, spreadsheets (and in some cases automated tools) are used for capturing measurement data and computing metrics. Although once rare, comprehensive tools for process measurement are now becoming much more common. Among other reasons for using spreadsheets extensively, two reasons are because only a few "right" tools are available and the cost of available tools is very high. As a result, in many organizations, the process of collating, computing, and analysis of metrics is largely manual or the tools are self-developed.

CLASSIFYING METRICS

In the software development industry, metrics basically fall into five categories:

- Productivity metrics
- Quality (defect) metrics
- Schedule metrics
- Effort metrics
- Resource utilization metrics

Let's now discuss each one of these categories in greater detail.

Productivity Metrics

Appendix D provided a discussion of the concept of productivity for SPMs. Appendix D should therefore be reviewed before proceeding with this section. Productivity metrics assist us:

- During the project acquisition stage to estimate the effort needed for cost estimation
- During the project planning stage to estimate the resources needed for the project, for scheduling the project, and for making delivery commitments
- In setting targets for people when allocating work
- In assessing the performance of resources and the fair dispensation of rewards
- In performing benchmarking with other projects within the organization or with other organizations

Productivity metrics are therefore important metrics used and derived during project execution. To derive productivity metrics we need data:

- The size of the work package
- The effort in person-days

Size. The concept of sizing conceptual items such as software elicits significant confusion and passion. LOC (lines of code) has been a classic measure of size, but lack of universal acceptance of LOC on the treatment of inline documentation and the possibility of the same functionality being achievable in lesser or more numbers of lines have made use of LOC contentious. The advent of GUIs (graphical user interfaces), RDBMS (relational database management system), and multitier architectures have changed the paradigm of software development: size does not entirely depend on LOC alone and software does not lend itself to easy counting. Other popular measures of software size include function points, object points, software size units, story points, and use case points:

- *Function points*: As a size measure, function points have the largest following and are the easiest to derive, but as with all things, function points have critics.
- *Object points*: As a size measure, object points have not attained the level of acceptance of function points, although object points are a very good measure for determining software size.
- *Software size units*: SSUs are relatively new and yet to find roots.
- *Story points*: Story points are also new and used in agile project estimation. A commonly accepted methodology does not yet exist.
- *Use case points*: Use case points are also a good measure of size, particularly when use case and RUP (Rational Unified Process) methodologies are adopted.

As software developers and scientists look for better methods to size software, other size measures will likely evolve. Currently, all in all, there does not appear to be a single, universally acceptable size measure for the size of software to be developed. Our recommendation is that every organization should standardize a software size measure for the organization and then use it across all of its projects. Other size measures could be used if necessary, but a conversion factor can be developed and used to convert software size into the organization's standard size measure. No matter what size measure is accepted, having a formal work allocation process in place is necessary to obtain the size of the software to be developed.

Effort. To get effort in person-days, a robust time recording process needs to be in place. The time accounting process needs to capture time at the source. All team members must therefore diligently record the details of the time spent —

down to the level of developmental phases and tasks. Several productivity metrics can be derived:

- *Gross productivity for an entire project*: The gross productivity metric includes all project activities, including requirements analysis, software design, construction, and testing. The size of the delivered software product is used to produce all of these measures. Size measures recommended for use in determining gross productivity are function points, use case points, object points, software size units (SSUs), or some similar measure. We can also derive productivity as person-hours per size measure, which assists us in software estimation for projects and to benchmark the project against other projects.

- *Requirements analysis productivity for a project*: The requirements analysis metric includes all activities in requirements analysis, including interviewing of executives, requirements gathering from secondary sources of information, preparation of documentation, and peer review. We can use the delivered software product size to derive productivity, the number of requirements, or the number of pages of the requirements document. If we use *the size of the software product*, we recommend using one of the functional measures: function points, use case points, object points, or SSUs. If we use (as some organizations do) *the number of requirements* as a size measure, use the finally approved requirements as the size and derive productivity in terms of person-hours per requirement. Probable, however, is that all requirements will not be of the same size. We might therefore have to normalize requirements using a normalization factor. For example, if we use the number of pages of the requirements document, we can derive the requirements analysis productivity as person-hours per page. (Productivity increases the more verbose a writer is!)

- *Software design productivity for a project*: The software design productivity metric includes all activities needed to convert the project requirements into artifacts that can be used for the construction of the software product. We can derive a gross productivity for the entire design activity or derive two metrics: one for the high-level design (also known as software requirements specification, functional design specification, software architecture, etc.) and another for the low-level design (also known as software design description, detailed design specification, program specifications, etc.) productivity. The gross productivity figure assists in determining software estimation. High-level and low-level design metrics (requirements analysis productivity and software design productivity) assist us in target setting and performance assessment. We can use either the delivered software product size or the number of pages of software design documents. Thus, we can derive software design productivity as person-hours per unit size measure or person-hours per page of software design documents.

- *Construction productivity for a project*: We can also derive gross productivity for the entire construction activity, including all activities such as table scripts, stored procedures (triggers, PL/SQL code segments, macros, and the list goes on), graphics, the code of different programming languages used in the project, and the build routines (make files). In the case of gross productivity derivation, we can use the size of the delivered software product. This gross productivity figure assists in software estimation for project acquisition and project planning. We can also derive productivity for each of the individual construction activities just mentioned by using the size measure appropriate for each activity. However, we will face challenges in measuring the size of GUI screens, the graphics used in Web pages, and reports developed using report-generator tools. Graphics are largely in the creativity arena and therefore depend on the graphic itself and the graphic artist. For screens, we can use the number of normalized controls used in the screen. We can take a text box as the base measure and normalize all other controls into text boxes, using a conversion figure for each set of controls. We might need to develop norms for such conversion figures at the organizational level for this purpose. For reports, we might need to use data items included on the report, including derived fields, control statistics, parameter fields, etc. We recommend using LOC as the size measure for programs (table scripts, stored procedures, triggers, programs, PL/SQL code segments, macros, etc.).

- *Testing productivity for the project*: We also need to derive productivity for each type of testing. Deriving gross productivity for the entire testing process will not yield a correct understanding because testing strategy differs from project to project (including the type of testing, the number of tests, regression testing strategy, and who conducts the tests, etc.). We recommend deriving productivity for unit testing, integration testing, system testing, and acceptance testing in the minimum. We can then use the number of test cases, test points, or software test units as the size measure for deriving the testing productivity. Testing productivity can be derived as person-hours per test case, person-hours per test point, or person-hours per software test unit using this data. (*Note*: Another book by Murali Chemuturi contains a detailed explanation of test effort estimation and productivity.[2])

For all of the productivity metrics just described, the formula for productivity is *productivity = size ÷ number of person hours*. The metrics for each project are derived periodically and reported to the PMO, quality department, or entity that is vested with the function of maintaining the organization's metrics repository. These metrics are used to compile the productivity metrics and to derive the organization's capability baseline. This baseline must be updated periodically in conformance with the organization's metrics process.

Quality Metrics

Quality metrics indicate the "state of quality" of software being developed in an organization. Quality metrics are derived from the number of defects "trapped" during software development as well as the number of delivered defects (usually defects that have been delivered to the customer). To get accurate data for computing quality metrics, a defect management process should be in place. The defect management process should include a formal recording of reported defects and a mechanism to track them through resolution. To be most effective, the defect management process should be developed and set at the organizational level. To be complete, the process needs to include defect reporting, defect analysis, defect resolution, defect resolution review, defect testing, and defect analysis functions. A range of quality metrics can be computed:

- *Defect density*: Defect density is a definition of the quality of the software developed in any organization. One method of computing defect density is using the *delivered defects*. Delivered defects are the residual defects remaining in a software product after all of the planned quality assurance activities have been performed and after the software product has been delivered to a customer. We more or less universally accept that some defects will lurk in software — even after extensive quality assurance procedures. (Organizations that achieve a six-sigma level of quality will still have three defects per one million opportunities.) So, to compute the defect density metric, we use the delivered software product size and the number of defects reported after delivery to the customer. (Here, *delivery* means the product has been placed in the hands of the customer.) Other versions of the defect density metric use the number of defects uncovered during other testing and review activities (which are viewed as *process* metrics). The size of software can be stated in LOC, function points, use case points, object points, or SSUs. The number of defects is taken from defect reports. The formula for computing defect density is *number of defects ÷ software size* and is expressed as one defect per unit of size. Should we include all defects irrespective of whether they are critical, major, or minor in nature? The answer is that different organizations take different stands. But one thing is certain: a defect, even if minor in nature, is still a defect. (Would you accept a new shirt from a vendor if it has a tiny hole in the tail — even if that part of the shirt could be tucked inside your pants when you wear the shirt?)

- *Defect injection rate*: In computations, the defect injection rate is similar to defect density except that the defect injection rate takes into consideration all of the defects uncovered during in-house quality assurance activities as well as those reported by the customer. The defect injection rate metric defines the ability of the organization's resources to produce quality software in the first iteration. The formula for computing the defect injection rate is *number of defects ÷ software size*, with the result being expressed a one defect per unit of software.

- *Defect removal efficiency*: The defect removal efficiency metric indicates the efficacy of the quality assurance activities being conducted in an organization. Although defect removal efficiency is computed for each quality assurance activity conducted in the organization, defect removal efficiency is generally computed and discussed at an organization level. The formula for computing this metric is *defects uncovered in the QA activity ÷ total defects uncovered in the software product in the subsequent QA activities*, with the result expressed as a percentage.

- *Cost of quality assurance*: Cost of quality assurance is computed as a percentage. The formula is *person hours spent on carrying out QA activities ÷ total person hours spent on software development, including QA*, with the result expressed as a percentage. Note that cost of QA can be computed using costs rather than effort, albeit using person-hours eliminates the impact of inflation, etc. during year-on-year comparison. The person-hours spent on QA do not include the person-hours spent on fixing defects. The person-hours spent include all of the effort spent on QA activities such as peer reviews and all types of testing (including regression testing). A trend analysis of the cost of QA can indicate whether a development process is improving or deteriorating. If the software development process is improving, the cost of QA should be declining. If the cost of QA is increasing, however, the indications are that the development process has problems that need attention.

- *Cost per defect*: Another important metric is cost per defect. The formula for cost per defect is *total person hours spent on uncovering defects and fixing them ÷ total number of defects uncovered*, with the

Table F.1. Interpretation of Defect Density and Defect Injection Rate

Defect Density	DIR	Inference	Necessary Action
High	High	Software development and QA activities are inefficient.	Improve software development and QA activities.
Low	Low	Software development and QA activities are efficient.	Maintain the status quo (the ideal scenario).
High	Low	Software development activities are efficient. QA activities are not as efficient as development activities. The organization is not spending adequate effort on QA activities.	Improve QA activities or processes and other relevant aspects.
Low	High	The organization is spending more effort on QA activities. QA activities are more efficient than development activities. Software development activities are not efficient.	Improve software development process, activities, and other relevant aspects to reduce the DIR.

result expressed as person-hours per defect (again this metric can be computed using cost, albeit using person-hours eliminates the impact of inflation, etc. during year-to-year comparison). Person-hours spent on uncovering and fixing defects includes all QA activities, including peer reviews, all types of testing, analyzing the defects, fixing the defects, peer review of the defect fixes, and regression testing of the defect fixes. The cost per defect metric can be computed periodically as well as at the end of a project. Trend analysis of the cost per defect metric is useful in gaining insight into the waste caused by defects during project execution. Costs that show an increasing trend suggest that the software development teams are not performing quality work.

From defect density and the defect injection rate, we can infer the capabilities of the development teams as well as the QA functions of the organization. Table F.1 illustrates some of the inferences that can be drawn from defect density and the defect injection rate.

Schedule Metrics

Schedule metrics provide information about an organization's capability to meet deadlines, carry out work, and conform to a preset schedule. Deriving accurate schedule metrics requires a number of processes to be in place, including planning, change management, and time recording processes. The planning process provides the scheduled dates, the change management process delivers information about changes in functionality and schedules, and the time recording process delivers actual dates. Schedule metrics are computed from this data. We also compute the metrics of schedule variance (SVM) and schedule conformance capability (SCCM) using this information. The formula for deriving the SVM is *number of days taken for delivery ÷ number of days originally scheduled for the delivery*, with the result expressed as a percentage. The formula for computing SCCM is *number of total schedules met ÷ total number of schedules*, with the result also expressed as a percentage. We recommend that the following schedule metrics be computed:

- *Schedule variance metric*: When multiple deliveries are to be made to a customer, the SVM for deliveries is calculated for each delivery. We recommend computing SVM for each delivery because any delay in delivery adversely affects customer satisfaction.

- *Schedule conformance capability metric*: The SCCM is calculated when multiple deliveries are effected to a customer. The formula is *number of deliveries effected within the schedule ÷ total number of deliveries effected*, with the result expressed as a percentage. In addition to providing information about the organization's ability to conform to delivery schedules, the SCCM also indicates the capability of an SPM to meet the schedules (and therefore can facilitate improved performance by SPMs). SCCM should be computed at multiple levels, including the organizational, project, and SPM levels, to better understand the ability to make deliveries on time.

- *Schedule variance metric for phase completion*: The SVM for phase completion is computed to show the schedule variance for completing various software development phases, e.g., requirements analysis, software design, construction, and testing. Trend analysis at the organizational level can detect if any phases are consistently not meeting the schedule. Organizational weaknesses at the phase level are revealed, which provides an opportunity to improve organizational capabilities.

- *Schedule conformance capability metric for phase completion*: The SCCM for phase completion is computed by phase at the organizational level. SCCM is computed for each software development phase. The formula is *number of times the phase was completed within schedule ÷ total number of times the phase was performed in the organization*, with the result expressed as a percentage. SCCM is computed periodically on completed phases. Combining the SCCM for phase completion with trend analysis allows the detection of organizational weaknesses in the performance of individual phases of software development — knowledge that permits an opportunity to improve organizational capabilities.

- *Schedule conformance capability metric for team members*: Based on data obtained about how team members are meeting the targets set for each allocation, the SCCM for each team member can be computed as work is allocated to them and they subsequently complete it. The formula used is *number of times schedule was met ÷ total number of allocations*, with the result expressed as a percentage. SCCM provides an insight into a team member's capability to meet the schedule. Combining the SCCM for team members with the defect injection rate and effort variance metrics provides an objective view of a team member's strengths and weaknesses. Analysis of the results of the SCCM for team members allows determination of the type of training a team member needs as well as effecting improvement of the team member's capabilities.

- *Schedule conformance capability metric for the project*: The SCCM for the project is a metric that provides important insight into why a delay in project completion occurred. The SCCM for the project provides insight into the question: was the delay due to an overriding cause or was it due to an overall delay in every activity? An overall delay in every activity (or most) could be due to poor planning or poor control during project execution. The formula for SCCM for the project is *total number of activities completed within schedule ÷ total number of activities performed in the project*, with the result expressed as a percentage. Table F.2 illustrates the inferences to be drawn from the SCCM for the project. An SCCM above 95% is considered to be high (and low otherwise).

Effort Metrics

Effort metrics are concerned with the efficacy of effort estimation as well as how effort is spent in an organization. Effort metrics tend to focus on the variance between the estimated effort and the actual effort spent on the activities and the relationship of the effort spent on various software development phases. Effort variance metrics allow drawing inferences about the efficacy of software estimation, estimation norms, and the effort control activities during project execution. Relative effort metrics tell us about the relative importance being placed on the various software development phases — which permits detection of too much effort being spent on any one phase (or phases). For example, the effort metric

Table F.2. Inferences from the SCCM Metric for the Project

SCCM	Project Completion	Inference	Necessary Action
High	On schedule	No concerns	No special action except analyzing the activities that could not meet the schedule
High	Overshot schedule	Could be a special cause; or a few activities could have caused the delay	Investigate the special cause for the delay or the activity that caused the delay and take corrective action
Low	On schedule	Possible only when a short cut is resorted to or overtime working is done during the final days	Investigate how the situation became possible and take necessary corrective action
Low	Overshot schedule	To be expected; also indicates poor progress monitoring	Investigate the reasons for not meeting the schedule (e.g., poor planning or poor control during execution) and take necessary corrective action

might reveal that most of the effort in projects is being spent on construction and that the requirements analysis and software design phases are being neglected. When anomalies such as these are uncovered, they can then be corrected. The recommended effort metrics for projects as well as organizations include:

- *Effort variance metric*: The EVM is generally computed for the entire project: for each software development phase and for each relevant work allocation. In all cases, the formula is *actual effort spent – estimated effort) ÷ estimated effort*, with the result expressed as a percentage. Effort can be measured in person-hours or person-days. *Project-level* EVM facilitates trend analysis at the organizational level to detect trends that can be used to take the necessary corrective actions. *Phase-level* EVM facilitates trend analysis and also uncovers tardy phases. For instance, if we were to discover that the same phase is consuming more effort than estimated in multiple projects, a root cause analysis could be conducted and necessary corrective actions could be put in place to prevent recurrence. *Work allocation-level* EVM facilitates uncovering chronic overshooting of estimated effort by resources. Work allocation-level analysis also facilitates uncovering specific types of activity that are repeatedly overshooting the estimated effort. The answer may be that the estimation norms are erroneous or the methods of performing the specific activity need improvement. Whatever the cause, these metrics help uncover problems and provide opportunities for improvement.

Table F.3. Correlation Analysis between Relative Effort Metric and Defects Traceable to Requirements Analysis

Project	REM of Requirements Analysis (%)	Number of Defects Traceable to Requirements Analysis
Project A	20	2
Project B	15	4
Project C	22	1
Project D	12	3
Project E	16	3
Note: Correlation coefficient is (–)0.822 (using CORREL function of MS Excel).		

- *Relative effort metric:* The REM is computed at the project level and at the organizational level. The REM facilitates the evaluation of effort spent on a particular software development phase vis-à-vis the value of that phase to the project. Obviously, effort spent on a particular software development phase should be commensurate with its value to the project. The REM can help us determine if we are effectively expending effort or wasting it. The formula for REM is *effort spent on a software development phase ÷ total effort spent on the project*, with the result expressed as percentage. Effort may be measured in person-hours or person-days. At an organizational level, REM provides a view of the activity that is receiving the most attention. The REM also indicates if effort is being spent in a balanced manner. If the REM indicates that effort is being spent in a lop-sided manner, the necessary corrective actions can be taken to rectify the situation. A correlation analysis of the REM with defect origins may reveal the reasons for defects in a software product. To elaborate a little more, consider the correlation between the REM of requirements analysis and the defects that originate in requirements analysis (i.e., are traceable to), which are shown in Table F.3.

Notice the very high negative correlation between columns two and three in Table F.3. From Table F.3, we can safely draw an inference: as we spend more relative effort on requirements analysis, the defects traceable to requirements analysis decrease. A positive correlation between two variables means that the dependent variable will increase (or decrease) with any increase (or decrease) in the base variable. A negative correlation means the dependent variable decreases (or increases) with an increase (or decrease) in the base variable. A positive correlation shows a direct proportion and a negative correlation shows an inverse proportion type of relationship between both sets of values. Remember another thing: correlation does not infer causality.

Resource Utilization Metrics

The resource utilization metric (RUM) provides data about the effectiveness of resource utilization. The RUM is computed in terms of revenue-earning and nonrevenue-earning activities as well as a gainfully employed resource or an idle resource.

Revenue-earning. The formula for computing the RUM for revenue earning is *person hours spent on revenue earning activities ÷ total person hours available*, with the result being expressed as a percentage. The RUM for revenue-earning activities provides a view of the extent of utilization of resources on internal activities. In all organizations, a certain amount of resource time needs to be spent on nonrevenue-earning activities, e.g., process definition and improvement, receiving and giving training, assisting the organization's HR department in recruitment activities, and assisting marketing in project acquisition (to name only a few).

Gainful utilization. The formula for RUM for gainful utilization is *person hours utilized on gainful work ÷ total person hours*, with the result being expressed as a percentage. Obtaining the accurate RUM for gainful utilization requires encouraging resources to book their idle time factually. Although allocated to projects, resources may need to be idle due to a host of reasons, e.g., waiting for inputs, approvals, or clarifications being a few. If the extent of idleness is known, corrective actions may be put in place to minimize such idleness.

Nonrevenue-earning. All time spent on nonrevenue-earning activities affects the profitability of an organization. RUMs give us a sense of whether (or not) revenue is being lost due to resource utilization gaps. If an increase in resource utilization for nonrevenue-earning activities is due to a lack of work, the focus should be on project acquisition. If projects are pending, however, and the time utilized for nonrevenue-earning activities is high, people should be shifted from nonrevenue-earning activities to revenue-earning activities. When the gap widens, we can correct the situation and increase utilization of resources on revenue-earning activities. Using the RUM as barometer can influence the bottom line positively.

WHEN TO DERIVE METRICS

Metrics are derived at the project level by the SPM and then collated at the organizational level. In many organizations, the QA department or the PMO is vested with the responsibility for deriving and maintaining organizational metrics. All metrics are to be maintained in an organization's metrics repository, which should be part of the organization's knowledge repository, or a repository for metrics alone.

Computing all of these metrics will consume a significant amount of time. Computing metrics every week and making them part of the weekly status report can place a considerable amount of overhead on an SPM. We recommend therefore that SPMs derive all metrics once a month and then report them in a separate metrics report. We also recommend finding automation tools to support the process.

PROCESSES CRITICAL TO AN EFFECTIVE METRICS PROGRAM

Our opinion is that for a metrics program to be effective, five organizational processes are critical. When these five processes (or groups of processes) are in place, a metrics program will enable organizations to derive the benefits of numeric or quantitative management:

- *Software estimation is a critical process for the metrics program*: If software estimation is conducted by conforming to a defined process, using organizational baselines for productivity, the estimation process is amenable to improvement. Many organizations, however, carry out ballpark estimation which does not lend itself to variance analysis, productivity computation, and improvement at a granular level. Yet, without having estimated values, variance analysis cannot be performed. Some organizations do not even estimate software size and therefore make deriving productivity impossible.

- *A formal work allocation process and tracking mechanism is essential to make data available in an organization*: A formal work allocation process allows classification of the effort spent on software development phases, peer reviews, various types of tests, and rework (including defect fixing) to name only a few areas of interest. Work allocation provides the information necessary for computing schedule metrics. A work allocation process also permits computation of effort metrics, resource utilization metrics, and schedule metrics at a granular level. Without a formal work allocation process and mechanism to track allocation, this vital data will not be available in an organization and many metrics cannot be computed.

- *Timesheets need to provide relevant data for computing metrics.* In many organizations, timesheets are focused on obtaining payroll data rather than on obtaining information for computing metrics. A timesheet needs to have a depth of seven levels: project, module, component, software development phase, software development task, type of task (fresh construction, change request, or defect fixing), and the date and start/end times for each activity. Having this information will permit the gathering of the data required for computing many metrics. For effort information to be relevant, all time must be recorded.

- *A defined metrics process is necessary to conduct useful metrics analysis*: A formal metrics process defines the metrics to be used in the organization, the procedure for gathering data and computing the metrics, how the metrics will be reported, and derivation of the organizational metrics. Defining how metrics analysis will be performed at the organizational level is also a very important component of the metrics program. By having a defined process, the metrics analysis activity receives an implied high level of importance within the organization, which helps ensure that metrics analysis is performed. Our opinion is that without a defined process, metrics analysis will be performed sporadically.
- *Centralization and control facilitate the effective use of data throughout an organization*: A metrics repository contains all of the metrics derived in the organization. These metrics should be maintained in a single location so that all concerned individuals in the organization can have controlled access to the information to retrieve it when required. Centralization and control facilitate the effective use of organizational data. The metrics repository can be a part of the organizational knowledge repository or a standalone. A repository lends itself to more effective usage when automated using a software interface and the data stored in an RDBMS.

IMPORTANT METRICS ANALYSES

Two basic types of analyses can be conducted on metrics data to aid decision-making: trend analysis and correlation analysis.

Trend Analysis

Trend analysis facilitates the detection of trends. Trend analysis is used for tracking the trends of productivity, defect injection rate, defect removal efficiency, defect density, and relative effort utilization to name a few. Many times trend analysis is a chronology-based analysis, meaning the data is arranged in chronological order and then analyzed (also known as time series analysis).

Table F.4. Defect Injection Rate of Projects

Project	Size (in Function Point)	Defects	DIR (Function Point per One Defect)
Project A	1250	67	18.66
Project B	1500	76	19.74
Project C	2200	111	19.82
Project D	3100	156	19.87
Project E	1100	57	19.30
Project F	4200	211	19.91
Project G	5200	256	20.31

To better understand trend analysis, let's consider an example of trend analysis. The defect injection rate in seven projects is depicted in Table F.4. When we plot this information on a graph, the trend can be seen graphically, as depicted in Figure F.1. As can easily be inferred, the DIR shows an increasing trend. If this trend were occurring in your organization, the scenario would be alarming. At the very least, a closer look at the software development process is required. Trend analysis conducted at the organizational level provides valuable information about the trends occurring in an organization and enables management to put actions in place actions to correct the trend.

Correlation Analysis

We often want to know if software size or team size has an impact on productivity. To determine this, we need to carry out correlation analysis. Correlation analysis allows the determination of whether (or not) a relationship exists between two sets of data, which is particularly helpful in the context of software estimation to establish if any of the following variables impact productivity:

- Software size
- Team size
- Average experience of team members
- Location of work (on-site or at a client's site)
- Programming language

When we establish that a relationship does exist, causal analysis can be used to determine if changes can be made to improve productivity. Correlation has three aspects: positive and negative; simple, partial, and multiple; and linear and nonlinear:

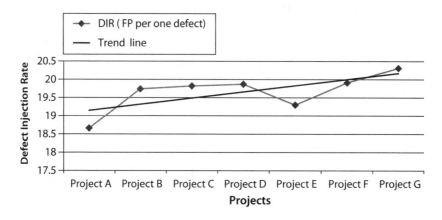

Figure F.1. Trend analysis of defect injection rate.

- Positive and negative correlation:
  - A positive correlation is a *directly* proportional correlation.
  - A negative is correlation is an *inversely* proportional correlation.
- Simple, partial, and multiple correlation:
  - A simple correlation refers to a relationship between *two* variables.
  - A multiple correlation refers to a relationship between *three or more* variables, studied simultaneously.
  - A partial correlation refers to a relationship between three or more variables, but studied between *two* variables, assuming that the other variables remain constant.
- Linear and nonlinear correlation:
  - A linear correlation is when the influence *is based* on a constant ratio.
  - A nonlinear correlation is when the influence *is not based* on a constant ratio.

Microsoft Excel has formulas for computing correlation that can be used directly. Table F.3 shows an example of correlation analysis between REM and the defects traceable to the requirements analysis phase.

Some final words. We have described the most important metrics that are relevant for SPMs at the project level and at the organizational level. IEEE Standards 982.1, 982.2, 1045, 1061, and SEI's guideline[1] provide greater details about of all the metrics that can be derived in software development organizations.

REFERENCES

1. William A. Florac, Robert E. Park, and Anita Carleton. *Practical Software Measurement: Measuring for Process Management and Improvement* 1977. CMU/SEI-97-HB-003. Pittsburgh: Software Engineering Institute/Carnegie Mellon University.
2. Murali Chemuturi. *Software Estimation Best Practices, Tools & Techniques: A Complete Guide for Software Project Estimators* 2009. Ft. Lauderdale: J. Ross Publishing.

APPENDIX G

MEASUREMENT AND MANAGEMENT OF CUSTOMER SATISFACTION

INTRODUCTION

Project-based organizations place a lot of emphasis on customer satisfaction and rightly so. Customer satisfaction is key for improving a company's internal processes in addition to its market reputation, repeat orders, and improved profitability. Customer satisfaction ratings (CSR) are often obtained through using a questionnaire (a customer satisfaction survey or CSS). But determining customer satisfaction in this manner has a drawback: customers are likely to be influenced by their emotions when filling out a CSS questionnaire. Why? The answer is because when filling out a CSS questionnaire, a customer can be extremely pleased about something or just the opposite. Naomi Karten, an expert on the subject of customer satisfaction, confirms this situation when she says, "People tend to rate service higher when delivered by people they like than by people they don't like.[1]" (Karten goes on to describe what one can do to be "likable!") So, more often than not, CSS ratings received from customers represent *perceived* feedback rather than impartial feedback. Sample form elements for a CSS are shown in Figure G.1.

Even with its limitations, a CSS is very important because, ultimately, customer perception is very important. But consider this scenario: often only one person in a customer's organization fills out a CSS, despite the fact that many people in the organization are using the product. When only one person is being surveyed, his expectations can be managed, making generation of the desired rating possible. And if only one person fills out the CSS, and we want all concerned individuals consulted, can we be sure that he actually does consult them before filling out the CSS? Ideally, he should, but more often than not, he will not. Yet, other users of the product may continue to unearth defects (and certainly do) in

---

Name of Organization Executing the Project:

Date:

Project Details:

Details of Person Filling Out Survey:

Instructions for Filling Out Survey:

- Rate each of the services provided using a five-point scale:
  - Quality of deliverables
  - On-schedule deliveries
  - Communication
  - Cooperation
- Elaborate on ratings.

Overall Satisfaction:

Provide Any Project-Related Observations:

Signature:

Name:

Date:

For Internal Use:

1. Received by:
2. Received on:
3. Progress report in which this information is included:

Figure G.1. Elements for a customer satisfaction survey form.

the product. Perhaps some of them are decision-makers. At some point, the person who filled out the CSS form might be shifted to another department or even leave the organization for greener pastures.

So, we recognize that responses to a CSS can be emotionally biased, that perception-based ratings alone cannot be relied upon, and that a customer is not one person, but everyone who is impacted. We also know that gaining an understanding of the true extent of customer satisfaction with the delivered software is important, which gives rise to the need for some way to accurately compute a customer satisfaction rating (CSR) based on internal data — data that is free from bias, accurate data that is available to us, and data that gives a realistic metric for customer satisfaction — in addition to the external perception of the customer.

THE USEFULNESS OF A CUSTOMER SATISFACTION SURVEY RATING

A CSS facilitates management of customer satisfaction by a project team. As already discussed, customer satisfaction management is very important for an organization: a satisfied customer is more likely to give a glowing reference about the capabilities of the organization to prospective customers. Remember a modernized version of a familiar adage: "An ounce of image is worth a pound of performance." If we combine that pound of performance with a "good" image and "wonderful" performance, the organization will go a long way along the road to success.

A good image, however, is inadequate for the long term. To really be successful in the long term, an organization needs to have a strong performance-based reputation — a reputation for efficient and effective project execution and for delivering a quality product. Having long-term success is where measurement of customer satisfaction comes into the picture.

SO, WHY MEASURE CUSTOMER SATISFACTION WITH INTERNAL DATA?

Consider three scenarios:

- *The customer is pragmatic.* He is not swayed by things such as the "recency" factor or the one-incident factor (a one-time occurrence of an unfortunate outcome, e.g., an error that negatively impacts a major function for a customer), prejudices of any kind, poor judgment, or some personal stake. He keeps meticulous project execution records and is an expert data analyst. Although having such a customer may be rare, his rating of customer service is likely to be a true reflection of a vendor's performance.

- *The customer is an average person.* Her rating is influenced by some of the factors in Scenario 1. Now assume that she rates this same vendor's performance as poor. If this low rating (which is biased) were accepted, the personnel in the organization involved in project execution would also receive low ratings as a result. They might, in turn, also receive lower pay increases and bonuses, if any at all — a situation that will lower motivation in these workers — when in fact they actually did a fairly good job and merit a better rating.

- *The customer is an average person.* His rating is influenced by some of the factors in Scenario 1. Assume that he rates this same vendor's performance as excellent. As a result, the personnel involved in the project execution might receive higher pay increases and bonuses, a situation that will further lower the motivation of the personnel in Scenario 2.

Scenarios 2 and 3 illustrate a phenomenon known as "rewarding the underperformers and punishing the better performers," a disastrous situation for any organization. An impact even more disastrous is that the organization does not have a realistic picture of how satisfied its customers really are. In this situation, any efforts to improve customer satisfaction can go in the wrong direction.

CRITICAL ASPECTS OF CUSTOMER SATISFACTION

A method based on five parameters that are critical to customer service can be used to derive a metric for customer service. (*Note*: One of the authors, Murali Chemuturi, developed this method based on internal data from organizations for which he provided consulting services. He developed the method through reverse engineering a vendor-rating metric that manufacturers use to rate their suppliers. He considers these five parameters to be essential for achieving high levels of customer satisfaction.) Each parameter is a *tangible* aspect of customer satisfaction that can be measured objectively:[1]

- *Quality*: Our opinion is that quality is first. The dictum that "customers forget the delays, but not the quality" aptly states the value of quality. Furthermore, customers usually forget everything else if (and only if) the quality delivered is superb.
- *On-time delivery*: Assuming that quality standards are met, nothing is more irritating for a customer than not receiving a delivery on the promised date. If a delivery is late, plans at the customer's end may have to be redrawn, resource allocations may have to be shifted, and subsequent actions may have to be rescheduled, which can cause significant inconvenience for the customer and potentially have a negative monetary impact.
- *Money*: Money in this instance refers to the money that a customer pays. Not uncommon is for escalation clauses to be built into contracts. So, when a vendor chooses to apply an escalation clause and to bill the customer for higher amount, the customer can be greatly impacted and inconvenienced. Often when the cost of a project increases, additional approvals also need to be obtained for the extra amount billed — besides having to answer many questions about the increase in cost. In short, price escalations irritate customers.

- *Issues*: Most projects have issue-resolution mechanisms (i.e., methods to solve problems). Some vendors, in an eagerness to always interpret the specifications accurately (and from fear that they might, in fact, misinterpret the specifications), raise issues in a manner that seems gratuitous. When valid issues are raised, a customer is usually more than willing to resolve them, but if the issues raised are perceived to be trivial, the customer is very likely to become annoyed.
- *Accommodation and cooperation*: Few projects are ever completed without changes being requested by a customer. When a customer requests a change, within reason, a vendor should cooperate with the customer and accommodate the change, implementing the change without postponing delivery and without increasing the price.

RATINGS

Five ratings are also critical to achieving customer satisfaction: quality, delivery schedule, price, issues, and cooperation.

The Quality Rating

No project is ever perfect, and most of the time, defects might not be detectable immediately upon delivery. Usually, a customer's expectation is "zero" defects, but all software quality professionals know that zero defects is rarely achieved. If an acceptable number of defects are detected during the warranty period, however, a customer likely will be happy (or as happy as he can be when a defect is discovered).

Sometimes, a customer specifies an acceptable defect density (the number of defects per number of opportunities for error). At other times, the acceptable defect density is implicit, e.g., when a customer selects a vendor based on their certifications or market reputation because the vendor's reputation alone does not lend itself to direct measurement. Using six-sigma philosophy, however, we can measure and specify the number of expected defects based on the "sigma" level of the vendor organization.

If an organization is at six-sigma level, expected defects from that organization will be three defects for every million opportunities. If the organization is at five-sigma level, expected defects will be three defects for every 100,000 opportunities; at four-sigma level, three defects for every 10,000 opportunities; at three-sigma level, three defects for every 1,000 opportunities. The expected number of defects delivered should be contrasted against the actual number of defects delivered. Usually, defect counting begins during the acceptance testing stage because defects can be discovered by the customer. An accounting of defects continues through the pilot runs, during live or production runs, and throughout the warranty period and afterward.

Defects can be classified in three categories: critical, major, and minor. One suggestion is to only count critical and major defects because minor defects are sometimes merely a difference in perception. For example, something that the customer perceives as a defect may not be considered to be a defect by the vendor.

Defect density is computed as defects per unit size or, conversely, as units of product per one defect. As already discussed, software size is measured as lines of code (LOC), function points (FPs), or some other size measure used in an organization. (What is important here is to select one unit of size and then to use it for all measurements.)

Use the following formula to compute a quality rating (QR) for customer satisfaction:

$$QR = (actual\ defect\ density - accepted\ defect\ density)$$
$$\div\ accepted\ defect\ density$$

If the actual defect density is *less than* the accepted defect density, then the QR metric is negative, meaning customer expectations have been exceeded. If the actual defect density is the *same as* the accepted defect density, then the QR metric is zero and customer expectations have been fully met. If the actual defect density is *more than* the accepted defect density, then the QR metric is positive, meaning customer expectations have not been fully met.

The Delivery Schedule Rating

Not receiving a delivery on the agreed-upon day can be very frustrating. Although the frustration might be eased a bit if the customer is called about the delivery being delayed, frustration will be there just the same. The funny thing is that even if the delay is the result of a change that the customer requested, the late delivery still frustrates the customer. Sometimes the customer seems to be thinking, "Can't they just accommodate this teeny-weeny change without postponing the delivery date? Vendors will take any opportunity they can to delay deliveries!"

On occasion vendors have been known to prefer compromising on quality rather than to delay a delivery. The philosophy these vendors espouse is that it will take the customer some period of time to discover a defect, but it will take no time at all for the customer to "come down heavy" on the vendor if a delivery is not on time. Sometimes, a simple statement can be quite convincing: "Sorry for the defect. Here's the corrected version. In our fervent effort to deliver on time, a defect crept in." Remember that in the long run, customers may forget a delayed delivery, but they will seldom forget poor quality. When asked for references, customers usually highlight the quality a vendor provides over the vendor's timeliness, which is the reason the aspect of the delivery is placed second in importance when determining customer satisfaction.

To compute the delivery rating (DR) metric, we contrast the accepted delivery with the actual delivery. But which date should be used as the accepted delivery date? To compute the highest rating possible for the organization, take the *latest approved* delivery date. To derive a true customer satisfaction rating, take the date that is on the purchase order. Some organizations use both: one for internal purposes and one for external purposes.

Use the following formula for computing a DR for customer satisfaction:

$$DR = (actual\ days\ taken\ for\ delivery - accepted\ days\ for\ delivery) \div accepted\ days\ for\ delivery$$

To determine the *actual days* taken for delivery, use the number of calendar days between the date of the purchase order and the date on which delivery was actually made. To determine the *accepted days* for delivery, use the number of calendar days between the date of the purchase order and the date of delivery specified on the purchase order.

If the actual delivery is made *before* the accepted delivery date, then the DR metric is negative, meaning customer expectations have been exceeded. If actual delivery is made *on* the accepted delivery date, then the DR metric is zero and customer expectations have been fully met. If actual delivery is made *later than* the accepted delivery date, then the DR metric is positive, meaning customer expectations have not been fully met.

The Price Rating

Obviously, no vendor can bill a customer for an amount that was not agreed to by the customer, particularly if the vendor expects his invoice to be paid in full and without issue. But why is the price rating important? Sometimes contracts are drawn up using an hourly rate with a maximum cap amount, which allows some amount of variance on either side. In such cases, the final billed amount can be lower or higher than the specified amount. At other times, e.g., when a price escalation clause is implemented or an additional payment is requested due to a change, negotiation will usually occur before the customer accepts the escalation. The amount accepted by the customer might not be the same as requested by the vendor. Requesting extra payment of money and the resultant negotiations can certainly frustrate customers, particularly if they have not been part of the discussion from the beginning. Whenever a customer has to pay more than the original purchase order amount, the customer can become dissatisfied. (Conversely, a customer is usually pleased when a vendor charges less money than the amount specified on the purchase order and also delivers what was promised!)

To compute the price rating (PR), use the price agreed upon (before taxes) on the original purchase order and the final amount billed. For the PR metric, use the formula for computing customer satisfaction:

$$PR = (actual\ amount\ billed - amount\ on\ the\ purchase\ order)$$
$$\div\ amount\ on\ the\ purchase\ order$$

If the actual amount billed is *less than* the purchase order amount, then the PR metric will be negative, meaning customer expectations have been exceeded. If the actual amount billed is *equal to* the purchase order price, then the PR metric is zero and customer expectations have been fully met. If the actual amount billed is *more than* the purchase order price, then the PR metric is positive, meaning customer expectations have not been fully met.

THE ISSUE RATING

Issues crop up during project execution mainly because the specifications are unclear, understanding of the specifications is lacking, or changes have occurred in business needs. Issues may also occur because of a conflict or an error in the requirements.

When a vendor raises an issue whose origin is attributable to the customer, the customer's satisfaction is not usually affected. The customer's satisfaction is affected, however, if the issues raised are due to the vendor's improper understanding of the requirements when an understanding should have existed. Customers usually expect any shortfall in exhaustive requirements specifications to be bridged by the vendor. Failure to meet a customer's expectations in bridging the gaps in the customer's requirements can cause dissatisfaction.

To compute an issue rating (IR), use the issue density (ID). Although the factor for ID can easily be computed, no standard measure exists for an acceptable ID. To calculate ID, use the number of issues and the software size. Although issues can directly relate to requirements, the number of requirements cannot be used because no common method for defining requirements exists, which means that size and granularity can vary significantly. Thus, ID is computed as follows:

$$ID = number\ of\ issues\ raised \div software\ size$$

Software size can be any software size measure, e.g., LOC or FP. Because no universal measure of ID exists, define an organizational standard and continuously improve it.

The formula for computing the IR component of customer satisfaction is as follows:

$$IR = (actual\ ID - standard\ ID) \div standard\ ID$$

If the actual ID is *less than* the standard ID, then the ID metric is negative, meaning customer expectations have been exceeded. If the actual ID is the *same as* the standard ID, then the ID metric is be zero, suggesting that customer expectations have been met. If the actual ID was *more than* the standard ID, then the ID metric will be positive, meaning customer expectations have not been fully met.

The Cooperation Rating

Most projects will not be completed without a few change requests from the customer. Because change requests are commonly implemented before delivery, how then do change requests rise give rise to customer dissatisfaction? The answer is that change requests cause additional work for a vendor. The impact on the vendor can be felt in two ways: a revised delivery schedule and potentially higher costs. Sometimes, the vendor can absorb both. At other times, the vendor absorbs the impact of the change by reducing their margin, but passes on the impact on the delivery schedule to the customer. In another scenario, the vendor absorbs the impact of the change to the delivery schedule, but passes on the impact on price to the customer. (The vendor may also reject the change request.)

Of course, to be expected is that a customer will be happy when all change requests are accepted, with no impact on the price or the delivery schedule. But because this situation is rarely practical, we compute a cooperation rating (CR) that has a formula:

$$CR = (number\ of\ change\ requests\ received - number\ of\ change\ requests$$
$$implemented\ without\ affecting\ delivery\ date\ or\ price) \div number\ of$$
$$change\ requests\ received$$

If the number of change requests received is the *same as* the number of change requests implemented, without affecting either delivery schedule or price, then the CR metric is zero, meaning customer expectations have been fully met. If the number of change requests received is *greater than* the number of change requests implemented, without affecting either delivery schedule or price, then the CR metric will be positive, meaning customer expectations have not been fully met. In the CR rating, there is no way to exceed customer expectations.

Table G.1. Weights for Ratings

Serial Number	Rating	Weight
1	Quality rating	w1 = 0.30
2	Delivery rating	w2 = 0.30
3	Price rating	w3 = 0.30
4	Issue rating	w4 = 0.05
5	Cooperation rating	w5 = 0.05
		Total weight = 1.00

The Composite Customer Satisfaction Rating

Having computed all of the five ratings that are critical to achieving customer satisfaction, the composite customer satisfaction rating (CCSR) can be computed. Obviously, in achieving customer satisfaction, all five of the ratings do not have the same importance. The ratings also vary from organization to organization, from customer to customer, and from project to project. Some customers may perceive quality as being the most important aspect of a product or a service, while some may perceive delivery as the most important aspect. For others, the highest importance may be placed on price. Given the differences in customer perceptions and preferences, assigning weights to each of the five ratings is necessary to arrive at a reasonably accurate CCSR.

To calculate a meaningful CCSR, the sum of all of the weights must equal 1.00. An example of how weights can be distributed is shown in Table G.1. Use this formula to compute CCSR:

$$CCSR = 5 - (QR \times w1 + DR \times w2 + PR \times w3 + IR \times w4 + CR \times w5)$$

This formula gives the CCSR on a five-point scale. It is possible for the CCSR to be greater than five in some cases. When this happens, customer expectations have been exceeded.

ANALYZING CUSTOMER SATISFACTION

Contrasting the CSS ratings with the CCSR allows organizations to improve their processes. Let's explore three scenarios:

- *Scenario 1*: The internal CCSR is *in agreement* with a CSS rating. The balance between the two metrics indicates that the customer's perception is in sync with the performance delivery and that customer expectations are being managed as they should be. The organization's strengths are equal in service and expectations management, giving a realistic picture to management. In this case, the organization only needs to take corrective action based on a rating that is poor.

- *Scenario 2*: The internal CCSR is *way below* the CSS rating, meaning that the customer's perception of the organization's service is better than the service level actually provided. This result sounds good, but it is of no benefit to the organization. If the organization continues to "sing its own praises" based on the customer's perception that the level of service is high, the organization will head downward. The resources will continue to place emphasis on expectations management rather than on service, thus never improving service. In this case, the resources need training to improve their levels of providing service (and other process changes may be required as well).
- *Scenario 3*: The internal CCSR is *way above* the CSS rating. In this case, the customer's perception of the organization's service is *worse* than the service measurements suggest. This situation suggests that the organization is concentrating on service with little concern for expectations management. The organization may also be neglecting interpersonal relations and communication with the customer. In this case, the resources may need training in expectations management.

There is room in the CCSR method to allow every organization to adapt the method to the organization's specific needs. For example, perhaps some of the five ratings could be dropped, substituted for, or even new categories could be added to suit a specific organization's needs. Our recommendation is to use the CSS and the CCSR to get a correct picture of the organization's level of customer satisfaction. Use them together to bring about improvement.

REFERENCE

1. Naomi Karten. Seminar: *Tales of Whoa and the Psychology of Customer Satisfaction* 2007. Randolph, MA: Karten Associates (www.nkarten.com).

APPENDIX H

AN INTRODUCTION TO PERT/CPM

Project managers have relied on PERT/CPM techniques to plan, schedule, and control projects for the last 60 years. PERT is an acronym for Program Evaluation and Review Technique. CPM is an acronym for Critical Path Method. PERT has its origins in research projects, but was successfully used in the development of the Polaris ballistic missile — a missile that would be launched from beneath the ocean's surface in 1960.[1,2] Owing to the success of the Polaris project, PERT gained popularity and was adopted in project-based manufacturing organizations. CPM had its origins in the construction industry.[3] PERT and CPM came on the scene in a big way after World War II.[4] Over a period of time, project managers have begun to combine the two techniques and use them together (known as PERT/CPM).[5]

A NETWORK DIAGRAM

The backbone of the PERT and CPM techniques is a network diagram. A network diagram graphically represents the relationships between the activities that are needed to execute and complete a project. Traditionally, a network diagram is composed of *events* (also referred to as milestones). An event denotes reaching of a milestone or the completion of an activity. These events are connected by arrows that represent *activities*.

Events. By definition, an event is the culmination of activity. An event does not consume resources. An event (or milestone) also represents a significant point in a project, e.g., the completion of a set of activities. In classic network diagrams, an event is represented by a circle.

Activities. An activity is the smallest unit of productive effort that can be planned, scheduled, and controlled. Activities are also referred to as tasks. An activity consumes resources: time, money, material, equipment, and information. In classic network diagrams, an activity is represented by an arrow. In more modern

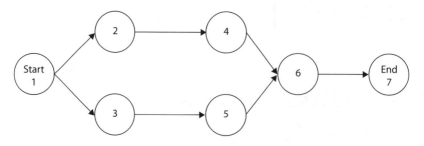

Figure H.1. The traditional network diagram.

network diagrams, an activity is represented by a circle or some other shape. In these diagrams, arrows are used to represent *precedence* relationships.

In a diagram, the entire network is embedded between two events: the *Start* event and the *End* event. The Start event signifies the start of the project; the End event signifies completion of the project. A traditional network diagram is shown in Figure H.1.

In Figure H.1, the circles represent events. In common usage, these circles are also referred to as *nodes*. Nodes are numbered, but they can also be named. The activities are represented by arrows and are referred by the predecessor event and the successor event. In Figure H.1, the activities are 1–2, 1–3, 2–4, 3–5, 4–6, 5–6, and 6–7.

With the passage of time, the orientation of network diagrams changed from event-oriented to activity-oriented. This activity orientation has shifted how activities are now represented (i.e., the circle in a modern network diagram). The arrows now represent the relationship between activities. Activity-oriented network diagrams are referred to as activity on node (AON) network diagrams or precedence network diagrams. Precedence network diagrams are predominantly used today. An AON network diagram is depicted in Figure H2.

CONSTRUCTION OF A NETWORK DIAGRAM

Develop the Work Breakdown Structure

The first step in constructing a network diagram is to develop the work breakdown structure (WBS) for the project. A WBS is a functional breakdown (or decomposition) of the project into successive levels of activities that need to be performed in order to complete the project. We will use a Start-End or End-Start approach to constructing a network diagram. In a Start-End approach, the steps include:

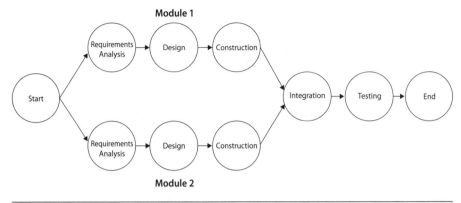

Figure H.2. An activity on node network diagram.

1. Enumerating all activities that are to be performed to begin the project
2. Enumerating all activities that are to be performed upon completion of the initial activities
3. Enumerating the next level of activities that are to be performed
4. Iterating Step 3 until all activities have been defined
5. A final listing of all activities (When all activities have been listed, the WBS is ready.)

This stepwise approach can be visualized as an upright triangle as shown in Figure H3.

The End-Start approach to building a WBS is exactly the opposite of the Start-End approach. The steps in an End-Start approach include:

1. Enumerating the last and final activities that need to be performed before completing the project
2. Enumerating the activities that need to be performed to enable beginning the last set of activities
3. Enumerating the activities that need to be performed to begin the next preceding set of activities
4. Iterating Step 3 until we reach a stage in which no previous set of activities exists (i.e., as long we can foresee the previous set of activities to be performed)
5. A finished WBS

This stepwise approach can be visualized as an inverted triangle as shown in Figure H4.

Once all activities have been identified, we establish the precedence relationships between the activities in the WBS. Remember that performing some

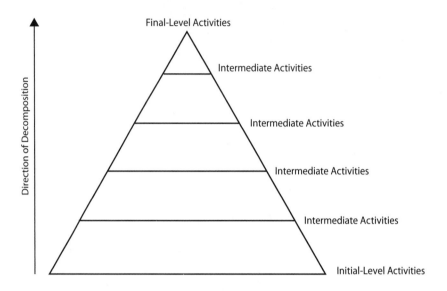

Figure H.3. The Start-End approach to a work breakdown structure.

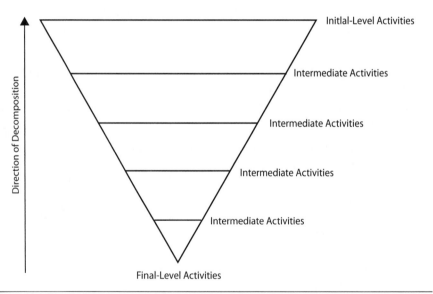

Figure H.4. The End-Start approach to a work breakdown structure.

Table H.1. Example of a Work Breakdown Structure

Activity ID	Activity Description	Predecessors	Successors
1	Start	None	1. Requirements analysis of Module 1 2. Requirements analysis of Module 2
2	Requirements analysis of Module 1	Start	Design of Module 1
3	Design of Module 1	Requirements analysis of Module 1	Construction of Module 1
4	Construction of Module 1	Design of Module 1	Integration
5	Requirements analysis of Module 2	Start	Design of Module 2
6	Design of Module 2	Requirements analysis of Module 2	Construction of Module 2
7	Construction of Module 2	Design of Module 2	Integration
8	Integration	1. Construction of Module 1 2. Construction of Module 2	Testing
9	Testing	Integration	End
10	End	Testing	None

activities in parallel with each other (concurrently) is possible and also that some activities have to be performed in sequence with each other activity (one after the other). In the diagram shown in Figure H2, the Module 1 and Module 2 activities can be performed concurrently, but Integration and Testing activities need to be performed in sequence. In other words, Testing can only be started after completion of the Integration activity. As an illustration, let's build a WBS that would generate the network diagram shown in Figure H2. This WBS is shown in Table H1.

Using the WBS in Table H.1, we can draw the network diagram shown in Figure H2. The following guidelines are helpful when drawing a network diagram:

1. Draw the Start node at the left-most place.
2. Add nodes to the right of the first node until the diagram is completed.
3. Number the nodes for easy identification/reference purposes, incrementing the node numbers from left to right and from top to bottom.
4. Do not cross the arrows unless doing so is unavoidable (shown in Figure H5).

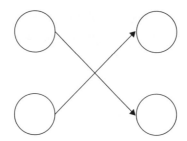

Figure H.5. Avoid crossing arrows in network diagrams.

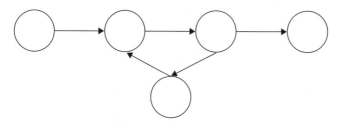

Figure H.6. Avoid loops in network diagrams.

5. Avoid loops in the network diagram (shown in Figure H6).
6. Distinguish each level of concurrent activities and draw the network diagram in tiers.
7. Allow no dangling activities. (Allowing no dangling activities means that every activity, with the exception of the Start and the End, should have a minimum of one predecessor and a minimum of one successor.)

Estimate the Duration for Each Activity

The next step in the PERT process is estimation of the duration for each of the activities. PERT recognizes the uncertainty inherent in estimation. PERT recommends estimating three values of duration for each activity:

- *Optimistic time*: Optimistic time (t_o) is the best-case-scenario duration: an expert performs the activity, all resources are available on time, no unforeseen incidents cause delays, etc. Optimistic time is the shortest duration in which an activity can be completed.
- *Pessimistic time*: Pessimistic time (t_p) is the worst-case-scenario duration: a novice performs the activity, all possible delays occur, resource availability is delayed, etc. Pessimistic time is the longest duration needed to complete an activity.

Table H.2. Data for Estimated Durations for Activities in Figure H.2

Activity ID	Activity Description	Optimistic Time	Pessimistic Time	Most Likely Time	Expected Time
1	Start	0	0	0	0
2	Requirements analysis of Module 1	4	8	6	6
3	Design of Module 1	5	11	8	8
4	Construction of Module 1	10	16	13	13
5	Requirements analysis of Module 2	3	7	5	5
6	Design of Module 2	4	10	7	7
7	Construction of Module 2	10	18	14	14
8	Integration	5	9	7	7
9	Testing	3	5	4	4
10	End	0	0	0	0

- *Most likely time*: Most likely time (t_m) is a normal-case-scenario duration: a person with average skills performs the operation, some delays occur, most resources are available on time, etc. Most likely time is the duration that will usually take place to complete an activity.

From these three duration values, the expected time (t_e) can be computed using a formula:

$$t_e = (t_o + 4t_m + t_p)/6$$

Table H.2 shows an example of computations of the expected times for the activities of the network diagram shown in Figure H.2.

Now let's calculate the duration required to complete the project. We compute this value using the t_e or the expected times of each activity. We do this from the network diagram shown in Figure H2. We place the values for Start and Finish near the node (shown in Figure H.7).

In Figure H.7, ES represents the earliest Start, which signifies the day on which the activity can begin, as counted from the first day on which the project began. EF represents earliest Finish time and signifies the day on which the activity can earliest finish, as calculated from the day on which the project began.

ES is computed as the earliest Finish day of the preceding activity. For example, the activity of design of Module 1 can be started on day 6. Day 6 is the day on which the preceding activity of Requirements analysis for Module 1 finishes. Now consider the Integration activity, which has two preceding activities: the construction of Module 1 and the construction of Module 2. Construction of

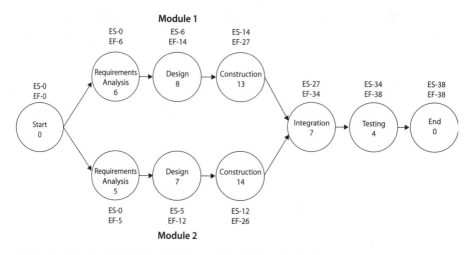

Figure H.7. Forward pass: a network diagram with earliest Start and Finish values for each activity.

Module 1 finishes on day 27, whereas the construction of Module 2 finishes on day 26. The Integration activity can therefore start only on day 27. Therefore, the rule for computing the ES for an activity is the last finish time of all of its predecessor activities. The rule for computing the EF for an activity is simply the ES of the activity plus its duration.

The method of computing project duration that we have just described is referred to as *forward pass* or the earliest time computation. Based on this computation, the End activity finishes on day 38, which is the earliest duration for the project completion.

We can now compute the durations for the activities by beginning from the End activity backward until we reach the Start activity. We compute the latest times for all the activities coming backward from the End activity to the Start activity. This method is referred to as *backward pass* (shown in Figure H.8).

In Figure H.8, LS represents the latest Start time for an activity. LS is the time at which an activity must start so that the successor activity will not be delayed. LF represents the latest Finish time for the activity.

To compute the latest times, we begin at the End activity and work backward. So, for the Testing activity, the LF should be day 38 so that the End activity is not delayed. The LS for the Testing activity is (LF – duration) or day 34. We work backward in this manner and compute the latest times for all activities.

The difference between the earliest time and the latest time for an activity is known as *slack* or *float*. For example, for the Design activity of Module 2, the ES is 5 and the LS is 6 (alternately, EF is 12 and LF is 13). Therefore, the slack for that

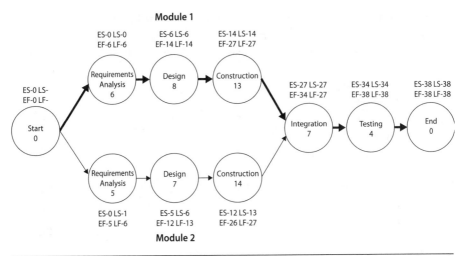

Figure H.8. Backward pass: a network diagram with the latest Start and Finish values for each activity.

activity is 1 (or 13 – 12). Slack is the amount of time by which the activity could be delayed without delaying its successor activities.

Notice in Figure H.8 that some activities have slack and some do not. Activities that have no slack are known as *critical* activities. Critical activities are those activities that are vital to the timely completion of the project. Any delay in completing a critical activity will directly and proportionately delay the project's completion.

The path from the Start activity to the End activity, which is connected by all of the critical activities, is known as the *critical path*. In a network diagram, all critical activities are normally connected by a red arrow. Notice in Figure H.8 that the critical activities are connected by a thicker line. To arrive at the duration of the project, simply sum up the duration of each of the activities on the critical path.

The critical path can also be derived by using an alternate way. We first trace all of the parallel the paths on the network diagram from the Start activity to the End activity and compute each of their durations. Notice in Figure H.8 that we have two paths: Path 1 and Path 2.

- Path 1 is Start–Requirements Analysis for Module 1–Design of Module 1–Construction of Module 1–Integration–Testing–End. The duration of this path is 38 days.
- Path 2 is Start–Requirements Analysis for Module 2–Design of Module 2–Construction of Module 2–Integration–Testing–End. The duration of this path is 37 days.

Table H.3. Data Illustrating the Computation of Standard Deviation

Activity ID	Activity Description	Optimistic Time	Pessimistic Time	Standard Deviation	Variance
1	Start	0	0	0.00	0.00
2	Requirements analysis of Module 1	4	8	0.67	0.44
3	Design of Module 1	5	11	1.00	1.00
4	Construction of Module 1	10	16	1.00	1.00
5	Requirements analysis of Module 2	3	7	0.67	0.44
6	Design of Module 2	4	10	1.00	1.00
7	Construction of Module 2	10	18	1.33	1.78
8	Integration	5	9	0.67	0.44
9	Testing	3	5	0.33	0.11
10	End	0	0	0.00	0.00

The critical path in a network is the path that has the longest duration from the Start activity to the End activity. Clearly, Path 1 has longer duration. Path 1 is therefore the critical path in Figure H.8.

PERT AND PROBABILITY

PERT acknowledges the uncertainty inherent in estimating the duration of projects and provides a methodology for estimating the probability for project completion for a given duration:

- The formula for computing the standard deviation for an activity is finding the difference between the optimistic time and the pessimistic time for the activity and then dividing the result by 6. The formula is *standard deviation* $= (t_p - t_o) \div 6$.
- Variance for an activity is the square of the standard deviation. We compute variance for all activities on the critical path.
- The standard deviation for the project is the square root of the sum of variances of the critical activities. The formula is *standard deviation for the project = square root* (sum of variances of all activities on the critical path).

Let's use the data in Table H.2 and compute the values, which are shown in Table H.3. The critical path, computed as discussed earlier and identified by the values in Table H.3, is 1, 2, 3, 4, 8, 9, and 10. The sum of their variances is (0 + 0.44 + 1

+ 1 + 0.44 + 0.11) = 2.99 or 3. Therefore, the standard deviation for the project is square root of 3 or 1.732.

To compute probability, we determine the value of Z using a formula:

$$Z = (D - t_e)/standard\ deviation$$

where:

D = the required due date for project completion

t_e = the expected time of completion of project according to the critical path

Then, we look up the probability for the value of Z (from probability tables that are available on the Internet, in mathematical tables, or in any book on statistics).

For the project shown in Figure H.8, let's now compute the *probability* of completing the project in 36 days:

$D = 36$
$t_e = 38$
Standard deviation = 1.732
$Z = (36 - 38)/1.732 = -1.15$

When we look up the value of Z from probability tables, we get a value of 0.12507 or about 12.507%. Thus we can say that the probability of executing the project (whose expected time of completion is 38 days) in 36 days, is about 12.5%.

CPM

As discussed earlier in this appendix, like PERT, CPM is also a network diagram-based technique, except in the matter of handling uncertainty. CPM treats the duration of activities as *deterministic*. Deterministic activities are those activities whose duration is known with certainty. CPM uses a single time estimate for each activity. CPM assumes the possibility, however, that by pumping in more resources, the duration of the activities can be reduced, within certain predefined limits, so that the total duration of the project can be reduced. This aspect of pumping in more resources to reduce the duration of activities, and thereby reducing the total duration of a project, is known as *crashing* the project. Crashing is the systematic reduction of the duration of an entire project, with the least possible increase in the cost of the project.

Before going any further, we need to answer a question: "Why would we need to resort to crashing the project?" (In other words, we are assuming that the project completion date arrived at using forward pass and backward pass computations will be acceptable to the client.) Often, however, the project completion date

Table H.4. Initial Data for a Crashing Example

Activity ID	Activity Description	Normal Time	Normal Cost ($)	Crash Time	Crash Cost ($)
1	Start	0	0	0	0
2	Requirements analysis of Module 1	6	9,000	4	12,000
3	Design of Module 1	8	12,000	7	15,000
4	Construction of Module 1	13	13,000	10	16,000
5	Requirements analysis of Module 2	5	7,500	4	10,000
6	Design of Module 2	7	10,500	6	14,000
7	Construction of Module 2	14	14,000	11	17,000
8	Integration	7	14,000	5	18,000
9	Testing	4	6,000	4	6,000
10	End	0	0	0	0

arrived at by our computations and the completion date demanded by the client are not the same. If the completion date demanded by the client is later than our date, all is well. But if the date demanded by the client occurs before our date, we are faced with a difficult situation. This situation is often a reality. Crashing can help us try to reduce the initial project completion date to meet client demands.

Each activity is associated with two sets of values: normal duration and normal cost and crash duration and crash cost. The relationship between these two sets of values is assumed to be linear. For example, say the Design activity of Module 1 has a normal duration of 5 days, with an associated normal cost of 1000. The activity's crash duration is 3 days and its crash cost is 1500. The activity's crash cost per day is then [(1500 − 1000) ÷ 2] = 250, a value that is known as *cost-time slope*.

Let's now look at an example of crashing using the project depicted in Figure H.8. The initial data for crashing is shown in Table H.4. Using the data in Table H.4, we can compute the number of *crashable* days and the cost-time slope for each activity, which is shown in Table H.5. Crashing is an iterative process because the process takes a number of iterations to achieve the objective. In this example, for a better understanding of the process, let's crash the project to its minimum possible duration.

In the first iteration, we will have two paths: Path 1 is 1–2–3–4–8–9–10, with duration of 38 days; Path 2 is 1–5–6–7–8–9–10, with duration of 37 days. Thus, we know the critical path is 1–2–3–4–8–9–10. To reduce the duration, we need to crash critical activities. So, we first consider the activity that has the least cost-time slope for crashing. We see in Table H.5 that Activity 4 (Construction of Module

Table H.5. Data for Crashable Days and Cost-Time Slope for a Crashing Example

Activity ID	Activity Description	Normal Time	Normal Cost ($)	Crash Time	Crash Cost ($)	Crashable days	Cost/ time slope
1	Start	0	0	0	0	0	0
2	Requirements analysis of Module 1	6	9,000	4	12,000	2	1,500
3	Design of Module 1	8	12,000	7	15,000	1	3,000
4	Construction of Module 1	13	13,000	10	16,000	3	1,000
5	Requirements analysis of Module 2	5	7,500	4	10,000	1	2,500
6	Design of Module 2	7	10,500	6	14,000	1	3,500
7	Construction of Module 2	14	14,000	11	17,000	3	1,000
8	Integration	7	14,000	5	18,000	2	2,000
9	Testing	4	6,000	4	6,000	0	0
10	End	0	0	0	0	0	0

1) has the least cost-time slope — 1000 per day. So, we will select this activity for crashing. Our next decision will be how much duration do we crash? We need to select duration such that the present critical path will not become shorter than any other path in the network diagram after crashing. We already know that the difference between the two paths is 1 day, so we can crash Activity 4 for 1 day.

From our discussion, we can now formulate the rules for crashing in the first iteration:

1. Select the activity on the critical path that has the least cost-time slope.
2. Select the duration such that the duration of the critical path after crashing is not less than any other paths in the network diagram.

Next, we need to redraw the network diagram using this new information. The new network diagram drawn after the first iteration of crashing is shown in Figure H.9.

Now, let's carry out the second iteration. As you can see from the new network diagram in Figure H.9, we now have two critical paths. When there is more than one critical path in a network diagram, the first rule in selecting the next

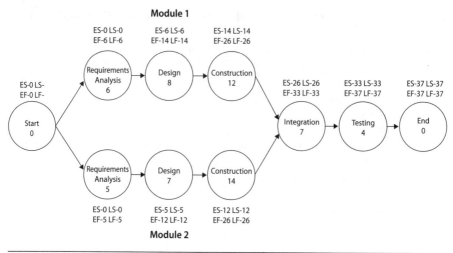

Figure H.9. A network diagram after the first iteration of crashing.

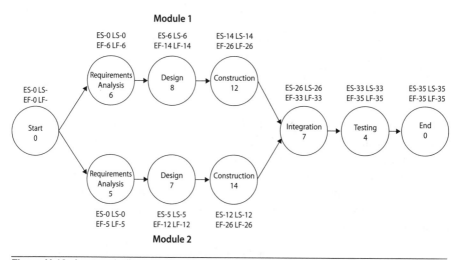

Figure H.10. A network diagram after the second iteration of crashing.

activity for crashing is to select activities that are common to all of the critical paths. In Figure H.9, we have two such activities: Integration and Testing. We already know that when we have multiple candidate activities for crashing that we need to select the one with the least cost-time slope. In our example, we have only one activity that can be crashed: Integration. Integration can be crashed by 2 days at an extra cost of 4000. But before crashing, a question needs to be answered: "Will full crashing (i.e., reducing the duration of the Integration activity fully to its minimum duration) reduce the entire project duration in the same linear amount? In this case: "Yes." So let's crash the Integration activity fully and redraw the network diagram. The revised network diagram is shown in Figure H.10.

Now, project duration is reduced to 35 days. Is further crashing possible? Let's look at the activities that can be crashed further:

- Activity 2 can be crashed by 2 days with a cost-time slope of 1500.
- Activity 3 can be crashed by 1 day with a cost-time slope of 3000.
- Activity 4 can be crashed by 2 days (because we have already crashed this activity by 1 day) with a cost-time slope of 1000.
- Activity 5 can be crashed by 1 day with a cost-time slope of 2500.
- Activity 6 can be crashed by 1 day with a cost-time slope of 3500.
- Activity 7 can be crashed by 3 days with a cost-time slope of 1000.

So, to reduce project duration by 1 day, we have to select one activity from both of the paths. As you can see, Activities 4 and 6 both have a least cost-time slope of 1000 per day. Activity 4 allows for crashing of 2 days, but activity 6 allows for crashing by 3 days. We can now draw one more network diagram by crashing these two activities, compute the critical path once more, and continue to iterate. But before doing that, we need to ask ourselves: "Has the desired duration been reached?" If so, we do not need to crash the schedule any further.

But because we have set the objective of crashing to reach the *limit* of possible reduction in duration, we need to check for the maximum possible amount of crashing. To do this, we enumerate all of the critical paths, along with their durations, and evaluate the extent possible for crashing. Let's look at it:

- Path 1–2–3–4–8–9–10 has a duration of 35 days, with a maximum crashability of 5 days (Activity 2 with 2 days, Activity 3 with 1 day, and Activity 4 with 2 days).
- Path 1–5–6–7–8–9–10 has a duration of 35 days, with a maximum crashability of 5 days (Activity 5 with 1 day, Activity 6 with 1 day, and Activity 7 with 3 days).

Notice that both paths allow a reduction of 5 days each, which is the limit to which this project can be crashed. So, let's draw a final network diagram, which is depicted in Figure H.11.

The project is now fully crashed, i.e., the minimum duration has been reached. No further crashing is possible. The final durations with costs are shown in Table H.6. From Table H.6, we can see that the normal duration is 38 days with a total cost of 86,000 and that the crashed duration is 32 days with a cost of 108,000.

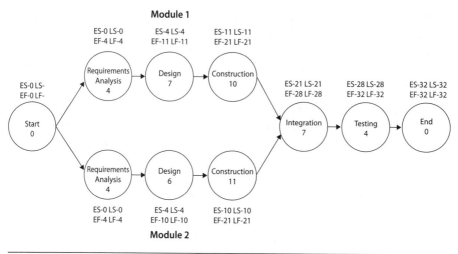

Figure H.11. A network diagram showing a fully crashed project.

So, summarizing the discussions on crashing:

1. Crashing is a systematic exercise to reduce the duration of a project with minimum increase in project cost.
2. Before attempting crashing, we need to set an objective for the reduction of project duration (or set the maximum permissible increase in project cost).
3. Crashing is an iterative process, which is iterated until the objective is met.
4. In any iteration, the rules for selecting the candidate activities for crashing are:
   a. If there are multiple critical paths, then the activities common to all critical paths are to be selected. Otherwise, all activities a on the critical path are candidates for crashing.
   b. In all the candidate activities for crashing, we need to select those activities that have the lease cost-time slope.
5. Crash the selected activities and recalculate the critical paths.
6. Check to see if the objectives have been met in terms of duration and cost.
7. If the objectives are met, redraw/update the network diagram and end the exercise. If the objectives are not met, reiterate Steps 4 to 6 until the objectives are met.

In practice, a manual crashing exercise for even a moderately large project having 500 activities may be impractical because a number of iterations are needed,

Table H.6. Data for a Fully Crashed Project

Activity ID	Activity Description	Normal Time	Normal Cost ($)	Crash Time	Crash Cost ($)
1	Start	0	0	0	0
2	Requirements analysis of Module 1	6	9,000	4	12,000
3	Design of Module 1	8	12,000	7	15,000
4	Construction of Module 1	13	13,000	10	16,000
5	Requirements analysis of Module 2	5	7,500	4	10,000
6	Design of Module 2	7	10,500	6	14,000
7	Construction of Module 2	14	14,000	11	17,000
8	Integration	7	14,000	5	18,000
9	Testing	4	6,000	4	6,000
10	End	0	0	0	0
	Total Cost		86,000		108,000

which requires a large number of computations. We therefore use computer-based tools such as Microsoft Project or Primavera to automate the process of crashing. Before using tools for crashing, understanding how the process actually works is important.

RESOURCE LEVELING

You might have noticed that we use duration when computing the critical path in our examples. A question may arise: "How was this duration derived?" PERT/CPM are duration-based techniques for arriving at a project's completion date. In both the techniques, the assumption is that all of the required resources are available for performing the activities when the activity is scheduled to start (e.g., the human, monetary, equipment, methods, material, and information resources, including the necessary approvals). But in reality, resources are often limited, particularly for costly resources that are shared by many projects and perhaps by many activities within the same project itself. If any of these required resources are unavailable, an activity will be delayed by the period that the resource is unavailable.

Resource leveling refers to the iterative exercise of systematically reducing the overload of the resources with the objective of maintaining the existing project completion date. If this is not possible, then the objective is to delay the project by the minimum (possible) extent. So, we follow several steps when computing the project completion date:

1. Initially we assume that all of the resources are available for all of the activities and compute the critical path and the project completion date.
2. Then we allocate the required resources to each activity.
3. Then we plot resource loading for each resource for the entire duration of the project by:
    a. Computing the number of hours of workload in terms of the activities to be performed by each resource
    b. Drawing a resource loading graph
4. Then we identify the resources that are overloaded. Overloaded resources include:
    a. Resources that have more than 8 hours of workload for the day (human resources and equipment resources)
    b. Resources that are not available or are in short supply (material and monetary resources)
5. Then we try to reduce the overloading of resources (human resources and equipment resources) by:
    a. Temporarily expanding capacity (the first consideration) by:
        i. Getting resources to work extra time for the required days and paying them overtime wages (or other incentives)
        ii. Hiring temporary workers for the required period
        iii. Subcontracting a portion of the work
    b. Providing all of the required resources to the critical activities and delaying the noncritical activities using each activity's available slack
    c. Computing the critical path to assess the impact on the project's completion date (We also recalculate resource loading for all of the resources for all days of project duration and assess the remaining resource overloading if any.)
    d. Performing Steps 5b and 5c iteratively until all overloading of resources is leveled to normal loading levels without delaying the project completion date
    e. Resorting to iterating Steps 5b and 5c and trying to minimize delay in the project's completion date when eliminating resource overloading is not possible without delaying the project's completion

When resources such as monetary and material resources are in short supply, we need to just go ahead and procure them. Otherwise, the resources in short supply will only delay the project by the amount of time procurement is delayed. Information resources also delay a project if their availability is delayed.

Monetary, material, and information resources, however, cannot be leveled by delaying the noncritical activities.

Just as crashing is an iterative process, so is resource leveling. For real-life projects that have 500 or more activities and 25 or more resources, resource leveling is very difficult and tedious. Usually computer-based tools such as Microsoft Project and Primavera are used for resource leveling, but these tools usually perform "resource-constrained" scheduling rather than leveling the resources. Our recommendation is that you do not commit to a project completion date until resource leveling or resource-constrained scheduling is performed.

Some closing words. We have presented a brief outline of the techniques of PERT/CPM. Even though introductory, this brief is adequate for software project managers who will use computer-based tools such as Microsoft Project and Primavera for scheduling of projects. The background information provided is to enable an SPM to perform scheduling effectively. Abundant literature is available for SPMs to learn more about PERT/CPM topics.

REFERENCES

1. http://en.wikipedia.org/wiki/UGM-27_Polaris
2. http://pert-chart.biz/tag/polaris-missile/
3. http://en.wikipedia.org/wiki/Critical_path_method
4. http://www.referenceforbusiness.com/encyclopedia/Per-Pro/Program-Evaluation-and-Review-Technique-PERT.html
5. http://www.interventions.org/pertcpm.html

APPENDIX I

ABBREVIATIONS

ABC	Always Better Control
ACWP	Actual cost of work performed
BCWP	Budgeted cost of work performed
BCWS	Budgeted cost of work scheduled
CC	Configuration controller
CCB	Configuration control board
CCSR	Composite customer satisfaction rating
CM	Configuration management
CMM	Capability Maturity Model
CMMI	Capability Maturity Model Integration
CMP	Configuration management plan
COCOMO	Constructive Cost Model
COTS	Commercial off-the-shelf
CPI	Cost performance index
CPM	Critical Path Method
CR	Change request
CR (Appendix G)	Cooperation rating
CRM	Customer relationship management
CSR	Customer satisfaction rating
CSS	Customer satisfaction survey
CV	Cost variance
DBA	Database administrator
DIR	Defect injection rate
DLL	Dynamic link library
DR	Delivery rating
EAI	Enterprise applications integration
EF	Earliest finish
ES	Earliest start
EVA	Earned value analysis
EVM	Effort variance metric
FF	Finish to finish
FP	Function point

FS	Finish to start
GUI	Graphical user interface
HR	Human resources
HTML	Hyper text markup language
ID	Issue density
IDE	Integrated development environment
IEEE	Institute of Electrical and Electronic Engineers
IP	Intellectual property
IPR	Intellectual property rights
IR	Issue rating
ISO	The International Organization for Standardization
IV&V	Independent verification and validation
JAD	Joint application development
LF	Latest finish
LOB	Line of balance
LOC	Line of code
LS	Latest start
MM	Meeting minutes
MOM	Minutes of meeting
MS	Microsoft
MWR	Maintenance work request
NC	Nonconformance
NCR	Nonconformance report
PC	Personal computer
PCR	Program change request
PD	Person-day
PERT	Program Evaluation and Review Technique
PI	Project initiation
PIN	Project initiation note
PL	Project leader
PL/SQL	Programming language/structured query language
PMO	Project management office
PMP	Project management plan
PMR	Program modification request
PPQA	Process and product quality assurance
PR	Price rating
QA	Quality assurance
QAP	Quality assurance plan
QC	Quality control
QR	Quality rating
RAD	Rapid application development

RAM	Random access memory
RDBMS	Relational database management system
REM	Relative effort metric
RFP	Request for proposal
RUM	Resource utilization metric
RUP	Rational Unified Process
SCCM	Schedule conformance capability metric
SCMP	Software configuration management plan
SDLC	Software development life cycle
SDP	Software development project
SEI	Software Engineering Institute
SEPG	Software engineering process group
SF	Start to finish
SLA	Service level agreement
SPI	Software performance index
SPM	Software project manager
SPMP	Software project management plan
SQA	Software quality assurance
SQAP	Software quality assurance plan
SQL	Structured query language
SRS	Software requirements specification
SS	Start to start
SSU	Software size unit
SV	Schedule variance
SVM	Schedule variance metric
TBD	To be decided
UI	User interface
UML	Unified modeling language
VED	Vital, Essential, Desirable
WBS	Work breakdown structure
XP	Extreme programming
Y2K	Year 2000

APPENDIX J

TEMPLATES FOR SOFTWARE PROJECT MANAGERS

Our thinking was that including multipage templates in the text of the chapters in the book would hinder the flow of the material. Therefore, we have provided a brief outline of the template contents within the corresponding book chapters. For convenience, more-detailed, multipage templates are presented in this appendix.

Exhibit 5.2. Template for a Software Project Management Plan

Exhibit 5.3. Template for a Configuration Management Plan

Exhibit 5.4. Template for a Quality Assurance Plan

Exhibit 5.5. Template for an Induction Training Plan

Exhibit 5.6. Template for a Risk Management Plan

Exhibit 5.7. Template for a Deployment Plan

Exhibit 7.2. Template for a Weekly Project Progress Report

Exhibit 8.1. Template for a Change Request Form

Exhibit G.1. Template for a Customer Satisfaction Survey Form

Software Project Management Plan for *Sample Project*

Name of Client

Revision History

Version Number	Date	Description of Changes	Prepared by	Approved by
Draft		Initial draft	XYZ	ABC
1.0		First release	XYZ	ABC

TABLE OF CONTENTS

1.0 Project Overview

1.1 Project Summary *<provide a brief description about the project's functionality, the client, target platform, etc.>*

1.2 Purpose, Scope, and Objectives *<describe the purpose, scope, and objectives set for this document>*

1.3 Deliverables *<describe all deliverables in a table as shown below>*

Deliverable	Soft Copy/ Hard Copy	Delivered to	Planned Date of Delivery	Comments
Source code	Soft	Systems Administration of Client		
Others				

1.4 Major Milestones

Milestone	Planned Date to Reach	Comments

2.0 References

Reference	Origin	Comments
	<Client/project team/organizational process/ IEEE standard/etc.>	

3.0 Definitions and Acronyms
<describe any definitions and acronyms that are unique to the project>

Term/Acronym	Definition/Full Form

4.0 Project Organization
4.1 Project Team *<provide an organizational chart and add any explanatory statements>*

4.2 Client Interfaces *<describe the organization at the customer's end for interfacing with the project team and escalation of issues>*

4.3 Roles and Responsibilities *<describe roles and responsibilities of the project team; organizational process may be referred to if it contains roles and responsibilities of project team; for such roles and responsibilities that are not contained in the organizational process, the table below may be used to describe these roles and responsibilities>*

Role	Primary Responsibilities	Secondary Responsibilities

5.0 Managerial Process
5.1 Project Start-Up

    5.1.1 Estimation Plan *<describe the events that trigger estimation, re-estimation, and revision of estimates>*

    5.1.2 Staffing Plan *<describe requirements of the different types of staff that are required along with the dates of their requirements and probable release dates>*

Type of Staff	Number Required	From Date	Probable Release Date

    5.1.3 Training Plan *<describe the list of training programs that need to be conducted for the project team or refer to the induction training program document>*

5.2 Project Execution

    5.2.1 Work Allocation and Control *<describe the methods used for allocating work to the staff, communicating work allocation to team members, reporting back progress and completion, target setting, etc.>*

    5.2.2 Quality Assurance Activities *<list the quality assurance activities planned for the project or give reference to the quality assurance plan document of the project>*

    5.2.3 Productivity Monitoring *<detail the productivity targets set for the project and the methods for measuring individual productivity and controlling it>*

    5.2.4 Effort Monitoring *<describe the method for estimating the effort required for each work allocation, target setting, and monitoring the same>*

5.3 Project Control

    5.3.1 Project Scope Control *<describe the requirements management methods or give reference to requirements management plan document>*

    5.3.2 Schedule Control *<describe reference to project schedule document and methods of monitoring it>*

    5.3.3 Cost Control *<describe cost control methods>*

    5.3.4 Quality Control *<describe the methods of quality monitoring>*

    5.3.5 Progress Reporting *<describe the periodicity of progress reporting along with reference to progress reporting formats, stakeholders to whom the report would be sent, etc.>*

    5.3.6 Metrics Reporting *<describe the metrics reporting, periodicity of reporting, stakeholders to whom the report would be sent, or make reference to metrics plan document>*

5.4 Risk Management

    5.4.1 Risk Identification *<if there is a separate risk management plan, make reference to it or describe the identified risks>*

    5.4.2 Risk Mitigation *<if there is a separate risk management plan, make reference to it or describe how the identified risks would be mitigated>*

5.5 Project Closure

    5.5.1 Release Resources *<describe the resource release activities along with probable dates>*

    5.5.2 Performance Appraisals *<describe the plan for conducting performance appraisals for the project team>*

    5.5.3 Document Best and Worst Practices *<describe the plan for documenting the best practices of the project>*

    5.5.4 Identify Reusable Components *<describe the plan for identifying reusable components>*

    5.5.5 Archive Project Artifacts *<describe the plan for archiving the project artifacts>*

    5.5.6 Project Postmortem *<describe the plan for conducting the project postmortem>*

    5.5.7 Project Closure Meeting *<describe the plan for conducting the project closure meeting>*

6.0 Technical Process

6.1 Software Development Life Cycle *<give reference to the organizational approved SDLCs and the SDLC selected for the project and the tailoring, if any, thereof for the project>*

6.2 Methods, Tools, and Techniques *<describe the methods, tools, and techniques of software engineering proposed for use in the project>*

6.3 Product Acceptance Plan *<describe the acceptance testing and customer sign-off process>*

7.0 Support Process Plans

7.1 Software Configuration Management Plan *<describe the software configuration management plan or make reference to the software configuration management plan>*

7.2 Software Quality Assurance Plan *<describe the software quality assurance plan or make reference to the software quality assurance plan>*

7.3 Process Improvement Plan *<describe the process improvement plan or make reference to the process improvement plan>*

7.4   Induction Training Plan *<describe the induction training plan or make reference to the induction training plan>*

7.5   Schedule *<make reference to the project schedule document here>*

7.6   Work Breakdown Structure *<make reference to the work register for the project here>*

7.7   Issue-Resolution Plan *<describe the issue-resolution activities of the project and make reference to change register document here>*

8.0   Any Additional Plans

8.1   Deployment Plan *<make reference to deployment plan document, if any, here>*

8.2   Warranty Support Plan *<make reference to warranty support plan document, if any, here>*

8.3   Data Migration Plan *<make reference to data migration plan document, if applicable, here>*

8.4   Any Other Plans

9.0   Annexes

<describe the list of appendices in a table>

Annex	Description of the Annex

10.0   Waivers

<list the process waivers obtained if any with references to approvals thereof>

Exhibit 5.2. Template for a software project management plan.

Software Configuration Management Plan for *Sample Project*

Name of Client

Revision History

Version Number	Date	Description of Changes	Prepared by	Approved by
Draft		Initial draft	XYZ	ABC
1.0		First release	XYZ	ABC

TABLE OF CONTENTS

1.0   Introduction

1.1   Scope *<describe briefly the scope of the plan, including the concerns, etc.>*

1.2   Objectives *<describe the objectives of this plan>*

1.3   Overview *<provide a brief overview of the project and the product>*

2.0   References

Reference	Origin	Comments
	<Client/project team/organizational process/ IEEE standard/etc.>	

3.0   Definitions and Acronyms

<describe any definitions and acronyms that are unique to the project>

Term/Acronym	Definition/Full Form

4.0   Organization of Configuration Management

- Roles and Responsibilities *<describe the roles and responsibilities of people performing the configuration management activities in the project>*
- Configuration Control Board Roles and Responsibilities *<describe the CCB, constitution, roles and responsibilities, etc. in granting approvals for change approvals for the project>*

5.0   Tools, Techniques, and Methodology

<describe the configuration management methodology for the project, tools and techniques used for managing the configuration, etc.>

6.0   Configuration Management Activities

- Identification of Configuration Items *<describe the types of items that will be brought under configuration management, including hardware, software and documentation>*
- List of Configuration Items *<make reference to the CI register document>*
- Naming Conventions *<detail the conventions to be followed for naming project artifacts, including documents, program names, database tables, table fields, program variables, constants, screens, reports, etc.>*
- Baseline Management *<identify the product baselines and how and when baselines are produced for all baselines, including development baselines, internal baselines, approved baselines, etc.>*
- Repositories *<detail the code repository and information repository giving directory structures with check-in/check-out procedures and authorities>*
- Configuration Management Software *<describe the software tool being used for managing the project configuration, if any; alternatively give reference to the tool documentation>*

7.0   Change Management
<describe the procedure to manage the configuration control, including procedures used for changing baselines, authorities for approvals for changing baselines, etc.>

- Change Control *<describe the methodology for controlling changes to CIs and baselines>*
- Change Requests and Change Register *<describe the methodology for evaluating change requests, approval/rejection of change requests, implementation of change requests, prioritization of change requests, tracking of change requests, and review and closure of change requests; make reference to formats of change requests and change register>*
- Release Management *<describe the methodology of releasing deliverables to the customer, preparing the build for release, release inspection, etc.>*
- Version Control *<describe the procedure to control the version of an artifact, version numbering system, the configuration management activities required for making modifications to a version-controlled artifact, etc.>*

8.0   Configuration Status and Accounting

- Storage and Release *<describe the policy of retention, backups, recovery plans, etc.>*
- Reports *<detail the reports for CI status, released CIs, change history of CIs, baselines, etc. with reference to report templates for each of the reports and periodicity of reporting>*
- Audits *<describe the proposed audits for configuration management activity, periodicity thereof, who would conduct the audits, closure of NCRs, audit results reporting, etc.>*

9.0   Training
<give reference to project induction training program if this topic is included or describe the training proposed for the project team on project configuration management and tools thereof>

10.0   Subcontractor Configuration Control Activities
<describe the configuration control activities at the subcontractor if any part of the software is subcontracted>

Exhibit 5.3. Template for a configuration management plan.

Software Quality Assurance Plan for *Sample Project*

Name of Client

Revision History

Version Number	Date	Description of Changes	Prepared by	Approved by
Draft		Initial draft	XYZ	ABC
1.0		First release	XYZ	ABC

TABLE OF CONTENTS

1.0   Introduction

    1.1   Scope *<describe briefly the scope of the plan, the areas of the project addressed by this plan, etc.>*

    1.2   Objectives *<describe the objectives of this plan>*

    1.3   Overview *<provide a brief overview of the project and the product>*

2.0   References

Reference	Origin	Comments
	<Client/project team/organizational process/ IEEE standard/etc.>	

3.0   Definitions and Acronyms

    <describe any definitions and acronyms that are unique to the project>

Term/Acronym	Definition/Full Form

4.0   Roles and Responsibilities

    <describe the roles and responsibilities of people performing quality assurance activities in the project as well as approval authorities, etc.>

5.0   Standards and Guidelines

    <list all the standards and guidelines proposed to be used in the project>

Project Area	Reference to Applicable Standard/Guideline

6.0   Quality Assurance Activities
<list all the quality assurance activities proposed for the project>

Proposed Reviews for Project
<list all the reviews proposed for the project against each type of artifact>

Project Artifact	Type of Review	Number and Type of Reviewer
Requirements documents	Guided walk-through/postal review/meeting review/ managerial review	
Design documents		
Source code		
Project plans		
Test plans		
Test cases		
Test results		
Table scripts		
User documentation		
Operations documentation		
Any Other		

Proposed Tests for the Project
<list all the proposed tests for the project against each test unit>

Project Test Unit	Type of Tests Proposed	Test Environment	Who Will Conduct Test	Pass/ Fail Criteria
Program unit	Unit test/ integration test/ system test/ functional test/ negative test/load test/stress test/ acceptance test, etc.	Development environment/ test environment/ target environment, etc.	Peer/PL/PM/ testing team/ client, etc.	
Sub-module				
Module				
Product				
Each customer release				
Product				
Any Other				

7.0 Metrics Proposed to Be Collected for the Project
<list all the metrics proposed to be collected with norms and permitted variance thereof>

Metrics	Norm for Project	Permitted Variance	Periodicity of Reporting
Productivity metrics		*<percentage or absolute value>*	*<weekly/monthly>*
Quality metrics			
Schedule variance			
Effort Variance			
Change metrics			
Any Other Metrics			

8.0 Tools, Techniques, and Methodologies
<describe the testing tools, testing techniques, and methodologies adopted in the project for carrying out the quality assurance activities; if automated testing tools are used, then give reference to the user guides of the proposed tools; methodologies for work allocation, progress reporting, test result evaluation, completion of testing may also be described>

9.0 Causal Analysis Proposed
<describe the causal analysis and defect analysis to be performed for defects unearthed during quality assurance activities; also describe the events/threshold levels that trigger causal analysis>

10.0 Quality Assurance of Subcontracted/Client-Supplied Products
<describe the methodology to carry out quality assurance activities for the part of software subcontracted, if any, including the activities and tests to be carried out as well as the activities to be carried out on the client-supplied product, if any>

11.0 Training
<describe the training necessary for carrying out the quality assurance activities described above and the plan to carry it out; if these topics are included in the induction training program, make reference to that document>

Exhibit 5.4. Template for a quality assurance plan.

Induction Training Plan for *Sample Project*

Name of Client

Revision History

Version Number	Date	Description of Changes	Prepared by	Approved by
Draft		Initial draft	XYZ	ABC
1.0		First release	XYZ	ABC

TABLE OF CONTENTS

1.0   Introduction
  1.1   Scope *<describe briefly the scope of the plan, the areas of the project addressed by this plan, etc.>*
  1.2   Objectives *<describe the objectives of this plan>*
  1.3   Overview *<provide a brief overview of the project and the product>*

2.0   References

Reference	Origin	Comments
	<Client/project team/organizational process/ IEEE standard/etc.>	

3.0   Definitions and Acronyms
<describe any definitions and acronyms that are unique to the project>

Term/Acronym	Definition/Full Form

4.0   Roles and Responsibilities
<describe the roles and responsibilities of people performing induction training activities in the project as well as approval authorities, etc.>

5.0   Training Approach
<describe the approach taken to impart the induction training, including classroom training, guided self-learning, on-the-job training, etc.>

6.0   Training Resources
<describe the training facilities, course outlines, course materials, self-learning materials, training slides, case studies, etc. that would be used for conducting induction training>

7.0 **Training Topics**

<describe the training topics to be covered in the induction training>

Topic	Duration	Faculty	Type of Training
Project plans	4 hours	PM/PL	Classroom
Configuration management tool	2 hours	PM/PL	Classroom
Testing tools	6 hours	Tool expert to be arranged by the training department	Classroom + hands-on
Any others			

8.0 **Project-Specific Skill Training**

<list the topics on which project-specific skill training may be required for the project>

Topic	Duration	Faculty	Type of Training
Programming language abc	24 hours	Language expert to be arranged by the training department	Classroom + hands-on
Any others			

9.0 **Training Evaluation**

<describe the methodology proposed for evaluating the training conducted for the project; if it is part of organizational process, make reference to it>

Exhibit 5.5. Template for an induction training plan.

Risk Management Plan for *Sample Project*

Name of Client

Revision History

Version Number	Date	Description of Changes	Prepared by	Approved by
Draft		Initial draft	XYZ	ABC
1.0		First release	XYZ	ABC

TABLE OF CONTENTS

1.0   Introduction

    1.1   Scope *<describe briefly the scope of the plan, the areas of the project addressed by this plan, etc.>*

    1.2   Objectives *<describe the objectives of this plan>*

    1.3   Overview *<provide a brief overview of the project and the product>*

2.0   References

Reference	Origin	Comments
	<Client/project team/organizational process/ IEEE standard/etc.>	

3.0   Definitions and Acronyms

<describe any definitions and acronyms that are unique to the project>

Term/Acronym	Definition/Full Form

4.0   Risk Management for the Project

    4.1   Overview *<describe the overview of the proposed risk management activities for the project>*

    4.2   Risk Identification *<describe the risks identified for the project, their impact, probability of occurrence, etc.; if a separate list is prepared, make reference to that list>*

    4.3   Risk Mitigation *<describe the proposed risk mitigation activities for the risks identified>*

    4.4   Risk Monitoring Activities *<describe the risk monitoring and reporting activities; if this is part of weekly status report, make reference to that document>*

4.5 Tools and Techniques <*describe the tools and techniques, if any, used for carrying out risk management activities in the project*>

5.0 Training

<*describe the training necessary for carrying out the deployment activities described above and the plan to carry it out; if these topics are included in the induction training program, give reference to that document*>

Exhibit 5.6. Template for a risk management plan.

Deployment Plan for *Sample Project*

Name of Client

Revision History

Version Number	Date	Description of Changes	Prepared by	Approved by
Draft		Initial draft	XYZ	ABC
1.0		First release	XYZ	ABC

TABLE OF CONTENTS

1.0   Introduction

1.1   Scope *<describe briefly the scope of the plan, the areas of the project addressed by this plan, etc.>*

1.2   Objectives *<describe the objectives of this plan>*

1.3   Overview *<provide a brief overview of the project and the product>*

2.0   References

Reference	Origin	Comments
	<Client/project team/organizational process/ IEEE standard/etc.>	

3.0   Definitions and Acronyms

<describe any definitions and acronyms that are unique to the project>

Term/Acronym	Definition/Full Form

4.0   Roles and Responsibilities

<describe the roles and responsibilities of the project team, the project support groups, and the client delineating the respective primary, secondary and support responsibilities as well as approval authorities, etc.>

5.0   Schedule of Deployment

<describe the schedule of the deployment activity; if this is included in the project schedule, give reference to that document here>

6.0 Resources Required for Deployment
<list the resources required for deploying the product; if a bill of materials is prepared, make reference to that document>

7.0 Facilities
<describe the required facilities, including building rooms, power requirements, privacy and security requirements, etc.; if there is an engineering drawing prepared for this purpose, make reference to it>

8.0 Hardware
<list the hardware, including the model, version, and configuration, required for deploying the product; if a bill of materials is prepared, make reference to that document>

9.0 Deployment Unit
<list the software and documentation that is provided as part of the delivery that is going to be deployed>

10.0 Support Necessary for Deployment
<describe the support necessary for deployment, including support software, documentation, and personnel>

11.0 Training
<describe the training necessary for carrying out the deployment activities described above and the plan to carry it out; if these topics are included in the induction training program, make reference to that document>

Exhibit 5.7. Template for a deployment plan.

Weekly Project Progress Report

Project Information:
1.1   Name of Project
1.2   Name of Project Manager
1.3   Reporting Period *<from mm/dd/yyyy to mm/dd/yyyy>*

Executive Summary:
<describe the highlights of the project such as overall progress, any significant events, etc.; briefly give the total picture of project progress>

Status of Project:

Overall Status

Module Name	Percentage Completion			
	Construction	Review	Unit Testing	Integration
Module Name 1				
Module Name 2				
Module Name n				

Tasks Completed During the Period

Module Name	Task Description	Start Date	End Date	Remarks
Module Name 1				
Module Name 2				
Module Name n				

Tasks Planned for the Next Period

Module Name	Task Description	Start Date	Scheduled End Date	Remarks
Module Name 1				
Module Name 2				
Module Name n				

Any Tasks that Are Outside Project Work

Task Description	Explanation of Need and Benefits Thereof
Tasks handled during the period:	
Tasks planned for next period:	

Resource Position:

Resource Name	Beginning of Period	Additions	Attritions	End of Week
SPM				
PL				
Module leaders				
Programmers				
DBAs				
Business analysts				

Issue-Resolution Status:

Pending With	Beginning of Period	Additions	Resolved	End of Week
Customer				
Systems Administration				
Human Resources				

Project Metrics:

<enumerate all metrics achieved until the end of the reporting period under these five heads>

Metric	Organizational Standard	Actual Achievement	Explanation for Variance
Productivity			
Defects			
Effort			
Schedule			
Changes			

Significant Events During Period:

<describe all significant events such as achievements and failures, including the circumstance that led to the event, if any action is required, from whom, etc.>

Description of Event	Explanation of Event	Action Required

Customer Interface:

Commendations Received

Date of Receipt	From Whom (Person Commending)	Description of Commendation	Name of Team Member Earning Commendation

Complaints Received

Date of Receipt	From Whom (Person Complaining)	Description of Complaint	Reasons for Origination of Complaint

Issues Needing Management Attention:

Project Support Group Issues

Description of Issue	Date of Origination	Pending With (Person)

Employee Grievances

Description of Issue	Date of Origination	Pending With (Person)

Any Interface Issues

Description of Issue	Date of Origination	Pending With (Person)

Best Practices/Pitfalls to Share with Organization:

Area Where Practice Is Applicable	Description of Best Practice/Pitfall

Process Improvement Suggestions:
<enumerate all suggestions>

Exhibit 7.2. Template for a weekly project progress report.

Change Request

Project Name:

Date:

Change Request Reference:

Initiator Information:

Name of Initiator	
Designation	
Contact Information	
• Telephone number	
• Email ID	
• Location	

Details of Change Requested:

Name of module affected by change request	
List of components affected by change request	
Description of the requested change (add additional sheets, if required)	
Reasons for change	
Priority (immediate implementation/when possible before completion of project/to be retrofitted at end of project)	

Implementation Information:

Aspect	Name of Person	Date of Completion
Analysis		
Approved for implementation		
Implementation		
Review		
Regression testing		
Closed on		

Exhibit 8.1. Template for a change request form.

Name of Organization Executing the Project
Customer Satisfaction Survey

Date:

Project Details:

Project ID	
Name of Project	
Project Initiation Date	
Project Completion Date	
Current Status of Project	
Name of Project Manager	
Name of Client Contact	

Person Filling Out Survey:

Name	
Designation	
Organization	
Role in Project	

Instructions for Filling in Aspect Ratings:

- Rate each aspect in the table below using the following five-point scale:
  1. Completely dissatisfied
  2. Does not meet expectations
  3. Just meets expectations
  4. Exceeds expectations
  5. Excellent service
- If possible, elaborate on your ratings in the **Comments** column.

Aspect	Rating	Comments
Quality of deliverables: 1. Overall product quality 2. Quality of Module A 3. Quality of Module B 4. Quality of Module n		
On-schedule deliveries: 1. Delivery A 2. Delivery B 3. Delivery n		

Aspect	Rating	Comments
Communication: 1. Progress reporting 2. Tele-conferences 3. Video conferences 4. Issue resolution		
Cooperation: 1. Courteous communications 2. Accommodations when necessary		
Overall Satisfaction		

Provide Any Project-Related Observations:

Signature: **Name:** **Date:**
For Internal Use: 1. Received by: 2. Received on: 3. Progress report in which this information is included:

Exhibit G.1. Template for a customer satisfaction survey form.

This book has free material available for download from the
Web Added Value™ resource center at *www.jrosspub.com*

INDEX

multiple registers, 101–102
single register, 100–101
Work sampling, 284, 286. *See also* Sampling
Workload, balanced, 216
Workplace. *See* Morale management

X

XP. *See* Extreme programming

Y

Y2K, as approach-driven software
development project, 11